T0311610

EXAMINING CREATIVITY IN THE WORKPLACE

This scholarly book explores the intersection of social cognition with a democratic philosophy of human resource management to advance a theory of workplace function that maximizes creativity. It examines how the work of Polanyi on tacit knowledge provides a useful theoretical structure for understanding person perception and self-fulfilling prophecy effects in the workplace, with a focus on gender, culture, and race as diversity variables. Based on a broad range of interdisciplinary empirical evidence and theories, this book provides a foundational set of concepts to build new applied intervention strategies. The authors create new, testable theories based on a synthesis of several major areas of research in social psychology and human resource management, moving beyond the narrow confines of trends in a particular subdomain. Part 1 offers a literature review of the field, ranging from theoretical, historical, and philosophical psychology to social psychology and neurocognition. Each chapter in this section offers a novel theory that is pertinent to workplace innovation, synthesized from existing evidence. Part 2 reveals applications of tacit knowledge to the field of human resource management, with a focus on cross-cultural applications for low- and high-power distance settings.

This insightful text presents the authors' original, qualitative research around workplace creativity and tacit knowledge and is valuable reading for scholars and advanced students in industrial-organizational psychology and human resource management.

Nahanni Freeman, PhD, is a professor of clinical psychology at George Fox University in Oregon in the United States. She serves as the director of research in the PsyD program. Nahanni completed her PhD at the Rose-mead School of Psychology at Biola University, USA. Her clinical experiences have been gained in a range of medical settings.

Bren Slusser, PhD, SHRM-SCP, has made a career in Human Resources as well as spent many years in higher education in the United States. Bren received her PhD in Organization and Management with an emphasis on Human Resource Management from Capella University and an MBA from the University of Phoenix, all while working full time and raising a family. Her BA in Japan Studies is from the University of Washington, USA.

EXAMINING CREATIVITY IN THE WORKPLACE

Applying Polanyi's Theory of Tacit Knowledge to Maximize Fulfillment at Work

Nahanni Freeman Ph.D., and
Bren Slusser Ph.D., SHRM-SCP

Routledge
Taylor & Francis Group

NEW YORK AND LONDON

Cover Image: © miroslav_1 via Getty Images

First published 2025
by Routledge
605 Third Avenue, New York, NY 10158

and by Routledge
4 Park Square, Milton Park, Abingdon, Oxon, OX14 4RN

Routledge is an imprint of the Taylor & Francis Group, an informa business

Library of Congress Cataloging-in-Publication Data
Names: Freeman, Nahanni, author. | Slusser, Bren, author.
Title: Examining creativity in the workplace : applying Polanyi's theory of tacit knowledge to maximize fulfillment at work / Nahanni Freeman and Bren Slusser.
Description: New York, NY : Routledge, 2025. | Includes bibliographical references and index.
Identifiers: LCCN 2024012775 (print) | LCCN 2024012776 (ebook) | ISBN 9781032345826 (hardback) | ISBN 9781032345772 (paperback) | ISBN 9781003322894 (ebook)
Subjects: LCSH: Quality of work life. | Creative ability. | Job satisfaction. | Corporate culture. | Organizational sociology.
Classification: LCC HD6955 .F684 2025 (print) | LCC HD6955 (ebook) | DDC 306.3/6—dc23/eng/20240321
LC record available at https://lccn.loc.gov/2024012775
LC ebook record available at https://lccn.loc.gov/2024012776

ISBN: 978-1-032-34582-6 (hbk)
ISBN: 978-1-032-34577-2 (pbk)
ISBN: 978-1-003-32289-4 (ebk)

DOI: 10.4324/9781003322894

Typeset in Optima
by codeMantra

To my dad, for his example of creative passion, to Tom, for modeling tolerance and humanism, and to my mother, for believing in my potential.

To Larry, for all the love, support, and encouragement throughout this process.

CONTENTS

ACKNOWLEDGMENTS

Nahanni

Life experience often underlies the academic passions that one pursues. I am thankful for resilience-enhancing moments, encountered in a range of contexts. Along my journey, I discovered signposts, collaborations, encouragers, and mentors who facilitated endurance. I am grateful to Aidan Freeman, Tom Michener, and Gary Warburton for many conversations that encouraged me to think about realities, the universe, philosophy, equality, and persons in new ways. I acknowledge Olivia Ball for her pure joy and mindfulness of the present, Jack Ball for his courage, loyalty, and optimism, and Craig Ball for his positive attitude and life coaching, orienting my compass towards new beginnings in the midst of facing adversity. I am grateful to Ann Michener for unwavering support and for contributions to models of leadership, educational theory and practice. I remain mindful of the many mentors at Rosemead and throughout my career who cast a vision and conveyed ethical ideals, enlisting critical thinking and deontological arguments. For the Freeman family, I am grateful for the camaraderie, the laughter, and the unconditional positive regard that brought me back to myself. In addition, there were the many students sitting in my office and talking about ideas and theories, sharing their questions and hypotheses, and blessing me with their cards and thoughtful offerings. This book was ultimately born from a series of lunchtime conversations between Bren and me—the vision of the tacit dimension I owe to her suggestion, and I will continue to explore this topic for many years to come.

Bren

After all the work that is put into completing a PhD program, you move on with life, working, raising a family, and anything else that can fit into a crazy schedule. This book is a long time coming. With years of working in Human Resources and higher education, having a practical application of material for training and development purposes is always welcomed and needed in an organization.

I wanted to deeply thank the individuals who agreed to be participants in the research survey conducted for the writing of this book, and an accompanying workbook was developed. Your insights and feedback are so valuable. I could not have done this without you, and for that, I am forever grateful.

I also want to thank Routledge and the reviewers of our proposal for seeing the need and value of the book.

I would be remiss if I did not mention my heartfelt thanks to my husband, who continues to push me to share my tacit knowledge with others, and for all the support from my friends and family who have been my cheerleaders throughout this process. This is a subject that is near and dear to my heart, and I am excited to be sharing it with the world.

ABOUT THE AUTHORS

Dr. Nahanni Freeman, PhD, completed her doctoral degree in psychology at Rosemead School of Psychology at Biola University and her predoctoral internship at the Doernbecher Children's Hospital, later going on to a post-doctoral fellowship in medical psychology at the Oregon Health Sciences University. She is a member of the Society for the Psychology of Aesthetics, Creativity and the Arts and the Society for Industrial and Organizational Psychology. Earlier in her career, Nahanni pursued a range of clinical experiences, working for a time on a medium security unit at the Oregon State Hospital as a psychologist. She also worked as a school psychologist in Colorado and offered clinical services to Denver area patients residing in elder care facilities. Dr. Freeman is currently the director of research and professor of clinical psychology at George Fox University, having previously been a professor of psychology at Colorado Christian University, within the undergraduate department. She began teaching for Colorado Christian University as an affiliate in 2001 and became a full-time assistant professor in 2004, an associate professor in 2008, and a full-time professor in 2022. While at Colorado Christian, Nahanni developed a research internship program, offering mentorship within an apprenticeship model to dozens of students and alumni. She has regularly presented collaborative research at the Rocky Mountain Psychological Association. Additionally, she has presented papers and/or posters at the American Scientific Affiliation, Southwestern Psychological Association, and Psychology and the Other. Additional affiliate teaching was completed at Regis University and Metropolitan State University of Denver.

Nahanni has published two prior books, both with Kendall-Hunt: *Social Neurocognition, Heuristics and the Psychology of Attitudes* (2022) and *Personality, Resilience and Development in Emerging Adulthood* (2022). Book chapters published recently include the following: American Cultural Symbolism of Rage and Resistance in Collective Trauma: Racially-influenced Political Myths, Counter-myths, Projective Identification, and the Evocation of Transcendent Humanity, in D.M. Goodman, E. Severeson, and H. Macdonald (Eds.) *Race, Rage, and Resistance: Philosophy, Psychology, and the Perils of Individualism* and Confessions and Quantum Uncertainties: The Violence of Language, Organismic Cells, and the Incarnation of Words in D.M. Goodman and M.M.C. Manalili (Eds), *Meaningless Suffering: Traumatic Marginalization & Ethical Responsibility*. Freeman is also the author of the article *Attitudes towards Mental Illness in American Evangelical Communities, Supernaturalism, and Stigmatization*.

Dr. Brenda "Bren" Slusser, SHRM-SCP, has made a career in Human Resources as well as spent many years in higher education. Humbly starting in an administrative capacity, Bren grew in knowledge and experience to become an executive director of HR for a school district, leaving that role in late 2023 to finish her book as well as travel with her husband for his employment, having been reminded that life is too precious and short, as we were reminded of from the sudden passing of our brother-in-law in 2023.

Bren received her PhD in Organization and Management with an emphasis on Human Resource Management from Capella University and her MBA from the University of Phoenix, all while working full time and raising a family. Her BA in Japan Studies is from the University of Washington. While this book is her first published works since the completion of her doctorate, the process has re-ignited a fire to research and write more, specifically on tacit knowledge and how it impacts organizations, through different subjects such as AI, DE&I, cross-generational teams, and the changing landscape of remote and hybrid work schedules.

She is looking forward to continuing to use her tacit knowledge gained through years of working in Human Resources, helping other organizations identify the tacit knowledge that resides within their organizations. This is seen by learning how best to utilize this tacit knowledge to maximize the organization's performance through the creativity and innovation that flourishes from the transfer of tacit knowledge and the development of solid social networks, which aid in the growth and development of an organization's greatest asset, their employees.

PART 1

The Psychology and Philosophy of Workplace Creativity

1

CONTEMPORARY SOCIAL NEUROCOGNITION AND TACIT DIMENSIONS OF PERSON PERCEPTION IN THE WORKPLACE ENVIRONMENT

Nahanni Freeman

Introduction

Catalysts for workplace creativity include democratic power structures, perspective-taking, and the power to harness the adaptive unconscious. Due to the tendency to internalize projections from the social mirror, vulnerable creatives and disadvantaged groups may experience significant damage to their self-efficacy in workplace environments that sustain system-justifying myths and social dominance hierarchies. Distortions in person-perception avert collective attention away from the creative potential captured in each employee or manager; unfortunately, these interpersonal distortions are often internalized by the individual in ways that undermine creativity, competency motivation, persistence, and human potential. Threats to self-concept increase cognitive load, impacting executive functions of the mind, priming threat detection systems, and recruiting selective attention towards the restoration of interpersonal safety.

Diversity is known to enhance workplace innovation, yet management of bias in person-perception remains challenging. This arises in part due to primitive and evolutionarily prepared neural systems that aim to reduce threat and diminish ambiguity and stimulus overload. Simplification strategies, sensitivity to contrast effects, and uncertainty avoidance are arguably hard-wired into the brain and can become habitual patterns through reinforcement, motivated cognitive processes, and chronic accessibility, which allows the individual to easily draw stereotypes to mind with minimal effort. In a power-distant workplace, the need for closure is high, and ambivalence is undermined in favor of certitude, expediency, mechanistic

DOI: 10.4324/9781003322894-2

efficiency, and precision. The systematic preference for consistency and avoidance of change, the confirmation bias applied to personnel decisions, and the impact of implicit prejudice on source credibility estimates will often be seen in workplaces that favor a social dominance orientation.

The brain is organized to provide selective attention to information that is salient, survival-oriented, emotionally significant, or personally relevant. Biases such as halo effects, memory anomalies, and inadequate surveillance of alternatives are not surprising in light of the human need to predict, simplify, and exert minimal effort while engaged in rapid, automatic processing. The unconscious can readily be primed, altering human observations and thought accessibility. Not only is sensory information processed early using feature detectors, but person perception and impressions form readily based on very limited data. Over time, distortions in person perception can be maintained through late processes that are enfolded in expectancies and perceptual sets. Top-down processes govern what people perceive and how they interpret, the potential of others. Sadly, many employees with great creative potential are subject to self-doubt, easily introjecting the reflected appraisals of their inadequacies that arrive with biased person perception; this is especially apparent for women in the workplace when they are embedded in contexts that sustain system-justifying myths related to sexist ideologies.

However, enriched workplaces can foster creativity by expanding the tacit knowledge that is gained through intuition, the adaptive unconscious, and covert processing, as described by Michael Polanyi (1966) in his philosophical work. By valuing the tacit knowledge that is gained over prolonged employment stability and recognizing the generative value of creating mentorship systems for new employees, supervisors and managers can better access the available talent in their workplace. Enriched workplaces will foster Janusian reasoning, which values the dialectical exchange of diverse ideas, debates, and consideration of what is opposite to the dominant paradigm. The invisible or disadvantaged members of the workplace community can come to be resilient provocateurs, challenging system-justifying myths and seeking to promote greater diversity of personnel, knowledge, ideas, and visions. By moving from surface-level processing of persons into more rational and inclusive analyses, power-distant workplaces can be transformed into places of equality where social exchange enlists the entire local community.

Nonconscious Processing in the Work of Michael Polanyi

A workplace environment may be enhanced or constrained through forms of nonconscious processing that are evoked within individuals, and as a part of the group mind. Below awareness, truth claims often attach to values in ways that can arrest or illuminate creative process. An epistemology, or theory of knowledge, will influence the level of weight assigned to the ambiguities that are inherent in person perception. Michael Polanyi (1966) argues in his work, *The Tacit Dimension*, that "we know more than we can tell" (p. 4). This thesis on human perception capitalizes on the notion that forms of understanding that resonate below the surface of awareness may yield a sophisticated epistemology, fostering resilience in social and organizational worlds. Insight regarding the *cues* in the environment or workplace that guide perception may be unnecessary, for workers perceive and learn organizational competence through non-conscious avenues. Awareness of the perceptual cues that inform social and workplace knowledge may be only minimally processed, and individuals may struggle to name the specific features that contribute to a whole (Polanyi, 1966, pp. 4-6).

A theory of knowledge often includes consideration of the accuracy and accessibility of human perception, memory, attention, and reasoning. Polanyi's (1966) work conceptualizes epistemology through non-conscious processing, with special relevance for workplace person perception. Polanyi provides a series of evidences to support the existence of tacit knowledge, including the ability to adopt either subject or object roles (p. 8). Non-conscious processing may alter a person's perception through a range of mechanisms, including biologically selected contrast sensitivity. Tacit knowledge may be a domain-specific developmental mechanism that is preprogrammed and canalized, or developmentally protected. A canalized trait will remain relatively invariant, despite a range of environments. In other words, the trait will persist unless very powerful intervening forces prevent its occurrence.

This chapter will address neuropsychological and social factors that are proposed to contribute to and maintain the cognitive and perceptual mechanisms that underlie tacit knowledge, which is felt to sustain creativity. Neuropsychological processes involved in distorted person perception and cognitive shortcuts will be examined in view of the human threat detection system and tendencies towards selective attention and recall. The impact of distorted person perception on the individual will be evaluated, with hypotheses regarding how to transcend, rather than merely endure, discriminatory bias.

Theory of Creative Canalization and Threat Detection Systems

When applied to the workplace, tacit knowledge sharing advocates for the importance of employee retention, intrapsychic resilience, insight into nonconscious assumptions/reactions, and interpersonal health. The current proposal builds on Polanyi's work on tacit knowledge, suggesting a synthesized *Theory of Creative Canalization* (TCC). According to TCC, workplace creativity follows a biologically prepared, interactionist path, whereby the organism confronts and neutralizes psychosocial threats in ways that either enhance or reduce access to facilitative unconscious processes. In a hostile, power-distant workplace culture, creative cognition meets with threat, which may be minimally evaluated by effortful consciousness but is rapidly processed by hypervigilant threat detection systems (TDS). These TDS operate to avoid and reduce uncertainty and are expressed through: enhanced contrast sensitivity, heuristics, egocentric bias towards the personally relevant, selective attention, early selection for person perception, and omission.

TDS can promote internalization of negative workplace projections for those with high neurotic vulnerability, a biologically influenced trait (Costa & McCrae, 1992), by interacting with the sociocultural context, increasing the activation of system justification (Jost et al., 2004), social dominance orientation (Sidanius & Pratto, 2001), and belief in a just world (Lerner, 1980). These factors reinforce existing hegemonies, provoke gender tokenism (Kanter, 1977b), and silence power-endurers. Within the hostile power-distant workplace, there will also emerge resilient provocateurs (RPs). RPs use attributional reframes and benefit from bias preparation, yielding suffering-derived creativity. RPs may also follow the route of resistance to projection, employing Janusian reasoning (Rothenberg, 1996) and maintaining allegiance to epistemic motivation as an embedded moral commitment.

Background Literature

Enriched Workplaces and Threat Neutralization

For workers who are fortunate enough to reside within an enriched workspace, creative cognition is enhanced through social collaborations, inter-disciplinary engagement, and participatory decision-making. The enriched workspace neutralizes threat, activating the adaptive unconscious (Wegner, 2002; Hofmann & Wilson, 2010) and promoting tacit knowledge. In the enriched workspace, social teams are encouraged, motivation and job involvement are enhanced by an environment built on cooperation rather than competition, and workers perceive fairness, equality, and a beneficial social exchange process. The current chapter will address the foundations of TCC in social neurocognition and traditional social psychology. TCC presumes the powerful influence of expectancy sets (Vroom, 1964) upon self-efficacy (Bandura, 1982), with the internalization of negative projections severing the creative connection to the adaptive unconscious, in the absence of *provocative resistance*.

Contrast Sensitivity and Person Perception

Interpersonal exchanges in the workplace are impacted by awareness of contrast, which underwrites truth claims. Contrast sensitivity involves the ability to distinguish between two or more objects in one's environment, which is important for adaptation and survival in hostile and power-distant organizations, but also fosters resilience in biophilous workplaces that enrich creativity. The ability to distinguish between two or more stimuli may be due to the meaning attributed to each, variations in the acuity of the human sensory systems in response to different stimuli, or activation in the threat-detection centers of the brain (Webb & Hibbard, 2019). Humans show a remarkable ability to quickly detect fear in the faces of others, which may have significance for how people respond to workplace threats. Both the human ability to detect changes in the sensory world and the importance of salience for attentional focus, impact contrast sensitivity. Salience occurs when a stimulus grabs attention, causing focus to be directed towards that stimulus. Social events that become salient are significant for workplace interactions and may affect equality and competitiveness. Strategic social exchanges appear to prompt activation in brain regions involved in attention, including the dorsolateral and dorsomedial prefrontal cortex (McDonald et al., 2020).

Cognitive Selectivity and Tacit Perception

Workplace person perception and competencies require the ability to be cognitively and emotionally *selective,* ready to detect changes in social and structural rituals. Tacit perception may involve many features that interact in multi-directional spirals, including the capacity for discrimination between similar stimuli. For example, accurate decoding of facial expressions in the workplace environment can foster rapport, while paranoid and rejection-sensitive decoding styles heighten vigilance for signs of threat. The ability to identify differences between two or more states can be facilitated when there is greater contrast sensitivity, or awareness of distinctive aspects of each stimulus.

Humans are oriented towards a particular fascination with the facial expressions of others, but cultural differences can affect the regions of activation during facial processing (Goh et al., 2010). In fact, differences in activation in the fusiform face area (FFA) of the brain were observed when Westerners were compared to East Asians on facial processing tasks. Cultural differences, even when subtle, can impact the way that contrast sensitivity functions when humans see images resembling a face (Pavlova et al., 2018).

Each workplace develops a quasi-culture, with social norms, hierarchies, and power dynamics. Culture also influences the expression of power distance between supervisors and subordinates, and cultural variation mediates mechanisms used to avoid uncertainty through inflexible rules, formalism, and dependence on authority (Hofstede, 1980). Tacit processes that govern human perception in the workplace may attach to instinctual drives for self-preservation and fear avoidance, which are unconsciously processed in ways that can stilt creativity in colleagues and subordinates.

The awareness that enhances contrast sensitivity may occur when attention appears to be focused elsewhere, such as with covert attention. Covert attentional processes may sharpen contrast sensitivity and acuity in the visual processing system (Phelps et al., 2006). The enhanced contrast sensitivity for fearful faces may occur, regardless of whether the individual directs covert attention towards the face or not. Contrast sensitivity is enhanced by the mere presence of a fearful face, and early visual processing is magnified through emotion. When covert attention is present, even if it is transient, it can potentiate these effects. One threat detection area in the brain is the amygdala, which is part of a set of structures important to emotion processing—the limbic system. The amygdala's role in contrast sensitivity suggests that there may be survival value attached to the processing of environmental novelty, including that which occurs in the social field. Novelty in the workplace can signal a threat to economic survival and can generate awareness of the hypercompetitive attitudes that tend to surface when it appears that power is relegated to the chosen few.

Contrast sensitivity is important for distinguishing changes in the environment that signal danger. Social novelty can signify threat, which may underlie the remarkable human capacity for rapid discrimination of emotion in the faces of others. Competing theories in cognitive neuroscience explore whether enhanced cortical sensitivity following novelty is transient or representative of enduring change (Gazzaniga et al., 2014, pp. 446–447). Emotional salience can be processed rapidly prior to conscious awareness, which may be in part due to the action of the amygdala (Amaral et al., 2003). While the human attentional system often fails to attend to the range of available signals in the environment, particularly when these data are presented in rapid succession while attention is diverted to a target stimulus (attentional blink or blindness), these errors in processing can be mediated by the heightened emotional valence of the stimuli (Andersen, 2005).

Top-Down Processes in Workplace Person Perception

Perception appears to have both top-down and bottom-up processes, both of which can impact and distort workplace perceptions and evaluations. Top-down processes occur when expectations and scripts strengthen awareness of sensations or other stimuli, sometimes producing perceptual biases, a high level of selectivity that causes individuals to ignore impor-tant features in their environment, perceptual sets that restrict creativity and conceptual openness, or even hallucinations. High motivation, such as might be seen following threats to self-esteem or safety, can alter the mechanisms linked to top-down processing.

With bottom-up processing, sensations cause a person to attend to changes in the environment. These sensations are later perceived and sub-jectively labeled. Prior to conscious attention being directed to a target, bottom-up processing may enhance the detection of stimuli, possibly due to a lower threshold for awareness with less reliance on typical memory encoding. When the threshold for detecting threats is low, as would occur in a workplace culture of fear, hypervigilant attention and exaggerated emotional responses may emerge, compromising creativity, constrain-ing interpersonal trust, and prompting social obsessions. In consideration of the affective persistence of some sensations, Andersen (2005, p. 171) writes, "perceptual representations of arousing events may burn brighter and longer relative to competing neutral distractor events." Heightened emotion may cause some features of attention and memory to sharpen and others to level. When the heightened emotion is founded on hypercom-petitive attitudes, high power distance, and workplace inequality, threats to cognitive processes can emerge and decrease workplace competence.

Uncertainty Avoidance in the Workplace and Perceptual Biases

Veiled exchanges in the workplace tend to increase ambiguity, triggering uncertainty avoidance strategies. Uncertainty avoidance primes the indi-vidual to notice ideas and people who deviate from the collective. Prim-ing may alert an individual to attend to particular concepts, causing an exclusion of attention that may render invalid performance appraisals in the workplace. When the social and economic data in the workplace are complex, and there is qualitative or quantitative overload (French et al., 1982), a greater strain is placed on cognitive load, and processing speed and efficiency may be decreased due to the divided attention that accom-panies anxious preoccupation.

Implied in Polanyi's (1966) work is the importance of selective attention in the processing of subliminal and veiled social messages. Selective atten-tion allows the individual to ignore aspects of the environment that might be distracting or irrelevant, focusing attention on those matters that have value for adaptation or survival. Selective attention appears to be impacted by: cognitive load and capacity, personal relevance, goals, arousal states, and reflexive responses to sudden changes in the environment that could signify some kind of physical or psychological threat (Gazzaniga et al.,

2014, p. 274). Selective attention is particularly adaptive to use when divided attention is called for, such as in the information-rich, ambiguous and stratified mosaic of the social world.

The work of Corbetta et al. (1991) reveals that sensitive identification of visual features is greater for singular than divided attention, with discriminatory proficiency related to activation of specialized areas of the extrastriate cortex. Thus, centers of visual processing show altered functions in response to selective attention, which may be affected by priming and environmental cues. Selective attention to spatial locations and filtering out irrelevant information appear to occur in the pulvinar nucleus of the thalamus (Desimone et al., 1989), an area of the brain that is also impacted by motivational factors and need states. Corbetta et al. (1991) found that attentional selection and filtering may also drive feature detection, or the ability to discriminate the shapes and outlines of objects. The authors suggest that top-down processes may prompt attention to regular sensory awareness, acting as a prime to visual regions in the cortex. In addition, selective and divided attentional strategies seem to activate unique brain regions, respectively. Selectivity can sharpen focus in the workplace in ways that either enhance efficiency or lead to omission errors. Divided attention typically reduces comprehension for the ignored line of incoming data while enhancing attention for the area of focus.

Humans rapidly form assumptions about others. In fact, Ambady and Rosenthal (1993) found that students form impressions of their professors within about 30 seconds of meeting them, and these impressions tend to correlate highly with end-of-semester evaluations. Perhaps top-down processes and perceptual sets govern such evaluative processes, reminiscent of halo effects (Beckwith & Lehmann, 1975; Rosenberg et al., 1960), which interfere with complete data processing. When selective attention colors visual perceptions, the alterations that occur in visual processing for selective information occur prior to the comprehensive scrutiny of the stimulus. Attention to spatial information occurs even earlier than attention to feature-specific details within the visual system (Schoenfeld et al., 2007), which makes evolutionary sense in terms of threat detection. If the spatial location of an object is not attended to, feature detectors are suppressed for the object that was not attended to.

Inattentiveness can lead to significant omission errors connected to workplace inequalities. The contributions of some employees or managers may be emphasized and sharpened, while leveling and retrieval failures may prevent other workers from advancement. As with figure-ground phenomena in visual perception, workplace hierarchies may cause some contributors to be eclipsed. The selectivity of the visual and attentional systems may also impact impression management and the ability to accurately decode facial expressions, contributing to the unconscious tacit knowledge that Polanyi (1966) refers to. Schoenfeld et al. (2017) found that attentional selection of an entire feature (color and motion) increased activation in visual cortex areas more rapidly than discrimination within a feature (such as discriminating two colors from each other). The features of an object that one attends to bind together, forming a perceptual unity. In sum, the authors conclude that visual processing of color is modulated by selective attention, and neuronal activation speed depends on the type of selective attention being used. When color is discriminated from motion, neural activation begins early. When a feature is deemed irrelevant, the neural activation takes longer to occur, and the finer details of the object may not be readily apparent.

These findings may have metaphorical relevance for interpersonal discrimination, which is often implicit and subject to early processing based on subtle nonverbal cues. Cast-offs in the workplace are deemed irrelevant to supervisory goals in high power-distance cultures. Consistent with evidence on discriminatory processes, biased person perceptions are more likely when credentials or liabilities are in the moderate range, introducing ambiguity that makes it more difficult to discern the difference between objects or persons, as shown with the case of McClesky vs Kemp (Wrightsman, 2001). Early selectivity in person perception can lead to abusive effects of the toxic organizational culture, causing some workers to feel dismissed, devalued, disrespected, and undermined.

Divided Attention and the Limits of the Human Attentional Capacity

Attentional shifts impact creative cognition, as well as self-conscious and interpersonal forms of awareness. Divided attention occurs when a person focuses on more than one stimulus at a time, which reduces memory encoding and efficiency. In the ambiguous and variegated context of the social and workplace environment, divided attention is common. Applied to Polanyi's (1966) work, the reviewed research implies that divided attention may be less specific and slower than selective attention. Selective attention is the dominant perceptual approach, as it simplifies the informational field. Selectivity may provoke the tendency to notice the most salient social cues while prompting the failure to detect a range of additional social features that are present during divided attention. Perhaps social engagement is invariably a form of divided attention, due to the array of inputs involved. Nevertheless, when presented with an array of competing social inputs, humans will gravitate towards selectively attending to particular features, such as facial expressions and body language, particularly orienting towards individuals who are socially dominant or threatening.

The susceptibility of the human memory system to error is well documented and includes the misinformation effect, false memory paradigms, imagination inflation, and source misattribution (Nichols & Loftus, 2019). While prior research has shown that those with higher fantasy-proneness, a higher need for cognition, lower working memory capacity, and dissociative susceptibility may be more likely to exhibit some of these effects, there are also studies that fail to report such individual differences (Nichols & Loftus, 2019). Furthermore, there does not appear to be an identifiable pattern of traits that reliably predict memory accuracy. Nevertheless, only *accurate* episodic memories seem to be processed by the hippocampus, while familiarity recall appears not to be (Aggleton & Brown, 1999). While judgments based on whether a stimulus is familiar involve the perihinal cortex of the temporal lobe and the medial dorsal nucleus of the thalamus, episodic memories, which are bound to time and place, are processed by the diencephalon and hippocampus. Eventually, neuroimaging data may assist with distinguishing familiarity-based recognition from actual memories; for now, it is hypothesized that the former often govern human action and can become conflated with certitude. In sum, familiarity operates in different brain regions than actual recall, and it seems probable that much of human social processing relies on a vague sense of recognition, which would be aligned with Polanyi's (1966) notion of tacit knowledge.

Under conditions of threat to the self, derogation of outgroups is more likely, which appears to be mediated in part by retrieval-induced forgetting (Pica et al., 2016). Modifications in recall may result from attentional adjustments that are present in the face of a threat, disrupting encoding. In a nonclinical sample, Sagliano et al. (2018) found that participants showed difficulty decreasing attentional focus on threats after recalling fear-related autobiographical details. Memory anomalies such as retrieval-induced forgetting signify the contextual forces that influence human perception and may contribute to decreased creativity for under-represented and under-valued employees. When the self is threatened, this may yield implications not only for the target's cognitive processing but also for the observer.

Unconscious Processing and Primes

Workplace primes include a range of stimuli that trigger implicit assumptions, threat, reward, and interpersonal bias. Polanyi's (1966) work coincides with psychology's historical interest in the significance of subliminal processing. Recent work in the study of neural activation patterns in networks of cells suggests that unconscious processing may be the most significant form of consciousness, showing high resilience even as pairings between simultaneously firing neurons decline (Lucinia et al., 2019).

Subliminal priming with human faces, regardless of affective valence, tends to heighten attention to the facial expressions of subsequent faces (Huang et al., 2019).

People are prone to focusing on the features of faces that resemble their own faces, as shown by studies of egocentrically oriented facial priming. However, exposure to egocentrically oriented facial priming tends to decrease the subsequent ability to accurately decode the facial expression in additional images. This suggests a lingering effect of self-relevant information, which may decrease visual memory encoding. Faces that look like one's own capture attention, which is consistent with other findings in social psychology on the salience effects of personal relevance. In conditions of threat, people will tend to focus more on protecting self-esteem, leading to distressing self-focused attention that undermines the availability of other cognitive and creative processes. Subliminal information also has the potential to alter executive functions of the mind, including the ability to change attentional focus, understand the meaning or significance of events, and engage in goal-directed acts (Ansorge et al., 2014). It is argued in the current chapter that social perception is largely subliminal, and the impact of preconscious data on the ability to focus and solve workplace problems may be significant.

Nevertheless, while Polanyi (1966) and others emphasize the importance of unconscious person perception, other authors remain skeptical of subliminal consciousness, de-emphasizing it as a major feature of human social and cognitive perception. It is possible that the unconscious contains greater awareness and accessibility than was once believed. For example, the *feeling-of-knowing* may be *consciously* mediated, assisting with problem solving in tasks that present subliminal visual details (Dongart & Kyllingsbeak, 2019). Subliminal processing studies often use masked primes, where a stimulus is embedded within a sequence in order to make it invisible (Ansorge et al., 2014). Whether the *feeling-of-knowing* contains aspects of conscious processing or not, it is likely a different cognitive form than effortful control, and it may be more prone to the types of egocentric bias that pervade many heuristics. The role of heuristic processing in workplace creativity remains elusive, but it is hypothesized that it may primarily serve to constrain creativity, despite the thesis that unconscious processes are generally expansive for the creative impulse.

Motivated Processing and Egocentric Phenomena

Human cognitive processes are prone to many forms of bias and error, including the tendency to struggle with seeing other people's perspectives, an issue referred to as *egocentric bias*. There is a quality to human cognition that excessively orients thinking towards one's own point of view, prompting inaccuracies in attempts to understand other people's minds. Egocentric bias is often revealed in the unique cognitive processes that surround personally relevant information, serving to enhance motivation, a known element of workplace success.

Polanyi (1966) discusses how tacit knowledge is goal-oriented and centered around personally relevant material (p. 10). When information is self-relevant, it is likely to be more carefully scrutinized (Petty & Cacioppo, 1986). Dual processing theories, such as the elaboration likelihood model (Petty & Cacioppo, 1986), predict that messages may be evaluated through deep cognitive analysis (central processing) or through the more common peripheral processes that focus on surface features (Chaiken, 1987; Chaiken & Trope, 1999; Smith & DeCoster, 2000). The likelihood of engaging in central processing is altered by situational variables that impact one's motivation or ability to evaluate a message, leading to either an increase or decrease in scrutiny of the message (Petty & Cacioppo, 1986). The thought processes that surround the issue become biased in line with the motivational and ability-related factors.

According to the elaboration likelihood model, when motivation and ability decrease, peripheral cues become paramount (Petty & Cacioppo, 1986). With heuristic (peripheral) processing, opinions can be forged rapidly, but with minimal depth of processing (Chaiken, 1987). These opinions are susceptible to variations in audience and communicator traits, being malleable and based on surface qualities of arguments, such as the sheer *quantity* of arguments made. Chaiken (1987) points out that persuasion may occur without perceived effortful control, and individuals may not be consciously aware of the types of rules they are using to make decisions.

The role of social memory, attention, and processing is highly relevant for the workplace, which tends to favor cooperative engagement and teams. Smith and De Coster (2000), based on a synthesis of neuropsychological data within social cognition, concluded that humans have at least two memory systems. The rule-based system relies on effortful and intentional retrieval and uses symbolism and cultural representations. The associative processing mode, in contrast, relies on learned connections, engaging in pattern completion. The two memory systems differ in the extent to which they rely on neural activation in the hippocampus, which is now known to play an important role in binding information to context (Gazzaniga et al., 2014). The rule-based system may enhance the formal structures needed for creativity, while the associative mode may accelerate early processing and brainstorming.

Motivated Processing, Hegemony, and Hierarchy

Motivated processing captures an important driver of completion and the dissemination of creative work, yet it may also constrain the scope of creative investigation. Within a workplace setting, which is often structured around hierarchy, power-holders and power-endurers are susceptible to persuasive implicit messages that decrease innovative expectations for workers with subordinate power. The irrational processes that yield original ideas also limit person perception and openness to innovative proposals, maintaining existing workplace hegemonies. Power structures are typically arranged to principally support the egocentric claims and objectives of the power holders.

In a study that manipulated the personal relevance of presented arguments, Petty and Cacioppo (1984) found that susceptibility to being persuaded by surface qualities of arguments was greater when the information being evaluated was of low personal relevance. Argument quality had a larger impact on persuasion when issue involvement was high due to personal relevance. This study provided support for the dual processing model that was articulated in the elaboration likelihood model. It would not be unreasonable to assume that epistemic motivation, such as the desire for accuracy in terms of person perception, may be enhanced in situations that are deemed personally relevant, capturing greater attentional resources and effortful control. Polanyi (1966) discusses how greater effort goes into interpretation when individuals attend to the end goal (p. 11). It would behoove power-holders to mark specialized attention towards proposals that appear to lack personal relevance for their own departmental objectives, and one method of shoring up consideration of the implausible-yet-inspired is to build interdisciplinary teams and programs.

Dual Processing Theories of Cognition and the Unconscious

While traditional theories of cognition contribute to a rich conversation about workplace creativity and interpersonal dynamics, more recent theoretical considerations in dual processing theories challenge some of the notions proposed by earlier models. For example, Baumeister and Bargh (2014) point out that, while prior discussions of the unconscious tended to consider controllability and awareness, it could also be the case that the unconscious mind resembles the conscious more than previously acknowledged. These authors contend that intentionality may not be the best way to distinguish conscious from unconscious processing. Some contemporary models de-emphasize conscious/non-conscious competition, arguing for complementary processes that can be distinguished through awareness and the ability to report.

Baumeister and Bargh (2014) acknowledge the pervasive evidence for nonconscious processing, even suggesting that conscious experience is derived from the unconscious. The authors argue that Libet's (2006) research on conscious control of motor behavior has been often misunderstood. In Libet's (2006) paper, he explores the interaction between mind and brain, suggesting that the mind is the subjective aspect of cognition called the 'cerebral mental field' or CMF. Sensory awareness is processed with a delay, so that the CMF is aware of sensory detail after it has already transpired. Libet points out that, "unconscious cerebral processes precede a subjective sensory experience" (p. 322). Libet's research also shows that, when an intention to move occurs, it has already been predicted by neural firing. While some may interpret these findings as evidence for material monism, or the notion that mental events are due to deterministic physical causes , the data could also indicate that conscious awareness is controlled by a partially volitional unconscious.

Distal and Proximal Cues and the Unconscious

Creative disruption, and constructive group dynamics, are affected by the direction and intensity of attention. When perceiving something in close proximity or in recent time in one's memory, hyperfixation on details can obscure a global understanding and central coherence. Close-up, salient social cues grab attention and become the central focus, while more distant cues may still influence the perceiver through the unconscious. If persons focus too closely on the parts of an object, their other sensory awareness may detour. Intuitive awareness of primes can also obscure attention to distal details while altering the probability of responses. According to findings on the weapons effect, for example, people will show stronger aggressive behaviors in the mere presence of a weapon (Jacques-Philippe-Leyens & Parke, 1975). Furthermore, victims under stress will tend to focus so much on the imminent threat of a weapon, that they will fail to notice the features of the assailant's face.

In some cases, the focus on the proximate obscures the identification of a configuration. This awareness can shift as the underlying goal becomes clearer over time. As awareness of distant cues related to social meaning and goals sharpens, attention will be shuttled away from the proximal cues. Dörfler and Ackermann (2012) provide an example of trying to find one's way around in a dark room by using a stick. Initially, one may be aware of the end of the stick in the hand, using it to probe the room. But eventually the focus shifts to the imagined layout of the room, and attention to the stick wanes. Likewise, writers will often attend first to meaning, which is the distal purpose of writing, but this draws attention away from mechanics, spelling, and grammar. Polanyi (1966) provides the example of how people gain an overall gestalt (completed perception) of a face without being able to think of the close-up features out of context. Proximal workplace cues are difficult to draw into conscious awareness; we may know them only when they serve to help us understand the whole.

Tacit workplace knowledge is functional because it directs us towards an aerial view of objectives, missions, and performance appraisal gestalts. Nevertheless, it would be misleading to assert that proximal cues and distal evaluations represent an objective external reality. The functional element of tacit knowledge implies that we only know the proximal cues because they help us to identify or predict the distal end (Polanyi, 1966, p. 10). Humans do not directly experience the distal stimulus, and "the object as perceived is not equal to the stimuli that are actually in contact with the person" (Heider, 1958, p. 28).

The contrast between internal perceptual realities and external realities, which evades naïve realism (seeing as believing), is a principle discussed in Heider's (1958) work, which was influenced by Gestalt research in perception, including the work of Wolfgang Köhler and Kurt Lewin. Heider's interpersonal theory is rooted in a broad tradition of early social cognition, such as perspectives of person perception advanced by Bruner and Tagiuri, which include consideration of the limited accuracy of human person perception, processes guiding perceptions, and emotion decoding (Heider, 1958, p. 22). Like Egon Brunswik, Heider acknowledges similarities in the processes used for the perception of human and inanimate objects (p. 23), while showing that the distal stimulus is mediated through sensory organs; the proximal stimulus is directly near the individual or may be internal. Polanyi's (1966) incorporation of distal and proximal cues in perception advances the theory of tacit perception, yet he does not adequately attribute his ideas to forerunners in his work.

Projections and Attitude Consistency

Projective processes catapult internal states, deficiency needs and nonconscious bias towards the workplace Other, driving heuristics that rest on a default of inertia. Attitude consistency maintains a sense of workplace safety by facilitating uncertainty avoidance. This drive for certitude can also block innovation. Building on the tendency to perceive invariants in shape, size and color, Heider (1958) proposes a constancy principle for social perceptions, whereby one's views of other people's "wishes, needs, beliefs, abilities, affects, and personality traits" are unlikely to change, despite maturation in the Other (p. 28). Once impressions are formed of colleagues, managers, or subordinates, these attitudes will tend to resist change, even after many years of developmental change and intervening variables have transpired. In a sense, person perception in the workplace can become fixated in ways that hinder collective and individual growth, causing the other person to freeze.

A consideration of goal-directed elements of the social world is fundamental to evolutionary psychology. The foundational belief in natural selection causes evolutionary psychologists to consider the genesis of attributes that are specific to particular circumstances (domain-specific adaptations), useful for general adjustment (domain-general adaptations), and which represent social modifications (Greenberg et al., 2015). The goal-directed value of social behavior is underscored by the assertion that, "from birth on, human beings cannot survive without extensive relationships with other human beings" (Greenberg et al., 2015, p. 40). There is evolutionary value to being able to rapidly decode the intentions of other humans, and some of these translations may occur almost instantaneously, even with nonconscious processing.

The ability to detect aggressive intentions in others is important for survival, as is the act to neutralize threat. Subliminal processing of aggressive cues can increase the likelihood that people will view others as aggressive (Todorov & Bargh, 2002). Attitudes that are frequently entertained are also readily drawn to mind, making them chronically accessible for memory retrieval. Environmental primes for violence can produce chronically accessed schemas, or sets of beliefs (Todorov & Bargh, 2002), which prime a person to take self-protective action. Attentiveness to social cues can occur with very little conscious monitoring due to the survival value of detecting aggression in others, yet hypervigilance may also promote misattributions for ambiguous social cues, harming workplace relational quality. As projections from the distorted social mirror are internalized into the target, innovative output and motivation are both likely to decrease.

Interpersonal Trust in the Workplace

Creativity often emerges within a social context, and power differentials and person-perception processes may facilitate or obscure innovation in the workplace. In considering person perception in the workplace, it is important to evaluate the role of interpersonal trust between employees and administrators. In a study of 651 county employees in a suburban community, it was found that trust between administrators and employees was one of the factors most predictive of acceptance of performance-related feedback (Reinke, 2003). Performance analysis in the workplace is an inherently interpersonal process that is impacted by the employee's level of broad understanding of the evaluative systems in place. Perceptions of favoritism undermine trust in the objectivity of the system, and Reinke (2003) discusses the importance of this for appropriate workplace boundaries. Supervisory analysis of the performance appraisal process was much more predicted by the view of the practical utility of systems with interpersonal dimensions being de-emphasized. This highlights the distinctive areas of selective attention that are stimulated when workers adopt varying roles. The egocentrism bias limits the ability of supervisors and subordinates to fully consider each other's perspectives.

Power Distance and Appraisals of Performance Feedback

Power distance can vary by culture and organizational context, and refers to dynamics where subordinates are afraid to disagree with supervisors, show dependence on authority, prefer to receive detailed instructions, and favor managers who make autocratic, paternalistic decisions (Hofstede, 1980). In a study of acceptance of performance feedback in a high power-distance culture, Moon (2019) found that trust in the manager and the specificity of feedback affected job satisfaction, including positive emotions towards the workplace. Job satisfaction correlates highly with job involvement, defined as the tendency to connect the job to one's self-concept. Job satisfaction can promote organizational commitment, decrease turnover, and correlate with job performance (Brown & Peterson, 1993; Iaffaldano & Muckinsky, 1985).

A meta-analysis of job satisfaction among salespersons found highly consistent predictors across a range of studies and contexts (Brown & Peterseon, 1993). The best predictor of satisfaction was role perception, followed by supervisory behaviors and factors related to the job tasks. Role ambiguity predicted lower performance and higher turnover, while role conflict reduced organizational commitment. It is surprising to note the low correlations between career satisfaction and job performance, which have been examined through meta-analysis (Iaffaldano & Muchinsky, 1985). Nevertheless, many organizational theories include the goal of increasing worker satisfaction as a possible means towards increased productivity. While it may be difficult to demonstrate direct relationships between job satisfaction and creativity, it is hypothesized that overall well-being and work-life balance may prove fruitful for innovation. Awareness of the influence of intuitive and subliminal qualities of person perception may serve to advance interpersonal trust and job satisfaction. However, awareness of the tacit dimensions of person perception may not yield improvements in creativity unless this knowledge prompts a movement towards greater appreciation of diversity, movement into more democratic power structures, and elimination of passive aggression and overtly hostile exchanges.

Job Involvement and Social Exchange

Investment in, and commitment to, one's career would plausibly support innovation. Tacit forms of knowledge may potentially interact with both investment in, and commitment to, one's job and collegial context. Worker satisfaction predicts job involvement, as shown by a study of 150 staff members at a university in Nigeria (Akinbobola, 2011). Job involvement can be predicted by contingent rewards, positive relationships with co-workers, and satisfaction with supervision. The relationship between job satisfaction and improved job involvement may occur due to feelings of obligation associated with social exchange theory (Emerson, 1976) and reciprocity (Cropanzano & Mitchell, 2005). In the Homans (1958) propositions regarding social exchange, focus is placed upon how reinforcement stamps in associations, and satiation is thought to decrease the reward-behavior connection, while deprivation increases it (Emerson, 1976). Behavioral principles and contingencies may be beneficial for workplace motivation and task completion, but if rewards are used to justify creative efforts, intrinsic motivation may decrease, as shown by the over-justification effect (Deci, 1972).

Social balancing and tacit or explicit perceptions of fairness may influence an enriched climate where workplace creativity is maximized. Important also to social exchange is the notion of reciprocity, which includes the idea that people receive what they have earned (Goulder, 1960; Cropanzano & Mitchell, 2005), an underlying view important to just world theory (Lerner, 1980). The just world theory was influenced by a range of foundational concepts in social cognition, which demonstrated that it is aversive when beliefs are disconfirmed, and emotionally distressing when beliefs that are deemed to be important contradict other beliefs. The notion that people want to live in an ordered world, where they can take actions to mitigate their own suffering underlies the belief in a just world. When the perception of an ordered and fair workplace culture is undermined, workers may resort to self-protective hibernation rather than innovation, holding low expectations that effort will yield success and recognition, as predicted by Vroom's (1964) expectancy theory.

The role of social exchange theory for workplace creativity merits further investigation, and workers and supervisors may intuit the level of reciprocity in workplace systems, seeking to maintain homeostatic balance. Social exchange theory (SET) has been critiqued for having inadequately defined and not fully integrated theoretical components, making it difficult to test the various elements that comprise the theory (Cropanzano & Mitchell, 2005). Part of this challenge may be due to the fact that this theory has interdisciplinary roots, bringing together psychology and economics (Emerson,

1976), anthropological ideas going back to the 1920s, and sociological theories from the 1960s (Cropanzano & Mitchell, 2005). The critique of SET rests on the arguable assumption that psychological theories have mutually exclusive tenets and that the goal of research in social science is to disprove or sustain elements of such theories. In contrast, it may be more beneficial to consider the possibility of multiple layers of truth when examining human behavior and to have the goal of better systematizing the sets of contingencies and probabilities that facilitate rudimentary predictions of actions.

An important element of SET, which has relevance for the employment setting, is the importance of reinforcement. While overt awareness of incentives and punishments can motivate, reinforcers can also operate below the threshold of awareness in some cases, functioning as tacit knowledge. Homans (1961/1974) discusses how each individual serves as a stimulus for the other, pointing out that physical proximity and the expectation of reward can alter the sequence of interpersonal actions. If prompted by angry emotions, actions that harm the target may provide reward. Social punishment may be observed through the withholding of rewards. Avoidance of aggression or The Frustrating Other may also serve as a reinforcer. Although Homans admits that interactions may follow a homeostatic principle, consistent with Heider's (1958) theory, he is also critical of the model. Homans acknowledges that some individuals may tolerate more ambiguity than what Heider's Balance Theory would predict, and Homans dismisses the need for a separate theory. In contrast, Heider's (1958) theory uses mathematical models to reveal the forms of imbalance that can occur between two persons when they have different preferences regarding objects, ideas, persons, or other entities. A balanced state for Heider (1958) is one in which there "is no stress towards change" (p. 201). Indeed, workplace environments will tend to restrain innovation in favor of consistency, predictability, and homeostasis.

Building on the work of Homans (1961/1974), Emerson (1976) discusses elements that derive from social reinforcement, including the habituation to rewards (comparison levels used when thinking about one's fortune/misfortune), the decreasing value of rewards if they have been recently received (diminishing marginal utility, which may connect to need), cost (aversive social interactions or lost time and effort/opportunities), and preference hierarchies (level of value assigned to a given reward by an individual). After adapting to a given level of reinforcement, the *removal* of the reward will be much more aversive (and hence motivating), than the initial provision of the enticement. This principle is based on comparisons to recently received rewards. These adjustments relate to contrast effects and reference points, which are often tacitly impactful on attitudes, motivation, and self-appraisals.

Humans will work to maintain balance or homeostasis in social, psychological, and biological systems; the internal feedback loop of consistency can restrain the kind of revolutionary action and thought that is required for innovation. This orientation towards the moderate underlies the *satiation-deprivation principle*, which posits that the value assigned to a reward will diminish, based on the number of reward *units* recently earned (Emerson, 1976). If deprivation precedes the reward, the reinforcer will hold greater value and be more salient, as has been noted in prior research on the reinforcing effects of social approval for those who have been deprived of it (Erikson, 1962). The effects of deprivation on the activation in pleasure regions of the medial forebrain bundle have been noted in animal studies (Routtenberg & Lindy, 1965), and deep brain stimulation of the structure has been shown to reduce the anhedonic low pleasure seen in depression (Dandekar et al., 2019). Deprivation often occurs through tacit social agreements, creating a hunger for affirmation that preoccupies the vulnerable individual. Connections between the creative impulse and suffering are not unknown, but it is likely that strained cognitive load interferes with the kind of incubation needed for project completion, visionary thinking, and optimism.

Effort Justification and Rewards

Rewards can prompt initial motivation and stimulate workplace creativity, but may lose potency once satiation and habituation occur. For the human organism, the relationship of rewards to creative motivation is also mediated by attributions about why one pursues creative mastery and completion. The principles of diminishing marginal utility and habituation to rewards may have even more value when juxtaposed with the contentions of effort justification (Aronson & Mills, 1959) and cognitive dissonance (Festinger, 1957). In a foundational study on effort justification, females who had to undergo an embarrassing initiation ritual to join a group later reported that they found the group more attractive than females who had experienced a milder form of initiation (Aronson & Mills, 1959). This suggests that people come to value things more when they must sacrifice for them, for there is an internal process of attribution whereby individuals explain their own behaviors in light of the presence or absence of rewards. At times, attributional ambiguity in the workplace leaves employees in a state of uncertainty regarding the causes of their advancement or lack thereof. If the individual is tacitly reminded of a threat against their group affiliation, they may assign a discriminatory cause to foreclosed advancement. In addition, implicit reminders of one's attachment to a disadvantaged group may also decrease performance quality and persistence, consistent with the predictions of stereotype threat (Steele & Aronson, 2004).

Creative persistence in the workplace is likely a feature of organizational commitment. Job commitment factors may also be important considerations for productivity. This is in-part due to the advantage of tacit workplace knowledge that can only be developed with high employee retention. Job involvement predicts organizational commitment, performance, and the probability of longevity in the position (Brown, 1996; Zopatis et al., 2014). Job involvement connects to cognitive identification with the job, while job satisfaction relates to an emotional state of liking the job (Brown, 1996). In a meta-analysis of 212 studies on job involvement, Brown (1996) found that people with high job involvement are more likely to find their work to be meaningful, to report positive relationships with supervisors, and to view their career as challenging and complex. They are more likely to believe that they have a voice and contribute to decisions about how performance is measured. Job involvement may be a buffer for work related stress and conflicting role expectations, correlating highly with organizational commitment, which reflects attitudes and attachment to a particular agency.

Participative Decision-Making and Organizational Commitment

Participative decision-making is important to organizational commitment, and the latter predicts turnover intentions. Job satisfaction includes both intrinsic and extrinsic elements, and the former seem to more strongly connect to organizational commitment (Zopatis et al., 2014). Despite the longstanding connections between job involvement and organizational commitment and the suggestions often made in literature that the empowerment of employees in decision-making is essential, many organizational structures continue to operate in a top-down fashion (Zapatis et al., 2014). Hegemonies in the workplace may also silence the creatives whose work remains filed away, free from the constructive critique that is needed for the actualization of the work's paragon.

Epistemic Motivation in Leadership and the Confirmation Bias

In consideration of employee performance appraisals, epistemic motivation, or commitment to truth-seeking, is essential for an administrator. This epistemic motivation requires authentic engagement with data and a willingness to challenge one's preconceived notions pertaining to equity and reward. Epistemic motivation may be hindered by overconfidence, a mechanism that could evoke confirmation bias. While concerns about 'information foraging' in relation to online search processes lead researchers to investigate the potential role of overconfidence in processing blogs (Schweiger & Cress, 2019), these ideas could also be extrapolated to face-to-face workplace encounters, which carry their own version of 'social tagging.' Source credibility may impact the processing and selection of social tags, such that greater confidence in one's attitudes may promote confirmation bias, while high source credibility may lead to greater openness to messages that are not guided by prior attitudes (Schweiger & Cress, 2019). The confirmation bias is likely motivated by the desire to reduce the distressing emotions that arise when one is confronted with information contrary to an existing belief, as shown by Festinger's contention that, "the fact that people tend to associate with others who agree with them, the fact that people read newspapers which already support their existing views, etc., can all be seen as instances of dissonance reduction or as avoiding increase of dissonance" (Festinger, 1957, p. 203).

Power relationships in the workplace may connect to interpersonal trust and the perceived credibility of others, fostering self-fulfilling prophecy effects pertinent to innovation. Power dynamics in the workplace affect perceptions about who should be promoted or given power and who should be retained; these perceptions are likely to be influenced by confirmation bias in the administrator or selection team. Projective processes in the workplace and perceived source credibility may impact upward mobility, especially when the administrators who make choices about promotion are highly confident in their own ideas. The confirmation bias, which is also referred to as the congeniality bias, may be motivated by the desire to protect one's belief from competing views, and the avoidance of cognitive dissonance, which is a defensive motivation (Hart et al., 2009). This congeniality bias leads to selective exposure to information. Meta-analytic results have demonstrated that individuals who are highly confident that their own ideas are correct may show a weakened confirmation bias, which might appear counter-intuitive, but suggests that accuracy motivation is also at play (Hart et al., 2009). Congeniality effects may be lower when confidence is high and decisions can be reversed, and these effects are enhanced by defense motivation. The idea of reversible policies and projects may undermine commitment and motivation if workers believe that their efforts will be thrown away, yet the element of reversibility also decreases the threat of failure and can facilitate greater democratic engagement from a range of workers in the creative process.

Need for Closure and Frozen Attitudes

A collective cognitive style of low complexity in organizations may block innovation. The desire for definitive knowledge may be construed as the need for closure (Kruglanski & Webster, 1996). The need for closure may be driven by urgency, or the desire for rapid conclusion, and permanence, the goal of maintaining long-lasting solutions (Kruglanski & Webster, 1996).

When individuals have lower confidence and a high need for closure, but their attitudes are not yet crystallized, they are likely to rapidly seize upon ideas during an information search. However, when the need for closure is high and confidence is also high, it is more likely that individuals will attempt to freeze their attitudes in place, becoming more resistant to new information (Kruglanski & Webster, 1996). High confidence seems to impact information foraging and is also linked to the tendency to more favorably evaluate ideas that are consistent with one's own (Schweiger & Cress, 2019). Furthermore, the tendency to use prior attitudes during information foraging seems to be greater for those who perceive the target to have lower credibility.

Source Credibility and Projection

Source credibility, which can be influenced by the projective process and entrenched stereotypes, may impact the workplace by affecting the willingness of those in power to consider the proposals generated by those with less power. In a meta-analytic study that investigated a collection of empirical studies about the perceived credibility of user-generated content on health, source credibility did not have a major impact. But when variation among the studies was examined, it was determined that source credibility was more attached to the platform where the information was posted than to the individual author of the post. Content generated by experts for common websites was typically perceived to have high credibility. When internet users search blogs and discussion boards, they may have expectations of encountering layperson-generated responses. In such settings, the credibility of the information seems to be influenced by homophily or the preference for information that is consistent with pre-existing notions.

Janusian Reasoning and Openness to Change

The tendency to remain stuck with the status quo can shore up existing workplace power structures, preventing change and protecting those in hegemony from threat, but also hindering innovation. If the desire to seek out information that one agrees with is connected to an earlier stage of development in workplace branding, then closed-mindedness to innovation and experimentation should be highest in institutions that tightly control their personas. While homophily may guide perceptions of credibility (Ma & Atkin, 2017), the administrator with epistemic motivation should remain open to new perspectives, employing Janusian reasoning (Rothenberg, 1996). In a clever design, Rothenberg interviewed 22 Nobel laureates in physics, medicine, chemistry, and physiology, using a structured protocol. He also conducted a document analysis of notable innovators from the past, including Einstein, Planck, Yukawa, Bohr, Darwin, and Dirac. A thread that could be woven through all of these accounts of the creative process was the ability to simultaneously consider many opposite points of view (the Janusian process).

Four identifiable stages can be linked to the Janusian process (Rothenberg, 1996). In the motivational phase, the creative innovator shows a deliberate, intentional focus on work that is deemed to be of emotional significance. During this phase, competing perspectives are brought together in ways that could be "isomorphic with emotional conflicts and other psychological processes" (Rothenberg, 1996, p. 221). The second phase is one where the inventive deviates from the canon of traditional thought, developing polarities of viewpoint for comparison. In the third phase, the creative conceives of surprising possibilities as many opposing views are considered at the same time. The final phase involves theory construction. While this model of the creative process has been studied with respect to great individual achievements, it is generally true that these individuals are supported by a vast array of professional liaisons with colleagues, competitors, written mentors, guilds, creative friendships, and students or protégés. So, while these inventive prospectors seem to function independently, they actually have a rich engagement with others that could be considered as a creative team. In addition, while these examples are furnished by truly exceptional individuals, they may also resonate and apply to more mundane forms of the creative process, such as what is often observed in the workplace.

Gender Typing and Perceived Credibility

Gender typing may contribute to an undervaluing of female contributions to workplace innovation. Power dynamics and perceived credibility in the workplace are impacted by adherence to expected gender norms. For example, while men who exhibit anger in the workplace are awarded with higher status than men who express sadness, women who express anger in the workplace are often evaluated negatively (Brescoll & Uhlmann, 2008). In addition, female expressions of anger are likely to be attributed to internal and trait-based causes, while men's expressions of anger tend to be viewed as externally driven. According to the gender tokenism hypothesis (Kanter, 1977a), women who work in professions where their gender is under-represented will be more likely to show adverse effects on their job performance. Tokenism occurs in skewed groups where there is high homogeneity among the socially dominant members. The token members of a skewed group are often "treated as representatives of their category, as symbols rather than individuals" (Kanter 1977a, p. 208). The token status often promotes isolation for the highly visible and different one, such that they become a "stranger who intrudes upon an alien culture and may become self-estranged in the process of assimilation" (p. 207).

While widespread belief in gender tokenism exists, recent meta-analytic findings confirm that female job performance exceeds male performance, regardless of whether women are under-represented in their chosen profession (Brescoll & Uhlmann, 2008). Some forms of gender bias use positive-sounding language to seemingly elevate women while also supporting the notion that women would be better suited for alternative professions. This bias has been termed benevolent sexism by Glick and Fiske (1997), and is associated with hostile sexism and the belief that women are inferior. Opposition to gender-based affirmation is higher among those who show social dominance orientation, but lower among those with benevolent sexism, which may underscore the insidious nature of the latter, given its procurement of temporary benefits (Fraser et al., 2015).

Individuals who show a social dominance orientation (Sidanius & Pratto, 2001) are more likely to prefer organizational and social structures that are hierarchically arranged, where social inequalities prevail. Social dominance orientation is also associated with aversive beliefs about women in the workforce, including skepticism regarding women's employment and preference for traditional roles (Christopher & Wojda, 2008). The preference for the maintenance of traditional gender roles is also associated with higher levels of authoritarianism, which likely impedes workplace innovation, but may foster high allegiance and commitment to organizational policies, as well as slavish obedience.

Social Dominance Orientation in the Workplace

Within an organizational context, employees who score higher on social dominance orientation are more likely to endorse harsh tactics (Aiello et al., 2013). Socially dominant employees who work in organizations with hierarchical power structures may contribute to and maintain such structures through a process of legitimization (Aiello et al., 2013). Social dominance orientation (SDO) is associated with lower empathy and compassion (Martin et al., 2015; Sidanius et al., 2012), as well as a tendency to endorse hierarchy-enhancing myths and economic system justification (Sidanius et al., 2012), consistent with the predictions of system justification theory (Jost et al., 2004). According to system justification, people are motivated to maintain the status quo in political, economic, and organizational settings, wanting to retain hierarchies even when those exclude opportunities for some. Justifying myths are used to explain inequality, and disadvantaged groups are prone to also endorse the legitimizing narratives.

Social dominance orientation has been shown to be associated with reduced empathy, which is one of the potential explanations for why power holders fail to engage in perspective-taking towards disadvantaged and less powerful others. The effects of SDO empathy reduction tend to increase with time, while *increases* in empathy do not necessarily promote reductions in SDO (Sidanius et al., 2012). In cultures or organizations with high power distance, conformity, loyalty, and obedience are socially valued and emphasized; directive managers are preferred; and subordinates are closely supervised and monitored, which can foster lowered inter-collegial trust (Hofstede, 1980). The power holders in such environments think of subordinates as "of a different kind" (p. 122), believe that those in power *deserve* privileges regardless of legitimacy, and feel that only a select few should be independent. Within high power-distance organizations, activities are highly structured and formalized, power is centralized, and standardization is preferred.

Resilience and Bias Preparation

Resilience is a foundational principle for the completion and self-marketing needed in order to disseminate and apply creative work. Resilience in the face of inequity may be enhanced through bias preparation, which provides training and exposure to the types of inequalities and threats that may be encountered in discriminatory settings. Resilience may be impacted by the intensity of discrimination experienced. For example, in a study of women of color in the marines, it was found that resilience could still be observed with lower levels of race and gender-based discrimination, but that mental health symptoms were associated with these experiences (Foynes et al., 2013). In a study of African American males, it was found that the relationship between racial discrimination and increased risk of incarceration was mediated by depression, disengagement from conventional norms, and hostile relational attributions (Burt et al., 2012). Resilience in this group was promoted by familial protective strategies, such as ethnic racial socialization, which promotes pride and respect for black identity, as well as roles and behaviors for adaptation. Resilience was also promoted by cultural socialization, which was geared towards teaching children about their racial heritage. Lastly, preparation for bias and the development of coping strategies were features of resilience.

Conclusion

In sum, it is proposed that workplace creativity is an inherently social process, in which person perception can influence creative cognitions.

The internalization of reflected appraisals, arriving in the form of ambiguous social cues and power distant workplace policies, can truncate the initiation and completion of creative work, especially by those with neurotic vulnerabilities or reduced resilience.

Workplace creativity is also a biological process, tied to the threat-detection system, which can create a burdensome cognitive load when sympathetic nervous system arousal is elevated. Overly taxed cognitive load serves as a blockade for the advantageous tacit knowledge that could be harnessed for the creative process. Neutralization of social threat is a strongly canalized form of biological preparedness, which is often invoked in the hypercompetitive workplace context, where economic risk and self-concept deprivation are pervasive. Nevertheless, resistant provocateurs may enlist a range of strategies to promote resilience, including attributional reframes, deep investment in compensatory creative work, and bias preparation. The enriched workspace, in contrast, must be a place of systematic democracy, where unconsciously generated creativity is enhanced through participatory decision-making that includes *every* voice.

Works Cited

Aggleton, J. P., & Brown, M. W. (1999). Episodic memory amnesia and the hippocampal-anterior thalamic axis. *Behavioral and Brain Sciences, 22*, 425–444.

Aiello, A., Pratto, F., & Pierro, A. (2013). Framing social dominance orientation and power in organizational context. *Basic & Applied Social Psychology, 35*(5), 487–495. doi: 10.1080/01973533.2013.823614

Akinbobola, O. I. (2011). Conflict in human capital relationships: The impact of job satisfaction on job involvement in a workplace. *International Journal of Social Science and Humanity, 1*, 92–95.

Amaral, D. G., Behniea, H., & Kelly, J. L. (2003). Topographic organization of projections from the amygdala to the visual cortex in the macaque monkey. *Neuroscience, 118*, 1099–1120.

Ambady, N., & Rosenthal, R. (1993). Half a minute: Predicting teacher evaluations from thin slices of nonverbal behavior and physical attractiveness. *Journal of Personality and Social Psychology, 64*(3), 431–441. doi: 10.1037/0022-3514.64.3.431

Andersen, A. K. (2005). Affective information on the attentional dynamics supporting awareness. *Journal of Experimental Psychology General, 134*(2), 258–281.

Ansorge, U., Kunde, W., & Kiefer, M. (2014). Unconscious vision and executive control: How unconscious processing and conscious action control interact. *Consciousness and Cognition, 27*, 268–287. doi: 10.1016/j.concog.2014.05.009

Aronson, E., & Mills, J. (1959). The effect of severity of initiation on liking for a group. *Journal of Abnormal and Social Psychology, 59*, 177–181.

Bandura, A. (1982). Self-efficacy mechanism in human agency. *American Psychologist, 37*(2), 122–147. doi: 10.1037/0003-066X.37.2.122

Baumeister, R. F., & Bargh, J. A. (2014). Conscious and unconscious: Toward an integrative understanding of life and action. In J. Sherman, B. Gawronski, & Y. Trope (Eds.), *Dual-process theories of the social mind* (pp. 35–49). Guilford Press.

Beckwith, N. E., & Lehmann, D. R. (1975). The importance of halo effects in multi-attribute attitude models. *JMR, Journal of Marketing Research (Pre-1986), 12*(000003), 265. Retrieved from http://ezproxy.ccu.edu/login?url=https://www-proquest-com.ezproxy.ccu.edu/docview/208743365?accountid=10200

Brescoll, V. L., & Uhlmann, E. L. (2008). Can an angry woman get ahead? Status conferral, gender, and expression of emotion in the workplace. *Psychological Science, 19*(3), 268–275.

Brown, S. P. (1996). A meta-analysis and review of organizational research on job involvement. *Psychological Bulletin, 120,* 235–255.

Brown, S. P., & Peterson, R. A. (1993). Antecedents and consequences of salesperson job satisfaction: Meta Analysis and assessment of causal effects. *Journal of Marketing Research, 30,* 63–77.

Burt, C. H., Simons, R. L., & Gibbon, F. X. (2012). Racial discrimination, ethnic-racial socialization, and crime: A micro-sociological model of risk and resilience. *American Sociological Review, 77*(4), 648–677.

Chaiken, S. (1987). The heuristic model of persuasion. In M. P. Zanna, J. M. Olson, & C. P. Herman (Eds.), *Social influence: The Ontario symposium* (Vol. 5). Psychology Press. First published by Lawrence Erlbaum & Associates in 1987; Reprinted in 2014 by The Psychology Press.

Chaiken, S., & Trope, Y. (Eds.). (1999). *Dual-process theories in social psychology.* Guilford Press.

Christopher, A. N., & Wojda, M. R. (2008). Social dominance orientation, right-wing authoritarianism, sexism, and prejudice toward women in the workforce. *Psychology of Women Quarterly, 32,* 65–73.

Corbetta, M., Miezin, F. M., Dobmeyer, S., Shulman, G. L., & Petersen, S. E. (1991). Selective and divided attention during visual discriminations of shape, color, and speed: Functional anatomy by positron emission tomography, *Journal of Neuroscience, 11,* 2383–2402.

Costa Jr, P. T., & McCrae, R. R. (1992). The five-factor model of personality and its relevance to personality disorders. *Journal of Personality Disorders, 6*(4), 343–359.

Cropanzano, R., & Mitchell, M. S. (2005). Social exchange theory: An interdisciplinary review. *Journal of Management, 31,* 874–900.

Dandekar, M. P., Saxena, A., Scaini, G., Shin, J. H., Migut, A., Giridharan, V. V., … & Fenoy, A. J. (2019). Medial forebrain bundle deep brain stimulation reverses anhedonic-like behavior in a chronic model of depression: Importance of BDNF and inflammatory cytokines. *Molecular Neurobiology, 56*(6), 4364–4380. doi: 10.1007/s12035-018-1381-5

Deci, E. L. (1972). Intrinsic motivation, extrinsic reinforcement, and inequity. *Journal of Personality and Social Psychology, 22*(1), 113–120. doi: 10.1037/h003235

Desimone, R., Wessinger, M., & Schneider, W. (1989). Effects of deactivation of lateral pulvinar or superior colliculus on the ability to selectively attend to a visual stimulus. *Social Neuroscience Abstracts, 1,* 162.

Dongart, R., & Kyllingsbeak, S., (2019). Masked priming in a semantic selection task reveals 'feeling of knowing' experiences but no subliminal perception. *Journal of Consciousness Studies, 26*(5–6), 6–34.

Dörfler, V., & Ackermann, F. (2012). Understanding intuition: The case for two forms of intuition. *Management Learning, 43*(5), 545–564. doi: 10.1177/1350507611434686

Emerson, R. M. (1976). Social exchange theory. *Annual Review of Sociology, 2,* 335–362.

Erikson, M. T. (1962). Effects of social deprivation and satiation in verbal conditioning in children. *Journal of Comparative Physiological Psychology, 55,* 953–957.

Festinger, L. (1957). *A theory of cognitive dissonance.* Stanford University Press.

Fraser, G., Osborne, D., & Sibley, C. (2015). "We want you in the workplace, but only in a skirt!" Social dominance orientation, gender-based affirmative action and the moderating role of benevolent sexism. *Sex Roles, 73*(5–6), 231–244. doi: 10.1007/s11199-015-0515-8

French, J. R. P. Jr, Caplan, R. D., & Van Harrison, R. (1982). *The mechanism of job stress and strain.* Wiley.

Foynes, M. M., Shipherd, J. C., & Harrington, E. F. (2013). Race and gender discrimination in the Marines. *Cultural Diversity and Ethnic Minority Psychology, 19*(1), 111–119. doi: 10.1037/a0030567

Gazzaniga, M. S, Ivry, R. B., & Mangun, G. R. (2014). *Cognitive neuroscience: The biology of the mind,* 4th edition. Norton.

Glick, P., & Fiske, S. T. (1997). Hostile and benevolent sexism: Measuring ambivalent sexist attitudes toward women. *Psychology of Women Quarterly, 21*(1), 119–135. doi: 10.1111/j.1471-6402.1997.tb00104.x

Greenberg, J., Schmader, T., Arndt, J., & Landau, M. J. (2015). *Social psychology: The science of everyday life.* Worth Publishers.

Goh, J. O., Leshikar, E. D., Sutton, B. P., Tan, J. C., Sim, S. K., Hebrank, A. C., et al. (2010). Culture differences in neural processing of faces and houses in the ventral visual cortex. *Social Cognitive Affective Neuroscience, 5,* 227–235. doi: 10.1093/scan/nsq060 PMID: 20558408

Goulder, A. W. (1960). The norm of reciprocity: A preliminary statement. *American Sociological Review, 25,* 161–178.

Hart, W., Albarracín, D., Eagly, A. H., Brechan, I., Lindberg, M. J., & Merrill, L. (2009). Feeling validated versus being correct: A meta-analysis of selective exposure to information. *Psychological Bulletin, 135*(4), 555–588. doi: 10.1037/a0015701

Heider, F. (1958). *The psychology of interpersonal relations.* John Wiley & Sons. Reprinted in 2015, Martino Publishing.

Hofmann, W., & Wilson, T. D. (2010). Consciousness introspection and the adaptive unconscious. In B. Gawronski, & B. K. Payne (Eds.), *Handbook of implicit social cognition: Measurement, theory, and applications* (pp. 197–215). Guilford Press.

Hofstede, G. (1980). *Culture's consequences: International differences in work-related values* (vol. 5). Sage.

Homans, G. C. (1958). Social behavior as exchange. *American Journal of Sociology, 63,* 597–606.

Homans, G. C. (1961/1974). *Social behavior: Its elementary forms, revised edition.* Harcourt, Brace, Jovanovich, Inc.

Huang, M. A., Sun, H.-M., & Vaina, L. M. (2019). Visual attributes of subliminal priming images impact conscious perception of facial expressions. *Journal of Behavioral and Brain Science, 9,* 108–120. doi: 10.4236/jbbs.2019.93009

Iaffaldano, M. T., & Muckinsky, P. M. (1985). Job satisfaction and job performance: A meta- analysis. *Psychological Bulletin, 97,* 251–273.

Jacques-Philippe-Leyens, G., & Parke, R. D. (1975). Aggressive slides can induce a weapons effect. *European Journal of Social Psychology, 5*(2), 229–236. doi: 10.1002/ejsp.2420050207

Jost, J. T., Banaji, M. R., & Nosek, B. (2004). A decade of system justification theory: Accumulated evidence of conscious and unconscious bolstering of the status quo. *Political Psychology, 25*(6), 881–919.

Kanter, R. M. (1977a). *Men and women of the corporation.* Basic Books.

Kanter, R. M. (1977b). Some effects of proportions on group life: Skewed sex ratios and responses to token women. *American Journal of Sociology, 82,* 965–999.

Kruglanski, A. W., & Webster, D. M., (1996). Motivated closing of the mind: "seizing" and "freezing." *Psychological Review, 103,* 263–283.

Lerner, M. J. (1980). *The belief in a just world: A fundamental delusion.* Plenum.

Libet, B. (2006). Reflections on the interaction of the mind and brain. *Progress in Neurobiology 78(3–5),* 322–326. doi: 10.1016/j.pneurobio.2006.02.003

Lucinia, F. A., Del Ferraroa, G., Sigmanc, M., & Makse, H. A. (2019). How the brain transitions from conscious to subliminal perception. *Neuroscience.* Preprint downloaded from author.

Ma, J. T., & Atkin, D. (2017). User generated content and credibility evaluation of online health information: a meta-analytic study. Telemat Informatics. *Elsevier Ltd., 34,* 472–486.

Mackey, J. D., Roth, P. L., Van Iddekinge, C. H., & McFarland, L. A. (2019). A meta-analysis of gender proportionality effects on job performance. *Group & Organization Management, 44(3),* 578–610.

Martin, D., Seppala, E., Heineberg, Y., Rossomando, T., Doty, J., Zimbardo, P., … & Zhou, Y. (2015). Multiple facets of compassion: The impact of social dominance orientation and economic systems justification. *Journal of Business Ethics, 129,* 237–249. doi: 10.1007/s10551-014-2157-0

McDonald, K. R., Pearson, J. M., & Huettel, S. A. (2020). Dorsolateral and dorsomedial prefrontal cortex track distinct properties of dynamic social behavior. *Social Cognitive & Affective Neuroscience, 15*(4), 383–393. doi: 10.1093/scan/nsaa053

Moon, K. (2019). Specificity of performance appraisal feedback, trust in manager, and job attitudes: A serial mediation model. *Social Behavior and Personality: An International Journal, 47*(6), 1–12.

Nichols, R. M. & Loftus, E. F. (2019). Who is susceptible in three false memory tasks? *Memory, 27*(7), 962–984. doi: 10.1080/09658211.2019.1611862

Pavlova, M. A., Heiz, J., Sokolov, A. N., Fallgatter, A. J., & Barisnikov, K. (2018). Even subtle cultural differences affect face tuning. *PLoS ONE, 13*(6), 1–13. doi: 10.1371/journal.pone.0198299

Petty, R. E., & Cacioppo, J. T. (1984). The effects of involvement on responses to argument quantity and quality: Central and peripheral routes to persuasion. *Journal of Personality and Social Psychology, 46*, 69–81.

Petty, R. E., & Cacioppo, J. I. (1986). *Communication and persuasion: Central and peripheral routes to attitude change.* Springer-Verlag.

Phelps, E. A., Ling, S., & Carrasco, M. (2006). Emotion facilitates perception and potentiates the perceptual benefit of attention. *Psychological Science, 17*, 292–299.

Pica, G., Bélanger, J. J., Pantaleo, G., Pierro, A., & Kruglanski, A. W. (2016). Prejudice in person memory: Self-threat biases memories of stigmatized group members. *European Journal of Social Psychology, 46*(1), 124–131. doi: 10.1002/ejsp.2140

Polanyi, M. (1966). *The tacit dimension.* University of Chicago Press. Reprinted 2009.

Reinke, S. J. (2003). Does the form really matter? Leadership, trust, and acceptance of the performance appraisal process. *Review of Public Personnel Administration, 23*, 23–37.

Rosenberg, M. J., Hovland, C. I., McGuire, W. J., Abelson, R. P., & Brehm, J. W. (1960). *Attitude organization and change: An analysis of consistency among attitude components. (Yale studies in attitude and communication.).* Yale University Press.

Rothenberg, A. (1996). The janusian process in scientific creativity. *Creativity Research Journal, 9*(2,3), 207–231.

Routtenberg, A., & Linday, J. (1965). Effects of the availability of rewarding septal and hypothalamic stimulation on bar pressing for food under conditions of deprivation. *Journal of Comparative Psychology, 60*(2), 158–161.

Sagliano, L., Trojano, L., Di Mauro, V., Carnevale, P., Di Domenico, M., Cozzolino, C., & D'Olimpio, F. (2018). Attentional biases for threat after fear-related autobiographical recall. *Anxiety, Stress & Coping, 31*(1), 69–78. doi: 10.1080/10615806.2017.1362297

Schoenfeld, M., Hopf, J. M., Martinez, A., Mai, H. M., Sattler, C., Gasde, A., ... & Hillyard, S. A. (2007). Spatio-temporal analysis of feature-based attention. *Cerebral Cortex, 17*(10), 2468–2477.

Schweiger S, Cress U (2019). Attitude confidence and source credibility in information foraging with social tags. *PLoS One, 14*(1), e0210423. doi: 10.1371/journal.pone.0210423

Sidanius, J., & Pratto, F. (2001). *Social dominance: An intergroup theory of social hierarchy and oppression.* Cambridge University Press.

Sidanius, J., Kteily, N., Sheehy-Skeffington, J., Ho, A. K., Sibley, C., & Duriez, B. (2012). You're inferior and not worth our concern: The interface between empathy and social dominance orientation. *Journal of Personality, 81*, 313–323.

Smith, E. R., & DeCoster, J. (2000). Dual process models in social and cognitive psychology. *Personality and Social Psychology Review, 4*, 108–131.

Steele, C. M., & Aronson, J. A. (2004). Stereotype threat does not live by Steele and Aronson (1995) alone. *American Psychologist, 59*(1), 47–48. doi: 10.1037/0003-066X.59.1.47

Todorov, A., & Bargh, J. A. (2002). Automatic sources of aggression. *Aggression and Violent Behavior, 7*, 53–68.

Vroom, V. H. (1964). *Work and motivation*. Wiley.

Webb, A. L. M., & Hibbard, P. B. (2019). The effect of facial expression on contrast sensitivity: A behavioural investigation and extension of Hedger, Adams & Garner (2015). *PLoS One, 14*(11), 1–18. doi: 10.1371/journal.pone.0205621

Wegner, D. W. (2002). *The illusion of conscious will*. MIT Press.

Wrightsman, L. S. (2001). *Forensic psychology*. Wadsworth/Thompson.

Zopatis, A., Constanti, P., & Theocharous, A. L. (2014). Job involvement, commitment, satisfaction and turnover: Evidence from hotel employees in Cyprus. *Tourism Management, 41*, 129–140.

2

RESILIENCE

Internal and External Worlds and Flow in the Workplace

Nahanni Freeman

Developmental Factors, Context, and Individual Differences

Resilience is typically described as a capacity to overcome or manage adversity, showing adaptation and flexibility that are manifested in attention, behavior, coping, and cognition. Resilience can be organizational or individual and may be enhanced through tacit knowledge (Polanyi, 1966), which is ineffable, embodied, and integrated into perceptions and sensations through reenactment and indwelling (Stephens, 2020). The ability to recognize distal and proximal cues (Polanyi, 1966), mindfully attending to subtle cues and patterns, can enhance the capacity to reorganize and recalibrate in response to stress, challenge, and tribulation (Stephens, 2020).

In a path analysis that investigated adversity across two studies, Graham and Sinclair (2023) found that a history of childhood adversity was a significant risk factor for burnout, turnover intentions, counterproductive work behavior, and lower integrity on the job, but it was not predictive of organizational citizenship behavior (OCB). However, adult adversity did predict a lower OCB. Workplace environments that can facilitate resilient coping may allow employees to transform personal suffering into post-traumatic growth and teleological creativity. Resources such as autonomy, positive relationships, and feedback on performance can help to mitigate burnout (Bakker & Demerouti, 2016), a chronic stress response that includes exhaustion, a diminished sense of achievement, and cynicism (Maslach et al., 2001). Cognitive factors, such as the construal of greater psychological distance through time, social and spatial distality, and hypotheticals, can elicit more abstract, less detailed appraisals, influencing decision-making and

DOI: 10.4324/9781003322894-3

behaviors (Trope et al., 2007). Fostering constructive thinking and perspective may enhance resilience, which is predicted to also maximize creativity.

Preferential and affective valence, a field of forces,[1] and the expectancy that diligence will lead to valued rewards may optimize motivation (Vroom, 1964, pp. 17–23), impacting creative output. According to path-goal theory, non-authoritarian, supportive leaders who provide clarification about policies, objectives, and means of performance appraisal and who reduce role ambiguity may energize employee engagement, especially when workers have a voice and contribute to their job description (House, 1996). Effective leaders may model the kind of passionate persistence that is foundational to grit—the ability to stick with efforts towards long-term goals despite obstacles and boredom (Southwick et al., 2019). Organizational and personal grit may increase creativity through the mediator of work engagement (Gonlepa et al., 2023).

Flow, Autonomy, and Autotelic Workers

In his classic work on flow and optimizing the moments of life, Csikszentmihalyi (1990) describes case examples of autotelic workers who found purposeful and creative work through daily tasks, which were transformed into complex and developmental skills that strengthened the individual (p. 151). This mindful approach to work results in increased feelings of emancipation. By designing work that elicits the engrossment of flow states, the autotelic personality can create attainable goals and seize moments of activity that promote telos, or a sense of an end rather than a means. Flow is not identical to work engagement, and includes elements of freedom from concern with time, self, or rumination, while immersed in motivating work that requires full attention and sensed personal control (Yan & Donaldson, 2023).

According to self-determination theory (SDT), flourishing may be enhanced through a context that supports drives for relational connection, freedom, and competence (Ryan & Deci, 2018). In SDT, the self is construed phenomenologically as capable of non-conflictual volition, autonomy, self-regulation, and integration; these functions can be hindered through "need thwarting social contexts," which promote defensive maneuvers (Ryan & Deci, 2018, p. 8). Although humans may tend towards system justification as a way to reduce uncertainty by defending existing hierarchies (Jost, 2019), the rationalization of unjust or dysfunctional organizations can influence psychological safety (Porter et al., 2024) and decrease flourishing and resilience. System justification may help to explain the non-conscious internalization of derogatory self-beliefs (Jost et al., 2004), which is likely to undermine the free expression of self-determination.

Self-determination may be limited in settings where nonverbal dominance maintains hegemony, or when artifacts of power (Kenrick et al., 2005) seek to reinforce social cognitive maps. Technologies can be used to create distal power through surveillance, derived power through symbolic associations, and artifacts can delegate power to constrain movement (Brey, 2008). However, when a person is vitalized with volitional hope, she will detour the exercise of control power, which has been used to constrain growth and behavioral latitude (Brey, 2008).

Team Reflexivity and Organizational Resilience

Not only is the resilience of the individual important to creativity in the workplace, but collective adaptation and change are also significant to consider. The interplay between the individual and the group is chief, with emergent team states including collective beliefs and representations, motivated information processing, and shared emotional experiences (Zhou & Liu, 2023). One important form of organizational learning is team reflexivity, which includes problem solving, evaluation of progress towards goals, analysis of internal and external processes, and review of necessary adaptations suitable for the external world (Zhou & Liu, 2023). In a meta-analytic study, Zhou and Liu (2023) found that creativity and emergent states on teams were related to team reflexivity. Critical thinking, evaluation of routine systems, updating of information, and inter-team communication and knowledge sharing are fundamental to team reflexivity processes. Groups that engage in improvised collaboration may have the potential to move beyond groupthink into authentic complexity and innovation (Sawyer, 2017).

The creativity-enhancing effects of the group may be enlisted in settings where nonviolent solidarity can foster shared passion for justice, as shown by Martin Luther King's proclamation that "we're going to change the whole Jericho road!" (Oates, 1982, p. 391). With transformational leadership, the symbol of reformation can secure commitment to a cause that transcends self-interest; for example, King's vision of hope for a beloved community can foster the moral courage needed for creative resilience, and followers can concur with his words, "I march because I must, and because I'm a man, and because I'm a child of God" (Oates, 1982, p. 414). King carved a path that modeled the ethic that "freedom is participation in power" (Oates, 1982, p. 424).

Strategies to Enhance Workplace Resilience

Building from the Job-Demands-Resource Model (Bakker & Demourti, 2017), Stuart-Edwards (2023) found that mindfulness predicted job engagement, which was defined as being energized and motivated for one's work and finding immersion and satisfaction in job-related tasks. Increased engagement was also proposed to be shown through alterations in participant perceptions of conflict between work and home expectations, reduced belief that one's work demands were excessive, and greater ability to tolerate emotional demands. Mindfulness, an attention redirection strategy, was shown to not only to buffer high demands in the workplace, but also increase in response to these demands.

Assuming the need for relationships and self-efficacy (Ryan & Deci, 2018), altruism is likely to enhance well-being. Chong (2023) presents a theoretical model that proposes that volunteer work may enhance job absorption and creativity through a mechanism of increasing the ability to assimilate inconsistent information. The theory presents the idea that these effects will be greater when the individual attends to global and abstract aspects of the experience, rather than concrete features.

Limitations

The ineffable and nonreductive elements of tacit knowledge increase the challenge of discussing the integration of molecular social science with philosophy. It is important to delimit the boundary conditions of theoretical models while also designing tools that fit conceptually with novel theories, acknowledging implicit assumptions (House, 1996). Data collection methods will necessarily limit the generalizability and reliability of some information related to workplace resilience. For example, some data that is collected for research in industrial-organizational psychology is built from online platforms, which come with some risks related to inattention (Stuart-Edwards, 2023), BOTS, and the inability to verify demographic factors. However, there is also research available to support the use of online data collection (Stuart-Edwards, 2023). The attempt to transfer theoretical concepts to pragmatic conclusions remains elusive.

A Society of Explorers

Michael Polanyi describes a society of explorers as a free and transformative metaphysical reality, where "man is in thought" (Polanyi, 1966, p. 83). Rather than attenuating to "modern fanaticisms" or dogmatism, an extension of Polanyi's (1966, p. 83) work may manifest in orientations that seek organizational resilience through the reduction of system-justifying mythologies. Such a society might ask a series of questions: (a) Why does one who is disempowered unconsciously maintain existing hegemonies? (b) What reinforces unawareness? (c) Which types of awareness facilitate growth towards a goal (i.e. positive tacit knowledge), versus internalization of the message, *thou art the "weaker vessel?"*[2] (English Standard Version Bible, 2011, I Peter 3:7). The striving to explore in a beloved community will include the sense that one's efforts are valuable and irreplaceable, a setting that can maximize the Köhler motivation gain, but will remain influenced by contextual forces and the field (Kerr et al., 2007). Awareness of a disadvantaged status is likely to remain repressed, with artifacts of power preventing the threatening prospect of inclusion at the decision-making table.

The self-presentational style in high power-distance contexts will often call for self-promotion, yet it is difficult to be both liked and considered competent at the same time (Kenrick et al., 2005). The self-presentational dilemmas unique to the adoption of the feminine persona at work can confine the full expression of self-determination, which is significant for creative flourishing in many western ecologies. The distance between the "expected" and the "actual" impacts the level of cognitive dissonance experienced by the worker, who experiences discrepancies that can attach to work-based perfection striving.[3] The exaggeration or personalization of feedback can yield creative paralysis.

Within the low power-distance ecology, redeeming the workplace culture will lean towards the elimination of hierarchies, supporting democratic power structures, and the construction of an infrastructure to support self-determination within communities. The desire for closure and completion—being able to see something through to its end—will include tortoise and hare qualities. The tortoise may labor anonymously—mindful of the transformative power of team and citizenship. The hare will experience engrossment, aggrandizement, and flow, a self-organizing inertia.

Equality, Being-in-Relation, and the Democratic

Polanyi (1966) speaks of Term one and Term two as ways that objects and perceptions associate—in relation to each other. How can this inform us about being in relation to the systems and culture at work, the group, and the colleague? A beloved community receives a vision of justice and love, reducing the confines of binaries and seeing humans as light, rejecting the limiting representations of the Other. Collaboration, rather than competition and social comparison, can create psychological safety at work, a prerequisite for many creative expressions.

Coaching and mentorship can transform through manifesting an approach towards challenges that resists self-limiting internalizations, restores realistic goal-setting, and offers autonomous personal projects embedded into the existing structure. This transforming example is often rooted in not only flow but also commitment to values, resolve, and justice, as shown by the words of Martin Luther King, for "we're gonna march with the force of our souls…we're gonna move out with the weapons of courage. We're gonna put on the breastplate of righteousness and the whole armor of God. And we're gonna march" (Oates, 1982, p. 412).

Supervisory receptivity to change is fundamental, for the fear of change immobilizes creativity; this strangulation is often manifested in a limited view of how, when, and where work is completed. The creative workspace must be grounded in ethics. Whether this will represent the ethical idealism described by Rescher (1987), where values manifest in human action, remains to be seen. Rescher (1987) argues that "ideals can be pursued only within the limits of the possible" (p. 125). The resolve must not be neutral, for with MLK "we must say to ourselves and the world, 'I am somebody. I am a person. I am a man [woman, individual] with dignity and honor'" (Oates, 1982, p. 424).[4]

Notes

1 Vroom refers to Kurt Lewin's (1938, 1951) field of force.
2 I Peter 3:7. [7] Likewise, husbands, live with your wives in an understanding way, showing honor to the woman as the weaker vessel, since they are heirs with you[a] of the grace of life, so that your prayers may not be hindered.
3 These notions are influenced by Alfred Adler's work on perfection striving, Karen's Horney's Tyranny of the Shoulds, Sigmund Freud's excessive super-ego, and Tori Higgins' Self Discrepancy Theory.
4 Bracketed words added for contemporary context.

Works Cited

Bakker, A. B., & Demerouti, E. (2017). Job demands–resources theory: Taking stock and looking forward. *Journal of Occupational Health Psychology, 22*(3), 273.

Brey, P. (2008). The technological construction of social power. *Social Epistemology, 22*(1), 71–95.

Chong, S. (2023, April 19–22). *A conceptual model linking off-work volunteering with on-job creativity and voice* [Poster presentation]. Society for Industrial and Organizational Psychology (SIOP), 38th Annual Conference, Boston, MA.

Csikszentmihalyi, M. (1990). *Flow: The psychology of optimal experience.* Harper Perennial.

Gonlepa, M. K., Dilawar, S., & Amosun, T. S. (2023). Understanding employee creativity from the perspectives of grit, work engagement, person organization fit, and feedback. *Frontiers in Psychology, 13*, 1–14, 1012315.

Graham, B. A., & Sinclair, R. R. (2023, April 19–22). *A life course perspective on adversity and organizational attitudes and behaviors* [Poster presentation]. Society for Industrial and Organizational Psychology (SIOP), 38th Annual Conference, Boston, MA.

House, R. J. (1996). Path-goal theory of leadership: Lessons, legacy, and a reformulated theory. *Leadership Quarterly, 7*(3), 323–352.

Jost, J. T. (2019). A quarter century of system justification theory: Questions, answers, criticisms, and societal applications. *British Journal of Social Psychology, 58*(2), 263–314.

Jost, J. T., Banaji, M. R., & Nosek, B. A. (2004). A decade of system justification theory: Accumulated evidence of conscious and unconscious bolstering of the status quo. *Political psychology, 25*(6), 881–919.

Kenrick, D. T., Neuberg, S. L., & Cialdini, R. B. (2005). *Social psychology: Unraveling the mystery* (3rd ed.). Pearson Education New Zealand.

Kerr, N. L., Messé, L. A., Seok, D. H., Sambolec, E. J., Lount, R. B. Jr, & Park, E. S. (2007). Psychological mechanisms underlying the Köhler motivation gain. *Personality and Social Psychology Bulletin, 33*(6), 828–841.

Lewin, K. (1938). *The conceptual representation and measurement of psychological forces.* Duke University Press.

Lewin, K. (1951). *Field theory in social science.* Harper.

Maslach, C., Schaufeli, W. B., & Leiter, M. P. (2001). Job burnout. *Annual Reviews of Psychology, 52,* 397–422.

Oates, S. B. (1982). *Let the trumpet sound: The life of Martin Luther King, Jr.* Harper & Row Publishers.

Polanyi, M. (1966). *The tacit dimension.* University of Chicago Press.

Porter, T. H., Rathert, C., Ishqaidef, G., & Simmons, D. R. (2024). System justification theory as a foundation for understanding relations among toxic health care workplaces, bullying, and psychological safety. *Health Care Management Review, 49*(1), 59–67.

Rescher, N. (1987). *Ethical idealism.* University of California Press.

Ryan, R. M., & Deci, E. L. (2018). *Self-determination theory: Basic psychological needs in motivation, development, and wellness.* The Guilford Press.

Sawyer, K. (2017). *Group genius.* Basic Books.

Southwick, D. A., Tsay, C. J., & Duckworth, A. L. (2019). Grit at work. *Research in Organizational Behavior, 39,* 1–17, 100126.

Stephens, J. P. (2020). From parts to whole: a place for individual tacit knowledge in organizational adaptability and resilience. In E. H. Powley, B. B. Caza, & A. Caza (Eds.), *Research handbook on organizational resilience* (pp. 102–115). Edward Elgar Publishing.

Stuart-Edwards, A. (2023, April 19–22). *The multitude of relationships between mindfulness, job demands, and work engagement* [Poster presentation]. Society for Industrial and Organizational Psychology (SIOP), 38th Annual Conference, Boston, MA.

Trope, Y., Liberman, N., & Wakslak, C. (2007). Construal levels and psychological distance: Effects on representation, prediction, evaluation, and behavior. *Journal of Consumer Psychology, 17*(2), 83–95.

The English Standard Version Bible. (2001). I Peter 3:7. Crossway.

Vroom, V. (1964). *Work and motivation.* Jossey-Bass Inc. Reprinted 1995.

Yan, Q., & Donaldson, S. I. (2023). What are the differences between flow and work engagement? A systematic review of positive intervention research. *The Journal of Positive Psychology, 18*(3), 449–459.

Zhou, J., & Liu, Y. (2023, April 19–22). *Effect of team reflexivity on team performance: A meta-analysis* [Poster presentation]. Society for Industrial and Organizational Psychology (SIOP), 38th Annual Conference, Boston, MA.

3

PERSON PERCEPTION, LANGUAGE, AND PHENOMENOLOGY OF TACIT KNOWLEDGE

Nahanni Freeman

Democratic Structure, Language, and the Emergent Environment

Optimized workplace creativity emerges in adaptive environments that foster participation in decision-making, equality, support for self-efficacy, and leadership intrigue with novel ideas. Leadership attitudes towards innovation and change transmit through explicit and implicit channels, with the employee serving as an interpreter of subtle cues intuited beyond the supraliminal. Internalization of workplace cultural norms into the self-structure may impede progress towards unconscious rivers of creativity, check association chemistry, and deliver shut-down mechanisms in the face of disempowering language. Linguistic symbolism conducts the energy of status structures, giving rise to identities within knowledge workers. Supervisory and peer support for innovation can be ascertained through tacit awareness, offering a productive vista for illumination.

Polanyi (1966) discusses the semantic features of tacit knowledge, as humans produce meaning through attentional shift and interpretation of cues (pp. 10–12). The autonomy of will allows for the disruption of attention from the proximal cue toward the distal. The relation between cues resembles the connection between parts and whole, whereby the molecules contribute to, but do not fully encapsulate, the configuration. For example, imagine that it is possible to recognize a whole face, identifying the individual attached to that face and the emotions expressed therein. However, one may struggle to identify the facial features in isolation, such as by looking at a photograph of a mouth or an eye and identifying who

DOI: 10.4324/9781003322894-4

it belongs to. The facial features are recognized as a whole percept; it is difficult to take them away from the whole and preserve their meaning. The features are attended to on some level, because they are in a tacit or implicit relationship with the whole. In this example, the facial features are the proximal term, and the face as a whole is the distal term.

The understanding of the relationship between proximal and distal cues is also relevant to goal-directed actions, or the functional elements of tacit relationships between cues. For example, one can envision an entire athletic movement, such as a skilled tennis serve by a professional player. The tennis serve could be taken apart in a slow-motion video, allowing for the comprehension of a series of small variations in muscle movements. However, as an observer, one would attend to the distal relation between all of the movements taken as a whole, with the goal of evading the opponent's return play. The focus on the goal and how it brings together the disparate elements of small muscle movements (proximal cues) into a coordinated distal whole is termed the "functional structure of tacit knowledge" (Polanyi, 1966, p. 10), because it emphasizes a motivational and contingent relationship between parts.

On the other hand, unconscious awareness of proximal cues can also present as an intuitive sense of a thing, such as an apprehension that a threat is imminent (Polanyi, 1966, p. 11). Through conditioning, proximal cues can attach to a distal event, creating a preliminary aura that allows the individual to attend to the appearance of a cue as a disruption from a steady state. These cues then trigger an expectation attached to a meaning that emerges from the joining of the proximal and distal cues. Polanyi (1966, p. 11) refers to this appraisal of a cue as significant, meaningful, and personally relevant as the "phenomenal structure of the tacit knowledge."

Within a workplace setting, communication can be thought of as a relationship between distal and proximal cues, which signify hidden meaning structures that are presumed to attach to pending reinforcers or punishers. There is the outward message of the communication, the real event of sound waves emerging from muscular changes in a communicant, and the reception audition by the listener. Yet, this muscular transmission model of language does little to facilitate understanding of linguistic nuance and hidden meaning. Nevertheless, tacit cues are constantly interpreted in an interpersonal exchange, as one attends away from micro-expressions and minute variations in vocal pitch towards the distal meaning, motivations, and goals of the other person. Perceptions of the workplace Other can be modified due to the interpretation of distal cues, with nonconscious processes impacting awareness of proximal cues based on body language, vocal cadence, and muscular changes observed in others. Perceptions of self are also emergent within the exchange, being internalized into inner language as a result of a projective process within a dialogue.

Tacit Communication of Power and Dominance Hierarchies

Communication regarding power, dominance, and status can be ascertained through rapid judgments, with some cross-cultural similarities in terms of postural expansiveness, initiation of touch, and expressions of pride (Carney, 2020). Greater social status and dominance can also be correlated with education, social economic status, leadership orientation, the extensiveness of one's social network, and outward displays of confidence (Carney, 2020). Some studies demonstrate that higher warmth may be observed in individuals who possess greater levels of social influence, implying that outward displays of confidence may be a form of compensation (Carney, 2020). For example, higher levels of competition predicted lower levels of warmth in a study by Fiske et al. (1999).

Nonverbal behavior is a transmission that must be decoded by a recipient and is embedded within an array of additional messages and behaviors within a temporal and situational context (Harper, 1985, p. 30). The face can be thought of as an "end organ," which triggers a neural and emotional response in another person, regulating social exchange and the interpersonal space between individuals (Harper, 1985, p. 32). Body movements, eye contact, and facial expressions that signify arousal, threat, or submission, as well as paralinguistic behaviors such as speech volume and latency times, can help to establish dominance, which regulates the social hierarchy (Harper, 1985, pp. 33–39).

Power may serve as a protective factor, reducing constraint in ways that help advance creativity in the workplace (Hoever et al., 2023). The positive effects of wielding power can mediate susceptibility to conformity, which may present as an obstacle to the creative process (Galinsky et al., 2008). At the same time, the experience of power may also increase susceptibility to inner conflict and cognitive dissonance, while it also seems to allow for greater idiosyncratic latitude. One strategy to address the internalization of dominance hierarchies is to become competitive with oneself, setting up perfectionistic standards that allow one to maintain an outward image that does not defy expectations for submissiveness (Mavin & Yusupova, 2023), which are often subtly conveyed through proximal cues.

Subtle proximal cues in language and nonverbal behavior convey the hierarchical structure and social scripts related to subordination. This language of the oppressed is often internalized in ways that prompt an internal saboteur. Power Distance Orientation is defined as the "extent to which a person believes that it is appropriate for employees to question the authority of supervisors" (Bao et al., 2023, p. 110). The salience of power distant relationships in the workplace affects attention, shuttling the individual's consciousness into a position of self-preservation, deferential obedience, and conformity. Awareness of systemic injustice and oppression in the workplace may lead to internalized subordination, with resultant effects on mental health and self-esteem (Han &Lee, 2023). For example, when sexism is internalized, this can lead to the maintenance and reproduction of sexist ideologies, which connect to objectification, feelings of inferiority, and subordination of the creative impulse (Han & Lee, 2023).

The extent of congruence between leader and subordinate power distance orientation is important for workplace happiness and productivity (Bao et al., 2023). The level of match in expectations between leaders and workers is impacted by cultural values and the ways that team structures are communicated. Often, high power distance orientation is linked to poorer outcomes, more negative attitudes, and greater resistance to organizational goals. When power distance is low, this can facilitate greater awareness of shared values, which carves a path for increased group and relational identification (Bao et al., 2023).

Intrapreneurship and Communication

When employees contribute to workplace innovations within their organization in a proactive manner, this level of organizational commitment has been deemed as *intrapreneurship* (Ravina-Ripoll et al., 2023). Diverse factors can impact intrapreneurship, including a sense of internal control, institutional values, subjective well-being, organizational values, company structure, and supervisory style (Ravina-Ripoll et al., 2023). Symmetrical internal communication patterns that foster trust and collaboration may yield greater employee creativity.

Internal communication within an organization is lateral, bottom-up, top-down, and originates from leadership within a strategic form. Symmetrical communication has been generally shown to be superior, which allows employees to contribute to decision-making and provide feedback to management (Lee & Kim, 2021). Leadership communication patterns can ultimately impact creativity; this may be mediated by the relationship between internal communication and engagement, productivity, performance, feedback-seeking, and commitment (Lee & Kim, 2021). Leader support for creativity may bolster innovation in employees; this nurturing is signaled through the suppression of criticism, recognition, consultation, shoring up subordinate self-efficacy, monitoring with the provision of constructive feedback, and openness to novel ideas and approaches (Maliakkal & Reiter–Palmon, 2023). The current project will seek to examine the relationship between the interpretation of tacit cues and the construction of thought, with implied relevance for interpersonal and organizational relationships and consequential effects on creativity. The notion that language evokes a reality, meted out in the internal world of the employee, is one foundation for linguistic responsibility and nonverbal self-awareness.

Proximal Cues

Language is multi-functional, with inner speech and written forms signifying monologue, while verbal forms often belie dialogue (Vygotsky, 1934, p. 240). Speech is ultimately an abbreviation for thought. Dialogue may unfold in a series of replies, like a "chain of reactions" (Vygotsky, 1934, p. 242) that respond to cues that are both subliminal and supraliminal. Inner speech is guided by a process of planning that involves the construction of a "draft," which helps to organize thought (Vygotsky, 1934, p. 243), yet it arrives in response to an environmental antecedent that cues and calls for a response.

Multiformat communication is increasingly accessible in a technological society, where various platforms, modes of delivery, and audience variables are present (Moffett et al., 2021). In a society rich with complex communication forms, including artificial intelligence, multiformat modes are described as "personalized, bilateral, simultaneous communication through various channels" (Moffett et al., 2021, p. 441). Yet, these authors also indicate that proximal cues are only really offered in face-to-face contexts, and permit touch, proximity, and "atmospherics" (Moffett et al., 2021, p. 451). Social presence, which allows for greater exchange of intimacy, is facilitated through the synchronicity of nonverbals and other communicative channels and through the visual and auditory feedback that can be decoded in subtle ways in live interactions. Social information processing, behavioral coordination, and information complexity are variables that intersect with workplace interactions in ways that can present friction or compel the organization towards change. Dynamic proximal cues can amplify sensory involvement, facilitating experiential communication.

Proximal Cues and Nonverbal Behaviors: Decoding and Internalizing Tacit Communication to Energize Creativity

The interaction between internalized cognitive structures, nonverbal behavior and person perception can affect workplace relationships, job performance, and innovation. When considering "distal indicator cues," which are defined as measurable expressions that reflect an inward trait, emotion, or state, Burgoon et al. (1990, p. 143) conclude that "these distal cues are perceived by an observer and represented as proximal percepts in the observer's cognitive structures." Attributions and social judgments extend from detected distal cues, for proximal percepts "represent subjective judgments abstracted from objective cues" (Burgoon et al., 1990, p. 143). Using a Brunswikian Lens Model to organize their understanding of relevant literature on nonverbal behavior, source credibility, and persuasiveness, Burgoon et al. (1990) constructed a path model of expressions and their influence on impression formation. Composites of nonverbal behaviors yield identifiable recipient reactions, similar to behavioral pheromones. Trait-based attributions related to character, composure, pleasantness, and competence can be mapped onto external expressions and clusters of nonverbal behaviors; this may alter persuasion through adjustment to perceived source credibility. Administrative support for creative work may be a barometer for creativity enhancement via tacit, transmissible social messages, and expressive composites.

Models of communication interactivity suggest that proximal and distal cues interact in systematic ways with an array of variables, such as "interdependent message exchange" (Burgoon et al., 2002, p. 659). Contextual affordances can alter communication and social judgments, such as temporal synchronicity or the ability to interact in real time rather than through recorded or written messages (Burgoon et al., 2002). When the communicator's goals facilitate contingent results, this can propel social outcomes. The positionality of the communicator as observer versus participant can also regulate social exchange. Burgoon et al. (2002) describe the "processual sense" of interactivity (p. 660), which refers to the presence of emotional and cognitive involvement, mutuality or reciprocity, spontaneity, social desirability, and smooth interactive coordination. These forces can create an environmental press that may either produce enhanced communication or lead to distractors that increase susceptibility to heuristics.

Not only can social evaluations be impacted by interactivity, but task performance may also be mobilized (Burgoon et al., 2002), which could yield implications for workplace innovation. Although face-to-face interactions may lead to more positive social evaluations, they do not necessarily produce better decision-making strategies or increase perceived competence. In fact, human interactions may be less deterministic than what was initially posed by channel theories, which highlighted the notion that adult communication will generally defer to nonverbal cues when these are in conflict with verbal cues, suggesting primacy. While visual cues may predominate when available, auditory information will compensate in the absence of exposure to facial expression. Channel reliance studies seek to isolate the effects of modes of communication and often imply that exposure to the richest array of cues may be more beneficial to human communication than exposure to a technological setting that produces an "impoverished communication environment" (Burgoon et al., 2002, p. 658).

Extraversion, Individual Differences, and Distal Cues

Distal cues are sometimes perceptually represented in the mind of an observer, emerging from sensory and interpretive mechanisms (Scherer, 1978). These distal cues can be considered as "indicators" of an internal subjectivity, for "stable traits and transient states are externalized in the form of distal cues in an organism's appearance and behavior" (Scherer, 1978, p. 468). Some of these externalizations can include "voice energy cues," which reveal levels of vocal energy expenditure and dynamism in ways that affect the probability of being perceived as extraverted (Scherer, 1978, pp. 467–468, 484). It is very possible that "suppressor effects" interfere with emotion decoding accuracy in ways that interact with the receptive strategies employed by the observer. The potential inaccuracy of emotion decoding directs workplace person perception, influenced by cultural diversity and gender typing, with mystifying implications for self-concept clarity and creative resolutions.

Social Complexity, Dominance, and Proximal Cues

Comparative psychology may offer a unique vantage point for understanding human communication networks through the examination of animal analogs (Freeberg et al., 2012). For example, the social complexity hypothesis situates the greater need for complex systems of communication in the presence of exposure to a wide range of social structures. Complex groups allow for regular exposure to both dominant and submissive others, hierarchical and egalitarian processes, and varied roles; this adds to the need for a wide range of communicative signals (Freeberg et al., 2012). The competing demands of self-interest and collective agendas are vast in social species, and the resultant complexity of communicative signals can yield an expansive range of potential interpretations. Complex social signals can be deemed as conspicuous, which can attract predators. In humans, predation can manifest as relational aggressors vying for power. The complexity of communicative signals is infringed upon by various forces, for "the properties of the environment constrain the type of signals that will be readily detected and evaluated by receivers" (Freeberg et al., 2012, p. 1795). Workplace environments require sensitive social instruments to interpret distal communicative signals, which persevere despite the suppressive athletics of collective subordination to dominance hierarchies. Suppressed signals and stifled expressions also invoke an impoverished environment for recipients, who rely on uncertain cues to guide their own social responses.

Egon Brunswik and Representation

In his analysis of research design, Brunswik (1956) exposes the reader to an ecological perspective, pointing out that variables are collapsed into a universe of understanding, yet undergirded by bias. His employment of the term "ecology" references the habits, consistencies, and environments in which research projects are situated, and perceptions of the distant world are generalizations that rely on probabilities ascertained from cues, embedded in uncertainty (Brunswik, 1956, p. 140). He defines variables within an ecology, which proposes that there is a "natural or customary habitat, or surrounding universe of a species, culture, or individual, with all its inherent variation and co-variation of factors" (Brunswik, 1956, p. 5).

With respect to his lens model, Brunswik (1956) refers to William James, discussing the notion that "perception is of probable things" (p. 51). Likewise, he builds on Thurstone's conclusion that representations are "based on insufficient evidence" (p. 51). Thus, responses to distal objects are merely potentialities—reactions to cues that hold "response-eliciting power" (p. 51). Influenced by Hull's (1934, as cited in Brunswik, 1956, p. 50) work on habit hierarchies, Brunswik proposes that social cues can be vicariously experienced in expressive structures with substitutionary qualities. His "ratiomorphic" view of perception offers the observation that organisms modify what is observed in light of cost, risk, and utility (p. 141), focusing on what seems most vital and recruiting what has been learned from conditioning (p. 146). Perception will tend to make salient the distal qualities of an object, leaning towards stereotyped responses that reduce error in a compromise to control uncertainty. Environmental variables are perceived through psychological dimensions, creating prismatic perceptions; the subjective evaluations that are used in social discourse and science may or may not arise from sensory impressions or unconscious structures (Brunswik, 1956, p. 5). If the study of psycholinguistics is to move beyond the molecular approach, where the distal is eclipsed by the proximal, it must be acknowledged that multivariate procedures will seek to represent that which is ineffable (Brunswik, 1956, p. 4).

Emotion Communication

Bänziger et al. (2015) examined the utility of a path model to uncover the relationships among person perceptions and emotional expressions, using a Brunswikian Lens Model. These authors point out that, in the model proposed by Brunswik (1956), people attempt to understand the uncertainty of the world (the distal object) through the presence of clusters of proximal cues, using systems of inference and assumptions about probability. The goodness of fit between the external world and the subjective perceptions of the world was termed ecological validity by Brunswik (1956). Distal cues can also be represented as the speaker's emotion, which is encoded in an outward expression and later decoded by an interpreter. The decoding of proximal cues and the transmission of these signals can be influenced by a range of motivational and emotional variables. Bänziger et al. (2015) found that clusters of cues connect to families of emotions. Individuals may use rules of inference to decode these cues within particular emotion families.

Signaling Systems across Species

Comparative psychology offers insights into human signaling systems through comparisons with animal and insect populations. Otte (1974) considers the functional aspects of communication, which are presumed to be ubiquitous in most forms of organismic behavior and rooted in sensory experience. Within these communicative forms, goals that serve reproduction, adaptation, or survival are chief. There are also byproducts or effects of communication. Socially reciprocal examples include releasing stimuli, which trigger responses in the recipient, and chemoreception, where odors or chemical reactions in an observer are enlisted through autonomic communication channels. Communication can include behavioral sequences, deceit and misinformation transmission, defense mechanisms serving protective functions, evaluation of competitors, aggressive mimicry, and threat detection. Inaccurate decoding can install vulnerability to predation (Otte, 1974).

A functional approach to the understanding of proximal and distal cues in human beings might include an analysis of the ways that communication serves to protect psychological survival, neutralize threats, and prevent psychosocial and economic predation. The subtle forms of workplace communication can emulate the seemingly autonomous cycles observed in the behavioral sequences of other living organisms, operating below conscious awareness but following natural and species-specific regulatory patterns.

Gender Differences in Signaling

Proximal factors in emotion signaling are antecedents to an expression, while distal influences include biological predispositions related to survival and psychosocial reward (Hall et al., 2000). Ambiguities in communication arise in the presence of masking behaviors, with some individuals showing higher skill at the simulation of authentic affect (Hall et al., 2000).

Since humans rely on social data for smooth interactions and threat detection, the value of accurate decoding is primary. Meta-analytic studies have revealed that females show higher levels of smiling, more accurate decoding of facial expressions, and reveal more expression accuracy, or the ability to convey emotional information to others through interpersonal signaling (Hall et al., 2000). The greater accuracy of nonverbal evaluation among female observers has been demonstrated across many geographic regions in hundreds of studies.

Gender offers a powerful regulating mechanism for outward emotional displays, prescribing the division of social labor (Hall et al., 2000). Cultural scripts encourage the promotion of gendered affective displays, such as "gender affirmation," which is defined as "the need to signal gender to oneself and others" (Hall et al., 2000, p. 102). The tendency to conform to gendered expectations consistent with biological sex is one strategy to attempt to avoid social exclusion and punishment. In some research, females are more likely to be socially reinforced for outward displays of happiness, while socially approved expression for males favors anger. Cultural and social learning factors are foundational for the emergence of an array of gendered display rules.

The Signifier in Lacan

The perspective of language in the work of Jacques Lacan is influenced by the linguist Ferdinand de Saussure, whose work on decoding the structure of symbols in language illuminated the former's understanding of delusional speech. A meaningful foray into Lacan's esoteric work is difficult to briefly achieve, but may be enhanced through a restatement of some of the basic features of de Saussure's terminology. Within de Saussure's model, a signifier (S) is "the form which the sign takes," which often refers to a language symbol, such as a word (Chandler, 2019, p. 1). The signified (s) is defined as "the concept it represents," which suggests a meaning or a mental concept, and the sign (S/s) is "the whole," based on an immaterial association between the signifier and the signified (Chandler, 2019, p. 1). Ultimately, Lacan's work suggests the power of the signifier to take on new meanings, for "the signified inevitably 'slips beneath' the signifier" (Chandler, 2019, p. 1).

In Book III of *The Psychoses*, Lacan (1955) describes the signifier as "the material of language," pointing out that the signified are not objects in themselves but rather concern "another meaning," which does not perfectly point towards a reality (p. 32). Lacan (1955) argues that language can be divided into "the symbolic, the imaginary, and the real" (p. 53). The emergence of language, the signifier, is unknown and unknowable; it is not controlled by the individual but arrives as a pre-existing system regulated by rules and oppositions. Despite this ineffable quality of language, some will reconstruct the signifier, fusing the symbol with the object as if their idea is "the key to the world" (Lacan, 1955, p. 55).

Lacan's (1955) primary focus is on delusional language in psychotic conditions, yet his work can be meaningfully extended to language in the normative sense. He describes the irony that language exists at one point in time (synchronic), yet also emerges across time (diachronic). Language is dynamic and can morph into forms where "certain elements become isolated, laden, take on a value, a particular force of inertia, become charged with meaning..." (Lacan, 1955, p. 54). This quality of emphasis is referred to as "eroticization," and it may speak to the obscure and particular meaning that an individual will internalize from the environment, fusing the words received from others into the self-schema. Lacan identifies expressed speech (real speech) as a puppet, a symbol of an external country.

The usage of language in the works of Lacan is ambiguous, non-normative and subject to many interpretations; he has been described by Mehlman (1972) as a "verbal iconoclast" (p. 10). In referencing Edgar Allen's Poe's work, *The Purloined Letter*, Lacan seeks to provide a cognitive short-cut to the problematic search for the one correct interpretation, when language is a series of symbols that require contextualized interpretation (as cited in Mehlman, 1972). The anthropological work of Levi-Strauss and the impasse and reversals that are yielded from this work provide a forum into the paradox of what is known versus what is mysterious in one's attempt to analyze and understand another person, for "in this pivotal tourniquet...either the subject's knowledge or the object's fascination will be sacrificed in the vain quest for significant knowledge of the other" (Mehlman, 1972, p. 12). There is something to be gained from the quest to understand without appropriating the other; to apprehend the strangeness of the other person is to allow for the maintenance of adaptive mystery.

The notion that neither the real nor the imaginary can be reduced to a linguistic form is expressed by Lacan (Shepherdson, 2003, p. 118), for the unconscious hovers in a transcendent realm beyond the individual and outside of representation (p. 120). Signifiers resemble living organisms and create symbolic maps of mental life, yet they are incapable of capturing being (Shepherdson, 2003). Lacan's work suggests that, when a person enters a symbolic world, a detachment from being may erupt (Shepherdson, 2003, p. 120), for the signifier owns a unique logic (p. 116). Influenced by Hegel, Kant, Aristotle, Plato, Freud, Merleau-Ponty, and Heidegger, Lacan's work expanded on the notion that the ideal of a thing is not equivalent to the thing itself. As with Kant's analysis of the sublime, the ideal of beauty is not equivalent to a beautiful object (Shepherdson, 2003, p. 124). Hence, one might encounter language as distinct from existence, outside of and other than being.

Lacan (1955, p. 56) identifies several dimensions of the Other, including "the big Other," which conforms to the Signifier, or language symbol. The Other is beyond what is apparent and may become that whom "one addresses oneself to beyond" (p. 56). The Signifier can reference "the imaginary, the ego and the body" (Lacan, 1955, p. 56) and lies in a region "beyond that reality" (p. 51). The Other is also manifested as the unconscious. The Signifier is a puppet, and behind the puppet is a real human being, who takes up space. Nevertheless, the signified is beyond the reality of the person.

The human tendency is to reify—to take an abstract concept and constrain its edges into something concrete, tangible, and defined. This is hinted at in Lacan's (1955) discussion of language as a surrogate for a deontological argument, or a sense of duty that appeals to a universal standard, for language can be used in a way that "presupposes recognition by an absolute Other, aimed at beyond all you can know…beyond the known" (p. 51). He extends his argument to the claim that speech entails a commitment, requiring an act of compliance or repudiation, and ultimately lands in creation, for "something gets born there" (p. 51).

The Doctrine of Signs

A set of linguistic symbols synthesizes with an interpreter, and the social elements of language are encased within its forms. In his discussion of the manifestation of the interpretive community, Josiah Royce (1913) identifies the role of the beloved community in the creation of a symbolic world, suggesting that the real is a "universal community" (p. 343). The interpretive world is community possession, for "Not the self, not the Logos, not the One, and not the Many, but the Community will be the ruling category" for an ideal civilization (Royce, 1913, p. 344). The sign post points towards one mind, the "inquiring wayfarer" (Royce, 1913, p. 347). The one who creates the sign is yet another mind—one posing an intention. The one who observes and interprets the signpost is a third mind. Thus, three minds are involved in signification; real signs, when added to an interpretation, constitute a universe (p. 345).

Language, like a signpost, points *towards* a mind. This recipient mind may or may not enlist the powers of interpretation, or may defer to an interpretive community—a culture. If one envisions a sign as a mind, or a "quasi-mind" (Royce, p. 345), it is evident that the sign is both subjective and real in some individual, perceptive sense. Royce's (1913, p. 347) metaphysical thesis is that subjective experience, phenomenology, is "a realm of signs." In his model, associations, memories, and facts are sign posts, yet they cannot be fully known through sensation. In Royce's model, we cannot assume that pragmatism offers a full rendering of the meaning of signs—we cannot verify the accuracy of our propositions. Each sign is preceded by an infinite number of other signs and events, which lead to the summation. But reality is not entirely submerged, for "if the past and future and are realities, then they constitute a life which belongs to some real community, whose ideas of past and future are really interpreted" (Royce, 1913, p. 348).

One feature of language, or communication more broadly, is the expression of an attitude—a latent belief or cluster of ideas that is willed into maintenance. This emphasis on the volitional elements of mind was championed by Wilhelm Wundt, Schopenhauer, William James, and Nietzsche, albeit in various forms. According to Royce (1913, p. 349), "absolute voluntarism" is a position that sees attitudes exclusively within the context of free will, yet it asserts that there is one optimum attitude in terms of how one orients towards the world. This emphasis on freedom provides a foundation for a series of questions, built from Royce's work and applied towards an action agenda in the modern context (1913, pp. 348–349). These inquiries include the following: (a) How will we "stand in the presence of the universe?" (b) How will we "propose to bear ourselves towards the world?" (c) What are the rules that constantly guide our interpretations of life?" (d) If "the very being of the world consists in the truth of the interpretation" of sign posts, what is my responsibility for my will towards an attitude?

Language connects symbols to a prime attitude, which is a philosophy of life. This philosophy can be considered a "doctrine" in the sense that it "counsels us to bear ourselves towards our world *as if* our experience were…" (Royce, 1913, p. 349). Here Royce builds on the work of Hans Vaihinger in some respects but also diverts from him, for Royce (1913) does not view the "as if" as a systematic cluster of "convenient fictions" (p. 349).

Phenomenology and Intersubjectivity

Polanyi (1966) discusses the phenomenal structure of tacit knowledge (p. 11); within the context of his remark, it is evident that he references the relationship between tacit and consciously accessible knowledge. For example, Polanyi refers to the proximal term as tacit knowledge, which is known only through its association with the consciously accessible distal event or recollection. He discusses associations, whereby attention is diverted away from the tacit event *towards* the explicit event. Polanyi describes the functional association between proximal and distal events with these words, which highlight attentional shifting, "we are aware of that *from* which we are attending *to* another thing, in the appearance of that thing" (p. 11).

In typical usage, the word *phenomenal* connotes an experience of the sensory and perceptual ways that an individual apprehends the world. Thus, phenomenal elements of consciousness relate to the subjective qualities that are experienced internally and cannot be fully shared. These perceptions are built from sensations, correlated with neural events, and follow principles of pattern formation and holism. While some models of consciousness purport that patterns of neural activity give rise to consciousness, it is also difficult to reduce the qualitative features of perception to material events or brain states (Robinson, 2004, pp. 14, 207). The many parts of an organic system or perceptual world interact in dynamic and causal ways within a conscious experience that possesses continuity over time and space (Robinson, 2004, pp. 215, 218). The structure of the phenomenal aspects of consciousness includes attentional qualities, which tend to reveal a figure-ground principle based on salience (Watzl, 2017).

When considering relational linguistics, one encounters Edmund Husserl's notion of intersubjectivity, which includes the conscious and unconscious exchange of subjective experiences between persons, built from empathy and constrained by the unique vantage point of each mind (Cooper-White, 2014). Taking on various theories of intersubjectivity, Durt (2014) examines the possibility, expressed by Reddy (2010), that part of engagement between minds includes the sense of being recognized as an existing other by another human being. Persons may use their own internal states to simulate the minds of others, recruiting folk psychology and inference to construct and confirm implicit theories about others.

Durt (2014) points out that, while language may serve to structure the ambiguous, it is not necessarily required for phenomenal experience, which can be sensory or unconscious. Durt also questions the understanding of language which would elevate its ability to shape perception. Nevertheless, the notion of shared intentional engagement, likely a feature of intersubjectivity, occurs when people "relate together to an action, belief, idea, symbol, object, or other meaningful entity" (Durt, 2014, p. 2). The author points out that, while we cannot fully enter the world of another person through shared intentional engagement, we may be able to understand their experience on some meaningful level when that is communicated. Influenced by Wittgenstein, Durt (2014) argues that language rules and culture may influence the learning process that contributes to the possibility of shared intentional engagement, which is also constrained by neuropsychological features.

An enactive view of intersubjectivity emphasizes an active, volitional enterprise rather than passive reformulation of another person's experience through analogies. While theories of intersubjectivity often focus on the projective process in the attempt to simulate others' minds to procure action prediction, Fuchs and De Jaegher (2009) posit that the attempt to enter into another's mental world is an embodied and dynamic dance as individuals attempt to co-create meaning with intentions capable of transformation. Focusing on the mutuality and incorporation that are relevant to enactive intersubjectivity, Fuchs and De Jaegher (2009) see the coordinated efforts of each individual as agentic and goal-oriented, seeking to incorporate the experience of the Other. Their interactive view of intersubjectivity suggests that it has emergent, rather than representational, drivers. The process of deep encounter with another person is not based on an individual projection from the internal world, but rather a byproduct of the coordinated participation towards meaning construction, which changes from one moment to another. In contrast to this enactive view is the notion that there is an inseparable gulf between each human, which can only be surmised through a process of distal inference based on one's own point of view.

An enactive view of intersubjectivity presumes that individuals "participate in each other's sensemaking" (Fuchs & De Jaegher, 2009, p. 470). Building on the work of Lyons-Ruth et al. (1998), Fuchs and De Jaegher (2009) refer to the notion of implicit relational knowing, which they define as "a pre-reflective knowledge of how to deal with others—how to share pleasure, elicit attention, avoid rejection, re-establish contact," and so forth (p. 481). Likened to a musical form of knowledge, this ability allows for the spontaneous rhythm-seeking that is part of the co-construction of a social encounter.

Recognition by another person, the sense of a gaze being directed towards oneself, is a powerful center of mutuality that may give rise to the later emergence of joint attention towards external objects (Reddy, 2005). Dyadic attention does not imply that both persons share the same view of the apprehended Other; rather, this attending process is a continuous, unitary commitment that attaches to emotions (Reddy, 2005, p. 104). Before the emerging human can attend to external objects, he/she must exist in a state of fusion with the object, being perceived.

Before language develops and facilitates interpersonal encounters, the human child learns "implicit relational knowing," which includes a set of procedures, infused with emotions that are acquired through interactions (Lyons-Ruth et al., 1998, p. 284). These are pre-verbal representations of self and other that are not often translatable into the symbolic codes of language (p. 285). Implicit relational knowing is nonconscious, constructed through a dyadic encounter, and important to co-regulation between persons. It includes cognitive, affective, behavioral, and attentive processes, and serves as a substrate for the experience of intersubjectivity.

Proximal and Distal Cues and the Unconscious

Polanyi (1966) alludes to how proximal cues can signify something that one is only experientially aware of due to the connection to the distal term. Likewise, one may be aware of a proximal justification for a decision, while lacking awareness of the distal associations that influence action (Ingram & Prochownik, 2014). The traditional sense of the term unconscious does not necessarily imply inaccessibility (Ingram & Prochownik, 2014). Rather, it implies effortful retrieval, unlocking information not readily accessible, despite the motivationally powerful elements of association. Furthermore, proximal and distal cues need not be thought of as dichotomous; rather, these cues can dynamically interact, and either the proximal or distal cue (or both) could be consciously inaccessible.

Language Emergence, Minds, and Lev Vygotsky

According to some models of the mind, the unconscious is deemed to operate within unique laws not governed by logic or constraint. These laws of consciousness are fluid, derived from associations, constantly changing, and yet serving as a ground for explicit experiences in consciousness. Recapitulation within the unconscious seeks mastery, a form of problem solving. These notions of mind are also borne out in Vygotsky's (1934) theory of thought and language. From this perspective, word meaning is dynamic, evolving from a process of generalizations (Vygotsky, 1934, p. 217). The continuous exchange between thought and language represents movement, based on self-governing principles, which is guided by associations that seek to solve a problem (Vygotsky, 1934, p. 218). The physical and meaning-oriented planes of communication may indicate polarities, yet these develop together and are not independent. The unconscious elements of language diverge from mathematical precision, following an "imaginative harmony" (Vygotsky, 1934, p. 221).

Mendoza-García (2023) describes early dyadic communication with a triadic model that includes two minds and an external referent from the world, combined within a co-creative event rather than a passive transmission. Adults and infants may engage in co-regulation, incorporating joint attention and mutual gaze to interpret the world and co-constructing reality within a social, cognitive, and sensory set of processes. The development of a linguistic world appears to be multi-modal, serving to generate regions of meaning, embedded within a sociocultural context. Co-regulation and co-creation of organizational worlds may also require intersubjectivity and a mutual gaze.

When children begin to express language as one-word wholes, this attempt to represent the world with a vocal object derives from a "dim, amorphous whole" (Vygotsky, 1934, p. 219). Any feature of a sentence can come to be emphasized, expressing an agent involved in some action; however, the hidden meaning of two identical grammatical structures can vary significantly (Vygotsky, 1934, p. 221). Verbal forms emerge gradually, expressing mind-related constructs that lie behind the words, fused with speech sounds, opaque, and difficult to recognize or interpret. Differentiation between objects, words, significance, memories, and consciousness emerges gradually, with the dawn of rising cognitive faculties, for "inner speech [lies] beyond the semantic plane" (Vygotsky, 1934, pp. 222–224). The "whole interior" of speech includes the subvocal, the motives that exist before the words, and the inner language built from egocentrism (Vygotsky, 1934, pp. 225–226).

Social interaction is likely to precede the development of the mind, prefiguring the structure that will later emerge as language (Johnson, 2002). The early interactions with caregivers are embodied experiences, which afford infants the opportunity to learn coordinated social encounters that create a scaffold for later understanding of others' minds. Vygotsky (1934) identifies inner speech as an autonomous function of thought rather than the silencing of outward speech. Inner speech is intuitive rather than phonetic, incomprehensible to others, enforces problem solving, results in the death of words, and suggests a sense of meaning rather than an objective set of definitions. This means a conglomerate, where concepts adhere in a dynamic cabal, which Vygotsky refers to as the process of agglutination. The context of inner speech as "reduced sound" is enhanced by awareness of emphatic meaning, for "a single word is so saturated with sense that…it becomes a concentrate"… (Vygotsky, 1934, p. 247).

Self-Concept Clarity

The social construction of thought also contributes to an understanding of self that is rooted in a series of exchanges between the self and Other, whereby the face of the Other serves as a mirror and source of identification. Self-concept clarity refers to a structural element of the self, referencing an internally stable set of beliefs about oneself that are held without reservation (Campbell et al., 1996). Individuals who show lower levels of self-concept clarity are more likely to experience anxiety and depression, negative self-focused attention and self-doubt, and rumination. A chronic state of self-examination that is experienced as unpleasant and, ironically, a tendency to fail to attend to internal states and cues may characterize low self-concept clarity. The model of self-concept clarity builds on a trajectory of research that views self-construal as not only dynamic but also as a mode of processing incoming information and memory retrieval in line with expectations.

Self-concept clarity, as described by Campbell (1990, as cited in Lewandowski et al., 2010, p. 416), "involves a person's maintenance of a distinct, cohesive, and consistent conception of their characteristics." As relational closeness increases, the sense of defining oneself in relation to the intimate other tends to become paramount, which leads to the inclusion of other in the sense of self. Self-concept clarity connects with the consistency principle, for "individuals with high self-concept clarity have more consistent self-beliefs, are less likely to change their self-descriptions over time or endorse mutually exclusive self-descriptive traits" (Campbell et al., 1990, as cited in Lewandowski et al., 2010, p. 418). Relational satisfaction and intimacy may be connected to higher levels of self-concept clarity.

Limitations

Research in the social sciences has increasingly made use of cultural comparisons, which yield informative perspectives on human variation and group behaviors. Nevertheless, there remains a need to develop more sensitive local scales that can detect regional differences in subcultural variables, facilitating greater transferability of findings. Over time, research performed across contextual microcosms may offer greater insight into the strong situations that resist change and constrain human creativity. While much prior research has been based on an analysis of power dynamics, including exchanges between leaders and subordinates, more work can be done regarding lateral relationships and worker-consumer interactions, especially in the domain of understanding the ontogeny of work-relevant identities and organizational citizenship behaviors that serve, rather than confine, innovation.

Modern research into workplace linguistic realizations can benefit from ecologically valid models that conduct research in a "home-based" context, with local investigations of circumscribed organizational contexts. The goal of uncovering the dynamic process within a specific context may be a more attainable objective than an attempt to extract and define universal principles. Increasing awareness of the intervening variables of mental illness and neurotic vulnerability within a workplace context is essential to an understanding of equity and its advantages over equality. Ongoing examination of moderator variables and usage of path analyses could offer a range of new theoretical constructs, which will provide probabilistic menus of explanation rather than setting the criteria of science upon a confirmation-disconfirmation agenda. The pursuit of mundane realism in research remains elusive.

The Signaling Community: A Model for Workplace Language

The current review of literature reflects a need to understand the dynamic system of workplace communication, which survives as an "interpretive community" (Royce, 1913). This community exists with interactivity between the social world, the local context, and the creative identity of the group and the individual. The workplace serves as a beehive of signaling transmissions, which must be decoded in a place where the person tends to slip beneath the signal. Within a context of adaptive intersubjectivity, the employee, colleagues, and leadership thrive in the co-construction of meaning, fostering resilience and the emergence of enhanced self-concept clarity and group identity formation.

For the individual, atonement for self-injurious introjection of oppressive systems can be made through a commitment to manage workplace rumination, showing resilience and intimate relationship-seeking rather than the shaming and silencing that arrive with internalized projections from a toxic organizational culture. This can occur in a beloved community, a place of trust, collaboration, diversity, and equality, where the hidden meanings of linguistic and nonverbal symbols are accepted as non-representational sources of potential creativity. Signs can never fully contain being; the signifier is a place of lack. Active, volitional intersubjectivity causes the production of creativity despite a lack of clarity, and within a context of mutuality rather than competition. As sensitivity to "the nature of effective (and ineffective) coordination for any player in that class of interactions" (Johnson, 2002, p. 628) increases, the individual moves from novice towards expertise in social decoding in the attempt to gain a subordinate goal of mutuality, listening and thriving.[1] The game of language is not to be played as a competitive striving, but rather to inch us towards a humanistic creative space, yet the workplace remains lodged in a spider's web of human machinations, for "discourse…includes acts, steps, the contortions of puppets, yourselves included, caught up in the game" (Lacan, 1955, p. 51).

Note

1 Johnson refers to Ludwig Wittgenstein's model of language games, as described in his 1953 posthumous work, *Philosophical Investigations*.

Works Cited

Bänziger, T., Hosoya, G., & Scherer, K. R. (2015). Path models of vocal emotion communication. *PloS One*, *10*(9), 1–29, e0136675.
Bao, Y., Liao, S., Liao, J., Sun, F., & Gao, S. (2023). When does leader–subordinate (in) congruence in power distance orientation affect employees' work engagement?

The moderating effect of team structure clarity. *Human Performance, 36*(3), 109–131.

Brunswik, E. (1956). *Perception and the representative design of psychological experiments* (2nd ed.). University of California Press.

Burgoon, J. K., Birk, T., & Pfau, M. (1990). Nonverbal behaviors, persuasion, and credibility. *Human Communication Research, 17*(1), 140–169.

Burgoon, J. K., Bonito, J. A., Ramirez, A. Jr, Dunbar, N. E., Kam, K., & Fischer, J. (2002). Testing the interactivity principle: Effects of mediation, propinquity, and verbal and nonverbal modalities in interpersonal interaction. *Journal of Communication, 52*(3), 657–677.

Campbell, J. D., Trapnell, P. D., Heine, S. J., Katz, I. M., Lavallee, L. F., & Lehman, D. R. (1996). Self-concept clarity: Measurement, personality correlates, and cultural boundaries. *Journal of Personality and Social Psychology, 70*(1), 141.

Carney, D. R. (2020). The nonverbal expression of power, status, and dominance. *Current Opinion in Psychology, 33,* 256–264.

Chandler, D. (2019, July 21). Signs. In D. Chandler (Ed.) *Semiotics for beginners. An online version of semiotics: The basics* (4th ed). Routledge; 2022. (Chapter 2). Retrieved from https://www.cs.princeton.edu/~chazelle/courses/BIB/semio2.htm

Cooper-White, P. (2014). Intersubjectivity. In D. A. Leeming (Ed.), *Encyclopedia of psychology and religion* (pp. 882–886). Springer.

Durt, C. (2014). Shared intentional engagement through language and phenomenal experience. *Frontiers in Psychology, 5*(1016), 1–4.

Fiske, S. T., Xu, J., Cuddy, A. C., & Glick, P. (1999). (Dis) respecting versus (dis) liking: Status and interdependence predict ambivalent stereotypes of competence and warmth. *Journal of Social Issues, 55*(3), 473–489.

Freeberg, T. M., Dunbar, R. I., & Ord, T. J. (2012). Social complexity as a proximate and ultimate factor in communicative complexity. *Philosophical Transactions of the Royal Society B: Biological Sciences, 367*(1597), 1785–1801.

Fuchs, T., & De Jaegher, H. (2009). Enactive intersubjectivity: Participatory sense-making and mutual incorporation. *Phenomenology and the Cognitive Sciences, 8,* 465–486.

Galinsky, A. D., Magee, J. C., Gruenfeld, D. H., Whitson, J. A., & Liljenquist, K. A. (2008). Power reduces the press of the situation: Implications for creativity, conformity, and dissonance. *Journal of Personality and Social Psychology, 95*(6), 1450–1466.

Hall, J. A., Carter, J. D., & Horgan, T. G. (2000). Gender differences in nonverbal communication of emotion. In K. Oatley, A. Manstead, & A. H. Fischer (Eds.), *Gender and emotion: Social psychological perspectives* (pp. 97–117). Cambridge University Press.

Han, E., & Lee, I. (2023). Empowering women in counseling by dismantling internalized sexism: The Feminist-Multicultural Orientation and Social Justice Competencies. *Journal of Mental Health Counseling, 45*(3), 213-230.

Harper, R. G. (1985). Power, dominance, and nonverbal behavior: An overview. In S. L. Ellyson & J. F. Dovidio (Eds.), *Power, dominance, and nonverbal behavior* (pp. 29–48). Springer-Verlag.

Hoever, I. J., Betancourt, N. E., Chen, G., & Zhou, J. (2023). How others light the creative spark: Low power accentuates the benefits of diversity for individual inspiration and creativity. *Organizational Behavior and Human Decision Processes, 176*(1–18), 104248.

Ingram, G. P., & Prochownik, K. (2014). Restrictive and dynamic conceptions of the unconscious: Perspectives from moral and developmental psychology. *Behavioral and Brain Sciences, 37*(1), 34–35.

Johnson, C. M. (2002). The Vygotskian advantage in cognitive modeling: Participation precedes and thus prefigures understanding. *Behavioral and Brain Sciences, 25*(5), 628–629.

Lacan, J. (1955). The psychoses (1955–1956). In J. A. Miller (Ed.) and R. Grigg (Trans.), *The seminar of Jacques Lacan, Book III*. W.W. Norton and Company (1997).

Lee, Y., & Kim, J. (2021). Cultivating employee creativity through strategic internal communication: The role of leadership, symmetry, and feedback seeking behaviors. *Public Relations Review, 47*(1), 1–11, 101998.

Lewandowski, G. W. Jr, Nardone, N., & Raines, A. J. (2010). The role of self-concept clarity in relationship quality. *Self and Identity, 9*(4), 416–433.

Lyons-Ruth, K., Bruschweiler-Stern, N., Harrison, A. M., Morgan, A. C., Nahum, J. P., Sander, L., et al. (1998). Implicit relational knowing: Its role in development and psychoanalytic treatment. *Infant Mental Health Journal, 19*, 282–289.

Maliakkal, N. T., & Reiter-Palmon, R. (2023). The effects of leader support for creativity and leader gender on subordinate creative problem-solving performance. *The Journal of Creative Behavior, 57*(1), 109–126.

Mavin, S., & Yusupova, M. (2023). 'I'm competitive with myself': A study of women leaders navigating neoliberal patriarchal workplaces. *Gender, Work & Organization, 30*(3), 881–896.

Mehlman, J. (1972). The "floating signifier": from Lévi-Strauss to Lacan. *Yale French Studies, 48*, 10–37.

Mendoza-García, A., & Moreno-Núñez, A. (2023). Early triadic interactions in the first year of life: A systematic review on object-mediated shared encounters. *Frontiers in Psychology, 14*, 1205973.

Moffett, J. W., Folse, J. A. G., & Palmatier, R. W. (2021). A theory of multiformat communication: Mechanisms, dynamics, and strategies. *Journal of the Academy of Marketing Science, 49*, 441–461.

Otte, D. (1974). Effects and functions in the evolution of signaling systems. *Annual Review of Ecology and Systematics, 5*(1), 385–417.

Polanyi, M. (1966). *The tacit dimension*. University of Chicago Press. Reprinted 2009.

Ravina-Ripoll, R., Galvan-Vela, E., Sorzano-Rodríguez, D. M., & Ruíz-Corrales, M. (2023). Mapping intrapreneurship through the dimensions of happiness at work and internal communication. *Corporate Communications: An International Journal, 28*(2), 230–248.

Reddy, V. (2005). Before the 'Third Element': Understanding attention to self. In T. McCormack, C. Hoerl, J. Roessler, & N. Eilan (Eds.), *Joint attention: communication and other minds: Issues in philosophy and psychology* (pp. 85–109). Oxford University Press.

Reddy, V. (2010). *How infants know minds*. Harvard University Press.

Robinson, W. S. (2004). *Understanding phenomenal consciousness*. Cambridge University Press.

Royce, J. (2013). *The problem of Christianity*. The University of Chicago Press.

Scherer, K. R. (1978). Personality inference from voice quality: The loud voice of extroversion. *European Journal of Social Psychology, 8*(4), 467–487.

Shepherdson, C. (2003). Lacan and philosophy. In J. M. Rabaté (Ed.), *The Cambridge companion to Lacan* (pp. 116–152). Cambridge University Press.

Vygotsky, L. (1934). *Thought and language.* In A. Kozulin (Ed. And Trans.), *A newly revised and edited version.* MIT Press.

Watzl, S. (2017). Phenomenal structure: Center and periphery—fringe, field, and margin. In S. Watzl (Ed.), *Structuring the mind: The nature of attention and how it shapes consciousness.* (Section II, Chapter 9, ebook). Oxford University Press.

4

WORKPLACE CREATIVITY AND THE THEORIES OF CARL JUNG

Nahanni Freeman

Two Minds

Carl Gustav Jung (1912b) identifies two modes of thought—directed thought is the foundation of science—while fantasy is an attempt to apprehend the unrevealed and unknowable. In some creative pursuits, intellectual sublimation occurs, and these cognitive channels unite. Building upon and modifying the work of Sigmund Freud with his discussion of irrational primary processes oriented towards wish gratification, association, and access to symbolic reasoning, Seymour Epstein (1994) posited an experiential and a rational system of the mind (p. 709). The experiential system was described as a form of processing tied to emotion, holism, associations, life experiences, and crudely processed assumptions perceived within mental images (Epstein, 1994, p. 711).

In *Unconscious Thought Theory*, developed by Dijksterhuis and Nordgren (2006), creative processes can include both attentive and directed processes (conscious and explicit information) and unconscious processes that occur when attention is directed towards another object. For these authors, attention is the primary difference between the two states, and explicit consciousness arises out of nonconscious processes, being reliant upon them (Dijksterhuis & Nordgren, 2006, p. 96). The unconscious processes have a higher capacity, being less constrained by cognitive load limitations; in addition, they derive from bottom-up-processes and underlie intuition in the perspective taken by Dijksterhuis and Nordgren (2006, pp. 97, 103).

Likewise, Michael Polanyi (1966) identifies the importance of subliminal cues in the process of inquiry that leads to understanding (p. 31). In Polanyi's

DOI: 10.4324/9781003322894-5

(1966) discussion of tacit relations, he focuses on the importance of attending from the proximal features of an object and shifting gaze to the distal features, purposes, and movements of an entity (p. 10). This offers a view into double consciousness and its attentional elements. That which is nearest is not explicitly perceived in isolation but is known by relation to the distal terms through a tacit cognitive process that may manifest through the interiorization of language (Polanyi, 1966, p. 11).

Origin, Creative Ideas, and Impressions

Jung (1933) describes the interaction between external and internal sources for creative ideas, stating,

> Impressive ideas which are hailed as truths have something peculiar to themselves…they have always been timeless; they arise from that realm of procreative, psychic life out of which the ephemeral mind of the single human being grows…Ideas spring from a source that is not contained within one man's personal life. We do not create them; they create us.
>
> *(p. 115)*

Jung (1933) is willing to explore a broad spectrum of religious studies, finding expressions of asceticism, ritual, and initiation to be important manifestations of attempts to balance the inner psychic world (p. 119). Religious symbolism is often revealed in dreams and fantasies. The fleeting impressions and evanescent memories of conscious life can be "temporarily obscured," blocked by an "unpredictable eclipse…interference from the unconscious" (Jung, 1961, p. 19). The opaque data of consciousness has not been deleted; rather, incompatible information can be repressed, omitted, or weakened when emotional energy wanes (Jung, 1961, pp. 22–24). Jung (1961) claims that novel synergy can arise from subtle variations in subliminally derived meaning and emotional valence, with new knowledge forms surfacing from dreams, the "penumbra of uncertainty" and premonition through the spontaneous revelation of the collective unconscious (pp. 25–29). Unlike the personal conscious that builds from a phenomenology of experience and memory, the collective unconscious is hereditary, impersonal, and inaccessible through direct forms of reason (Jung, 1936, p. 42).

Creativity, Inspiration, and Transmission

In their research that examined creative work in poetry, scientific writing, fiction writing, and idea generation, Thrash et al. (2010) found elements of positive affect, openness to aesthetics and experience, effort, and inspiration were influential variables. Inspiration was defined as a state that includes "transcendence, evocation, and approach motivation," which can include transmission of light, which can be used to record spiritual insight, imitate and transform work, or actualize ideas once in nascent form (Thrash et al., 2010, pp. 469, 470). An integrated model of intuition has been proposed by Svenson et al. (2023), who propose that it may include heuristics, logical processes, anticipatory reactions, and nonconscious processes.

Creative insight may also be excited by archetypes, which are unconscious "images of the instincts," found in active imagination and dreams; these indigenous artifacts manifest as an "autochthonous revival of mythological motifs" (Jung, 1936, p. 44). Archetypes can be viewed as "categories of the imagination," which are revealed in the symbols of trance, dreams, and hypnosis, following a unique mental chemistry that cannot be reduced to brain-related potentials (Jung, 1936, p. 43).

Subjectivity and Perspective Taking

Jung (1933) argues in favor of the idea that some of the most meaningful truths are rooted in subjectivity (p. 116). Warning against remaining in a state of certitude, Jung (1933) explores the way that "subjective material presents itself" to the individual rather than exclusively being designed from the interior of a person (p. 116). It is within the dynamism of the internal world and the cosmos that creativity can emerge. Furthermore, the recognition that one is necessarily limited by unique dispositional forces and internal assumptions provides a window into the thought that openness to others' perspectives, as well as the literature and mythology of other cultures and eras, will be an important origin for creative work. By moving inside subjectivity while considering the very different vantage points of others, one may encounter a form of truth that moves beyond conventional constraints.

The value of perspective taking for creativity has also been examined in studies of teams, showing differential effects based on team composition (Hoever et al., 2012). For example, diverse teams were found to exhibit more creative benefit from perspective taking, possibly through the sharing of knowledge, elaboration of constructs, and constructive debate. Shared collective representations may be more plausible in workplace contexts where mindfulness is practiced at the individual and group levels (Dupree, 2023).

Archetypes, Cultural Transmissions, and Storytelling

An exploration of Jung's archetypal theories may offer the advantage of considering shared human and organizational narratives and values, which can provide a catalyst for creative work through enhanced salience of compelling examples, enriched by a symbolic language (de Souza Sant'Anna, 2023). Rogers (2023) defines role-meaning archetypes as intrapsychic stories that connect to felt meaning in one's workplace role; these were argued to serve as protective mechanisms in the face of workplace distress (p. 3). Storytelling within an organization may serve a powerful purpose, integrating and transmitting cultural perspectives and role models and affecting engagement and norms (Ameen Alharbi & Bhalla, 2023). While workplace archetypes of leadership may reinforce existing hegemonies, alternative models may enlist greater diversity, such as the Magnificat image or Mary as a young female with limited means who finds favor with God (Rothausen, 2023). Theoretical perspectives, such as post-colonial feminist frames, may help to contribute to the retrieval of underrecognized archetypes of how oppressed persons resist power, providing for "critique [of] the construct of a universal woman, which has produced exclusionary canons" (Jamjoom & Mills, 2023, p. 957).

Striving Towards the Light

Jung examines the notion of exploration through the poetry of Faust, connected to a case example. Within this model, there is a paradox expressed, for Faust hints at the evening sense of time and human perishability, lost capacity, as "the glow retreats"; this is contrasted with the desire to soar, looking upward towards the constellations—looking beneath to "a floor of waves" (Jung, 1912a, p. 89). This sense of something unreachable is also found in the case example of the client's poem about the song of a moth, who strives in the direction of an unreachable sun. In associating his patient's conflicts with Faust, Jung describes the way that longing for a transcendent and glittering beyond can also bring "a loathing for life" and a desire to retreat from the present (Jung, 1912a, p. 89). One solution is the "renunciation of the world" through asceticism, which Jung attributes to the Greek myth of Scylla, while another model of Charybdis includes acceptance. Beneath each is a desire to solve a conflict between longing and tragic pain or doubt. The internal process is creatively resolved or encountered through parallelism with myth.

In his reflection about how his work differs from Freud and Adler, Jung (1933) describes his orientation towards looking at health in humankind rather than creating a science of the diagnosis of pathology (p. 117). Westwood and Low (2003) normalize the human response as inherently creative, sharing an Eastern view of "circular conception," which emphasizes "creative acts...as reiterative and repeated configurations of a pre-established, holistic reality...not a newness but a rediscovery" (p. 239). This view of creativity instills revelation rather than origination, with elastic and polychronic estimations of time rather than idealization of linear progress and irrevocable loss (Westwood & Low, 2003, p. 239).

Polarities, Tension, and Projection

The divine syzygies are described by Jung (1954) as "male-female pairs of deities," like yin (feminine) and yang (masculine), in a harmonious balance of opposition. Like the antagonism of gravitational pull towards planetary orbs, or the sun and moon in corresponding alignment, an archetypal pair represents a nonreductive configuration, a potent metaphor for creative energies, constructive debate, and diverse teams. The othering of opposites can also include projection, "an unconscious, automatic process whereby a content…transfers itself to an object, so that it seems to belong to that object" (Jung, 1954, p. 60). Unlike transference, which is built from memory and experience, projection is inaccessible and subliminally derived.

Workplace projections can incorporate discriminatory attitudes based on race, gender, or other classifications, yet they largely remain inaccessible to consciousness. Evocations of archetypes within projective processes are potential headwaters. Jung (1954) describes the Anima as the "feminine and chthonic part of the soul," connoting an inhabitant of an underworld. The seductive power of the Anima is revealed in her ability to invoke erotic love or misogyny, infatuation, and maternal idealization, yet the Anima is found guilty, for "the entanglements are all her doing" (Jung, 1954, p. 71). Jung infers that archetypes are not primarily composites of parental Imagos or attachments; in contrast, they are powerful, repressed, and elusive—to dissect them is to instantiate mutation.

Intimation and Illumination

While the debate regarding the Dalton vs Higgins origin of atomic theory remains (Grossman, 2017), it is generally felt that these ideas surfaced in the early 19th century, well after Democritus (c. 460–c. 370 BC) first authored the notion of material and soul atoms. Jung (1954) advances the idea that this ancient Greek forerunner predicted the "minimal constitutive elements" through engagement with mythology and archetypal forms (p. 57), which resemble "transcendental intuitions," projections of abstract psychic content that are transformed ("hypostatized") into a tangible reality.

In his work, *The Art of Thought*, Graham Wallas (1926) builds a theory of creative realization from an analysis of case studies of Henri Poincaré, Hermann Helmholtz, and Varendonck's Psychology of Daydreams. Identifying stages of preparation, incubation, intimation, illumination, and verification, Wallas (1926) evinces the balance between the interface of the hard work of creativity and its sudden appearance as insight. For example, Poincaré discovered awareness during incubation, but these mathematical findings were more like portals than complete equations. Illumination is described as a flash or a click, an uncontrollable appearance that is preceded by an aura. The presentiment of epiphany is energized by thoughts that reside on the "fringe of consciousness which surrounds...focal consciousness as the sun's corona surrounds the disk of full luminosity" (Wallas, 1926, p. 47). The muse for Helmholtz materialized in incubation, for "happy ideas came...readily during the slow ascent of wooded hills on a sunny day" (Wallas, 1926, p. 37).[1]

Synchronicity

Jung (1960) describes synchronicity as "the simultaneous occurrence of two meaningfully but not causally connected events" (p. 25). Jung first introduced the term in 1930 in response to his reading of the I Ching, or Book of Changes. From this work, he derived the notion of coinciding things as different, yet as if the same. Synchronicity: this view is not representational and does not equate the psyche with brain events. Knowledge gained through synchronicity can offer "self-subsistent meaning" not derived from the senses, but gained from consciousness transcendent to space and time. Synchronous events reveal glimpses of order in a disharmonious world; they are necessary but not absolute, and show regularity but not predictability (Jung, 1960, p. 95). Rather than a pre-established harmony, Jung posits that psychic facts should be added to the list of time, space, and causation as separate and verifiable entities.

Limitations

Jung (1954) warns against a defensive empiricism in psychology that is built exclusively on a materialistic worldview. Arguing in favor of qualitative methods and clinical observation, Jung cautions that medical psychology often fails to acknowledge the theoretical roots of case formulations. Psychological research struggles to find longstanding replication across samples, which is probably due not only to variations in study methods and aims but also to the randomness associated with each human participant. Hoever et al. (2012) offer the point that ongoing meta-analytic studies are often needed to review the overall effects of assumed creativity predictors on outcome variables. The psychosocial field that is examined in ethnographic research can yield ambiguities that produce challenges for studying and expanding theories of the unconscious (Özdemir Kaya & Fotaki, 2023).

Studies of the impact of diversity and group processes on creativity and intuitive illumination can continue to deepen the range of contexts explored, including the forms that diversity may take. Team diversity can be considered in many ways, including both superficial (social categorization and demographics) and deep structural (informational and value-oriented) forms (Phillips & Loyd, 2006). In the same way that experts may demonstrate cognitive entrenchment through commitments to stable paradigms (Dane, 2010), work teams and managers should guard against research designs and interventions that show inflexible stability in adherence to popular trends. Extending work experiences across multiple domains and with a wider social network may be useful methods to work beyond the forms of entrenchment that constrain experimentation and adaptability (Dane, 2010). Ongoing research into how organizations either hinder or advance intuitive processes is warranted (Svenson et al., 2023).

A Canton of Pilgrims

Expanding on Michael Polyani's (1966) *Society of Explorers,* and Josiah Royce's (1918) *Interpretive Community*, the Canton of Pilgrims view espouses a borough where the unconscious is offered to the light of inquiry rather than dissection. Qualitative methods of exploration, dream interpretation, hypnosis, literary immersion, cross-cultural studies, interpretive teams, psychoanalysis, and creative imagination are technologies with potential to rupture homeostasis, opening gates to revelations beyond imitation. Following the rigor of preparation, incubation periods installed in the workplace day can enlist greater access to the adaptive unconscious, preceding the intimation that cannot be controlled or predicted by a pathfinder. Within the commonage, diverse teams share tacit knowledge, the interpretive products of living mentors, and the concentrated wisdom of the writings of human histories, confessors known only by the obscurity of their words and images, with intuition rising to the Camino of the venture wanderer—the entrepreneur.

Note

1 Wallas refers to Rignano's (1923) *Psychology of Reasoning*, which recounts a speech made by Helmholtz in 1891.

Works Cited

Ameen Alharbi, D. A. N., & Bhalla, P. (2023). Crafting cultural narratives: The influence of storytelling on organizational culture. *Journal of Research Administration, 5*(2), 7805–7821.

Dane, E. (2010). Reconsidering the trade-off between expertise and flexibility: A cognitive entrenchment perspective. *Academy of Management Review, 35*(4), 579–603.

de Souza Sant'Anna, A. (2023). *Bion and beyond: Assimilating psychoanalytic perspectives for leadership in contemporary organizational dynamics.* FGVneop—Núcleo de Estudos em Organizações e Pessoas, Brazil.

Dijksterhuis, A., & Nordgren, L. F. (2006). A theory of unconscious thought. *Perspectives on Psychological Science, 1*(2), 95–109.

Dupree, C. H. (2023). *Collective mindfulness in the workplace: A narrative research study exploring individual mindfulness practices and the influence on collective mindfulness practices of workgroups* (Doctoral dissertation, The George Washington University).

Epstein, S. (1994). Integration of the cognitive and the psychodynamic unconscious. *American Psychologist, 49*(8), 709–724.

Grossman, M. I. (2017). John Dalton and the origin of the atomic theory: Reassessing the influence of Bryan Higgins. *The British Journal for the History of Science, 50*(4), 657–676.

Hoever, I. J., Van Knippenberg, D., Van Ginkel, W. P., & Barkema, H. G. (2012). Fostering team creativity: Perspective taking as key to unlocking diversity's potential. *Journal of Applied Psychology, 97*(5), 982–996.

Jamjoom, L. A., & Mills, A. J. (2023). Narratives of workplace resistance: Reframing Saudi women in leadership. *Human Relations, 76*(7), 955–989.

Jung, C. G. (1912a). The song of the moth. In B. M. Hinckle (Trans.), *Psychology of the unconscious.* Translated to English 1915. Reprinted by Dover Publications, Inc. 2002.

Jung, C. G. (1912b). Concerning two kinds of thinking. In B. M. Hinckle (Trans.), *Psychology of the unconscious.* Translated to English 1915. Reprinted by Dover Publications, Inc. 2002.

Jung, C. G. (1933). *Modern man in search of a soul.* W. S. Bell and C. F. Baynes (Trans.). Harcourt Inc.

Jung, C. G. (1936). The concept of the collective unconscious. In R. F. C. Hull (Trans.), *The archetypes and the collective unconscious* (pp. 42–53). Bollingen Series. Princeton University Press.

Jung, C. G. (1954). Concerning the archetypes, with special relevance to the animal concept. In R. F. C. Hull (Trans.), *The archetypes and the collective unconscious* (pp. 54–74). Bollingen Series. Princeton University Press.

Jung, C. G. (1960). Synchronicity: An acausal connecting principle. In R. F. C. Hull (Trans.), *The collected works of Carl Gustav Jung* (Vol. 8). Bollingen Series XX. Princeton University Press. Reprinted 2010.

Jung, C. G. (1961). Approaching in the unconscious. In C. G. Jung, M. L. von Franz, J. L. Henderson, J. Jacobi, & A. Jaffé (Eds.), *Man and his symbols* (pp. 1–94). Dell Publishing. Published posthumously in 1964.

Özdemir Kaya, D. D., & Fotaki, M. (2023). Grounding in the unconscious: "The field" in psychosocial organizational ethnography. *Organization,* 1–23. doi: 10.1177/13505084221148640

Phillips, K. W., & Loyd, D. L. (2006). When surface and deep-level diversity collide: The effects on dissenting group members. *Organizational Behavior and Human Decision Processes, 99*(2), 143–160.

Polanyi, M. (1966). *The tacit dimension.* The University of Chicago Press. Reprinted 2009.

Rogers, B. A. (2023). *Distressing but meaningful: The buffering effect of role meaning archetypes* (Doctoral dissertation, The University of North Carolina at Chapel Hill).

Rothausen, T. J. (2023). Diverse, ethical, collaborative leadership through revitalized cultural archetype: The Mary alternative. *Journal of Business Ethics, 187*(3), 627–644.

Rignano, E. (1923). *The psychology of reasoning.* Routledge. Reprinted 2014.

Royce, J. (1918). *The problem of Christianity.* The University of Chicago Press.

Svenson, F., Pietrzak, P., & Launer, M. A. (2023). Different types of intuition at the workplace: An integrative review. *Business: Theory and Practice, 24*(2), 334–348.

Thrash, T. M., Maruskin, L. A., Cassidy, S. E., Fryer, J. W., & Ryan, R. M. (2010). Mediating between the muse and the masses: Inspiration and the actualization of creative ideas. *Journal of Personality and Social Psychology, 98*(3), 469.

Wallas, G. (1926). *The art of thought.* Solis Press. Reprinted 2014.

Westwood, R., & Low, D. R. (2003). The multicultural muse: Culture, creativity and innovation. *International Journal of Cross Cultural Management, 3*(2), 235–259.

5

INDWELLING, EMPATHY, AND NON-MECHANISTIC, NON-REDUCTIONISTIC CONCEPTS OF THE COLLEGIAL OTHER

Nahanni Freeman

Introduction

The relationship between internalization and creativity can be shown with knowledge-sharing, which can influence self-efficacy (Islam & Asad, 2024), incorporation of organizational culture, mindfulness, and transformational leadership (Batool et al., 2024; Srivastava et al., 2024), and interiorization of cross-cultural perspectives, creative cognition, and momentum (Reiter-Palmon & Hunter, 2023). The consumption of social attributions and contextual factors, which interact with individual differences in creative cognition and personality (Runco, 2023), may be an important consideration when imagining the role of indwelling in workplace creativity. Learning may be considered as a form of indwelling based on transfer, modeling, disruption, dissonance, reflection, and imitation. The role of human-centered educational practices, structured forms of design concept germination, improvisation, and leveraging of psychological capital may facilitate adaptive transformations in creative prospects (Meinel & Krohn, 2022).

Philosophical, Historical, and Psychological Features of Indwelling

A workplace environment has a peculiar ability to be materialized as a biopsychosocial incorporation, internalized into the psychological space of the employee. Organizational absorption is consuming for those prone to addictive and circular workplace thought patterns, supplemented by driven job behaviors such as workaholism. For these individuals, social and

DOI: 10.4324/9781003322894-6

familial functioning can become compromised as the rumination about work tasks, competence, and the judgments of others becomes incorporated into identity and the cognitive life space (Oates, 1971). Retention may be impacted by the interaction between internalized oppression, self-efficacy, prior efforts to change the context, and the receptivity of the environment. Ultimately, the level of indwelling in the workplace culture can prompt meritorious loyalty or soul-crushing neglect.

Workplace embodiment may stimulate skepticism about satisfaction, cost, risk, and the potential for growth. Hirschman (1970) proposed a theory of workplace dissatisfaction that argued for the presence of a sequence of turnover risk factors. The model examined how employees exercise their voice, attempting to correct an unfavorable work situation. Loyalty to the organization or workplace relationships was predicted to moderate the relationship between voice and turnover intentions, with some employees choosing to exit rather than face conflict or risk associated with change-seeking expressions. Hirschman's model cultivated a swath of responsive studies, including a meta-analysis by Farrell and Rusbult (1992) that found workplace behaviors clustering into dimensions of constructive/maladaptive or active/withdrawn; an additional outcome of dissatisfaction was neglect (Saunders, 1992). The Farrell and Rusbult (1992) meta-analysis uncovered a structure for how an appraisal of alternatives and satisfaction may interact with the level of investment an employee is willing to offer (Farrell & Rusbult, 1992; Saunders, 1992). In longitudinal work on the model performed by Withey and Cooper (1989), it was found that loyalty may sometimes resemble entrapment more than devotion. Expectations regarding the efficacy of voice can motivate or stall instrumental agency.

Workplace retention can be imagined as a form of membership, with the indwelling of organizational lifecycles and supervisory behaviors impacting dynamic attitudes regarding job satisfaction (Farrell & Rusbult, 1985). While degenerative spirals are sometimes presumed to be initiated by covert attitudinal shifts, it is important to acknowledge sources of repair. Voice may be more likely in situations where employees perceive that other alternatives are available, and constructive incremental change may connect with higher levels of intrinsic and tangible investment by both the employee and the organization. The level of commitment to an organization seems indelibly connected to expectations.

In an analysis of Michael Polanyi's work on implicit learning and tacit knowledge, Jones and Miller (2009) explore the notion of unconscious inference and its impact on perception, citing the way that light particles enter the retina as a model of receptivity (p. 6). Unconscious inference is identified as a primary medium of perceptual learning, and Polanyi may have assumed that "indwelling is the way in which we become entangled with those particular contexts which become our contexts" (Jones & Miller, 2009, p. 7). The entanglement is preceded by attunement, a shift in attention in the context of the trust that is required for commitment.

Polanyi (1966) states, "When we make a thing function as a proximal term of tacit knowing, we incorporate it in our body…we come to dwell in it" (p. 16). This internalization seems to enlist important notions of attachment and intersubjectivity relevant to Margaret Mahler's symbiotic fusion, a self-other merger discussed in the object relations literature. Polanyi (1966) discusses empathy as a form of indwelling, referencing Dilthey's work on representation (p. 16). Reminiscent of the ancient theory of the eidola as well as monadology, consumption of an environment creates a miniature copy within an observer, with digestion generating a microcosm and mind that reflect a habitat. Polanyi's (1966) view of coalescence states that we "interiorize bits of the universe," potentially recommending a sense of unity between mental and material elements (p. 35). Indwelling ignites awareness of the pervasive influence of workplace functions on adult well-being and adverse experiences (McGinnis, 2018). However, indwelling can also offer a portal into the unconscious and facilitative imagery, securing creativity resources that nurture resilience. Two potentials of indwelling are paradoxical, delivering a multiverse of emergent outcomes relevant to workplace functioning and overall well-being.

Dilthey and Representation as a Creative Response

Polanyi (1966) discusses a form of indwelling that builds on the work of the German philosopher, Wilhelm Dilthey. Referencing the Gesmmelte Schriften, Volume VII,[1] Polanyi states, "Dilthey taught that the mind of a person can be understood only by reliving its workings" (Polanyi, 1966, p. 16). Dilthey's (1882) perspective was influenced by Franz Brentano, Hermann Lotze, and Immanuel Kant; his viewpoint emphasizes the role of subjectivity and self-knowledge in perception, stating that "All facts have their existence only within consciousness…" (p. 277). Awareness of subjectivity can enhance workplace innovation by dislodging deterministic and constraining views of self, others, and context. For Dilthey, mental representations existed as a component of a psychic act, extraordinarily diverse and rooted in potentiality. Representation may be considered as a manifestation of indwelling, a merge between interior and exterior spaces.

Creativity in the workplace is emergent from consciousness and imagination. From Lotze,[2] Dilthey emphasizes the representational qualities of the human experience, also noting the persistence of images after objects disappear, which is influenced by Brentano's assertion of mental objects as floating into "intentional inexistence"[3] (Dilthey, 1882, p. 298). Dilthey quotes Immanuel Kant's perspective on representations, which were felt to be forms of knowledge, impacted by desire and pleasure-seeking, and formed in relation to the person as subject.[4] In addition, Kant claimed that representations are not merely observed in relation to other associations, but cause an object to form a reality in the psychic world, generally following the principle of the unity of consciousness. For Kant, representations followed idiosyncratic rules in order to maintain existence. When impacted by desire, representations denoted an expression of some future possibility and served as a form of self-determination. Dilthey implied that representations may not necessarily form a whole percept (1882, p. 300), but he did indicate the tendency to organize perception around a nexus (p. 279) and asserted that psychic acts are "irreducible" (p. 294). As with tacit knowledge, workplace creativity extends beyond the atomistic and economic variety, building on awareness of a concealed possibility yet to be manifested.

Theodor Lipps: Perceptual Fusion, Relativity, and Adaptation

A theory of aesthetics can hold particular relevance for the appreciation of creativity as a form of beauty in the workplace, connecting to the view of elegance that is connoted with the principle of parsimony in the sciences. Polanyi (1966) describes indwelling and its implications for the creative arts, expanding on the work of Theodor Lipps in Aesthetik, published in 1903. Polanyi states, "Lipps represented aesthetic appreciation as an entering into a work of art and thus indwelling in the mind of its creator" (Polanyi, 1966, p. 16). This perspective is likely a bridge from Lipps' work with studies of perception of tone and spatial qualities, which he argued tended towards principles of fusion of impressions and sensations (Lipps, 1905, p. 71). Workplace enrichment can afford exposure to a diversity of stimuli and novelty, expanding opportunities for indwelling and creative synthesis.

Diverse groups can facilitate divergent thinking in the workplace, quickening perceptual integration, cross-associational networks, and the insight emergent from preconscious material. For Theodor Lipps, the ideational process included nonconscious elements that contributed to perceptual fusion, a model adopted from Carl Stumpf (Lipps, 1905, p. 196). Lipps also integrated aspects of Wundt's theories but discharged some particulars. He seemed interested in perceptual convergence in a variety of ways, including the remark that physical vibrations of chords create "a feeling of consonance," which "takes place in the soul" (Lipps, 1905, p. 139). Perceptions were felt to "enter into manifold relations with one another," later meeting in the soul as spatial relations (Lipps, 1905, p. 127). The subjectivity and unique properties of perception are described by Lipps (1905) as he encounters Weber's Law, psychic relativity, adaptation, perceptual comparisons, reduction towards wholes, and projective processes with object perception, where the corporeal world is transformed into the mind's eye from a range of vantage points. Each of these encounters implies various forms of integration of the external and internal, with a transformative process that generates a creative impression.

Samuel Butler, Non-Mechanism, and Vitalism: Potential Forces Propelling Creativity

Mindful attention to the present moment in an unhurried and capacious workplace may maximize creative potential and constructive indwelling, especially when integration of the body and sensations is incorporated. Polanyi (1966) discusses the work of Samuel Butler, who described the way that objects can become a "sentient extension of our body" (p. 16). Polanyi describes this as a sense of generalization from the body, which extracts attention towards the object of interest and changes the appearance of the object. Rattray (1914) explores Butler's philosophy in terms of his perspectives on consciousness and the cosmos. These reflections include the notion of vitalism, which tends to imply a sense that living organisms operate according to unique principles that extend beyond physical and chemical processes, sometimes also including the notion that all matter is alive. Connection to a hidden vital source of creative impulse is observed across cultures and historical eras with the notion of a muse, divine inspiration, genius-as-gift, and indwelling spirit. The thought that creative forces may contain unique energetic and concealed properties is found within various models of the spontaneous emergence of works of art after prolonged rehearsal and study.

An understanding of philosophies of consciousness holds promise for an illumination model of creative impulse. According to Rattray (1914), Butler opposed mechanism, suggesting that both body and mind are "more controlled of the spirit...the spirit of life is not a product of mechanism, but mechanism is a product of life" (Rattray, 1914, p. 376). Butler emphasized consciousness as a property submerged in the hidden qualities of objects due to atomic movement, looked at the infinite aspects of consciousness, and discussed the fallacy of size in terms of the relative perspective that assertions of size rely upon, using this as a way to also understand mind-related phenomena (Rattray, 1914) as forms of possibility, subjective and grounded in comparison. The prospect of automaticity, which occurs after familiarity and shifts in attention, was a principle of Butler's theory (Rattray, 1914, p. 373) that remains engaged with Polanyi's views of tacit knowledge.

Awareness of the transcendent and entertaining the possibility of a creative source beyond and more powerful than the ego may impel innovative movement in the workplace. Samuel Butler's work, as portrayed in Rattray, implies a form of panentheism, or expression of the idea of interdependency between God and the world (Rattray, 1914, p. 373), which suggests a certain transcendent force potentially influential on human consciousness. This is revealed in Rattray's conclusion that "Our world is but the world of our self-consciousness: it is but a drop in the bucket of our real life: the rest is silence, for it is hid with Christ in God. The Universe is alive! And its soul is God" (Rattray, 1914, p. 26).

The notion of tacit knowledge is also implied by Rattray's (1914, p. 376) discussion of ancestral memories in the work of Robert Louis Stevenson and Sigmund Freud, which likely contributed to Carl Jung's construct of archetypes. Tacit knowledge could also be viewed within the model of intergenerational or instinctual human understanding, which can interface with experience within time. Connection to archetypal knowledge can be viewed as a form of indwelling that crosses the boundaries of generational wisdom and cultural narratives, fostering new revelations from old conscious material.

Interiorization and the Eidola

Polayni (1966, pp. 16–18) describes the process of interiorization, referencing sensory and aesthetic knowledge, moral principles, and science, adding that "we interiorize bits of the universe, and thus populate it with comprehensive entities" (p. 35). Considering metaphors for transformation, transmission, and imitation can be illuminating for an understanding of human communication and the complexities of workplace systems. On a metaphoric level, one may consider the Platonic aesthetic view of the eidola, which differs from the conception presented in Epicurus, Democritus, and Lucretius (Pappas, 2020). In the Platonic model, the source of living organisms is divine, yet there are also shadows, dreams, and images, or eidola, which are reflections of the real (Pappas, 2020). An eidola can be conceived as an imitation of something real, a tiny copy that contains part of the real yet remains external to the object of mimesis. A theory of creativity that is built from novel imitation could be useful, with rigorous study of historical and philosophical sources bringing new life that swells beyond the frozen elements of mechanistic and dehumanized forms of economics and marketing. Consciousness, change, movement, and the order of ethics can forge new creative worlds in an organizational system.

The notion of movement between beings and objects in the world is central to change. Some initiators of change are immaterial, concealed, or transitory. The metaphor of the eidola is useful in constructing a model of change that considers interactions between the sensory, perceptual, material, and spiritual features of existence. Kodera (2024) reviews Sir Kenelm Digby's (1603–1665) translation of Renaissance Neoplatonic panpsychism as synthesized with Christianity by Marsilio Ficino (Kodera, 2024). Generally, panpsychism transfers the idea that consciousness is foundational for reality and the physical world; this view has many different expressions as surfacing in the work of Wundt, William James, Gustav Fechner, Hermann Lotze, and others (Goff et al., 2022). In the work of Baruch Spinoza (1632–1677), for example, the role of consciousness in material reality is expressed in the scholium of his *Ethics,* as shown by words, quoted in Goff et al. (2022),

> A circle existing in nature and the idea of the existing circle, which is also in God, are one and the same thing … therefore, whether we conceive nature under the attribute of Extension, or under the attribute of Thought … we shall find one and the same order, or one and the same connection of causes….
>
> *(Goff et al., 2022, para. 7)*

Beyond mechanisms, outside of logarithms, one can encounter living creativity, which can be harnessed in an actualized workplace. One way that the limits of mechanism can be parceled out is through vitalism or the position that all of the physical world is alive; this was often presented during the Renaissance era, where spirits were viewed as evasive mediators, perhaps with agency (Kodera, 2024). Sensation, imagination, and memory were felt to have magnetic qualities, and the universe was conceived as sentient and alive. A spiritus philosophy held that ethereal forces were tied to natural changes, for spirits were instruments, porters, distributors, and transmitters, forging interactions between the imagination and the world soul. In the view of Ficino, the world soul housed a hierarchical and natural cosmos, created with spirits that had both material and immaterial qualities (Kodera, 2024). The spiritus model implies an interiorization of life.

The impression of indwelling can be expanded with the metaphor of an eidola, which was a shadow that represented a Platonic form, facilitating communication between the spiritual and the physical (Kodera, 2024). The eidola were viewed as "the precondition for the interaction between the stars and our bodies; they are emanations of a world soul" within Ficino's worldview (Kodera, 2024, p. 153). The view of eidola was also influenced by the Epicurean model, which emphasized the idea of tiny particles, emitting from objects in the world or living bodies, which could incorporate these atoms as a "tincture" (Kodera, 2024, p. 152). Changes in knowledge,

Being, light, and mental representation were attributed to the material and immaterial transfer from one being to another, or from one object to another, in an exchange of life force. This insemination in sentient beings is also housed in the internalization of micro-expressions, nonverbal atoms, and minute yet detectable modifications of voice. All are potentially internalized into the self-system, with an impact on the entire workplace microcosm. Adaptive internalizations are possible within humanistic workplace settings that emphasize individuality, freedom, and congruence.

A Person-Centered Approach to Employment Indwelling

A person-centered approach to a workplace environment may include the model of self-actualization proposed by Carl Rogers (1961). Within this perspective, the healthy individual will recede from facades and the attempt to meet cultural expectations, moving towards: creativity, self-direction, trust and acceptance of self and others, complexity, a fluid process of personal change, and openness to experience and the present moment (Rogers, 1961, pp. 167–175, 193). An increasing sense of internal freedom and awareness of the richness of life would accompany a clear sense of meaning in the person who orients towards congruence between internal realities and external presentations. Rogers' (1961) model envisions a healthy milieu as one where relationships are genuine because individuals are aware and accepting of their emotional experiences (p. 34). Respect for the separateness of others is conveyed within a space of warmth, empathy, and safety, where moral evaluation of others is absent and awareness of each person's drive for growth and self-actualization is not only recognized but encouraged (Rogers, 1961, pp. 34–36). Rogers (1961) advocated for the application of his theory towards an approach to organizational administration built on the assumption that workers will naturally move towards creativity, problem-solving, and cooperation within a healthy geography (p. 37). Ultimately, the greatest concern should be for an anthropology that champions the human being "as a person of unconditional self-worth" (Rogers, 1961, p. 34).

A theory of tacit knowledge insists that long-term retention of employees is essential, predicated on the assumption that experienced workers possess expertise that extends well beyond the narrow parameters of job duties. These vast stores of intuitive knowledge cannot be fully communicated but guide problem-solving, inhibition, social exchange, and improvisation. In light of concern regarding what has been deemed "the Great Resignation," employers and supervisors are wise to consider ways to prevent turnover intentions. An environment that nourishes self-actualization clarifies values, promoting adaptive internalization, commitment, and organizational identity.

A maladaptive form of indwelling is observed with the internalization of workplace shockwaves. While traditional models of turnover have focused on overall employee satisfaction and the presence of alternatives, the Unfolding Model proposed by Lee and Mitchell (1994) assumes that turnover deliberation decision paths are often instigated by the presence of shocks or unexpected negative events that trigger acute reactions. These authors suggest that a query into the dynamic events that unfold in the workplace may assist with prediction, rather than post-diction, with respect to turnover. Later evidence supports a context-specific model of turnover that takes industry trends, job specifications, and worker-job situational variables into consideration (Hom et al., 2017).

In an investigation that compared male and female STEM professionals, an inverted-U function was observed in job performance for those who developed turnover intentions (Wu et al., 2023). Performance increased rapidly, followed by a sharp decline. This pattern could indicate reactivity to work-related shocks. Wu et al. (2023) conclude that person-centered approaches may yield more utility than variable-driven models for abetting retention.

Person-centered approaches are also advocated by Conte and Harmata (2023), who describe the importance of seeing the employee holistically and as an individual in terms of multi-dimensional cognitive ability patterns, rather than relying on the traditional barometer of general intelligence as a unitary construct to predict job performance. Supervisor ratings of effort, discipline and peer leadership may vary depending on a range of different cognitive profiles, providing insight into the diversity of cognitive patterns that interact with workplace-employee fit (Conte & Harmata, 2023). Person-centered approaches to the workplace can include the fostering of belonging, social capital, long-term projects, and community-based teams, as well as the inclusion of an orientation towards matching people's knowledge, preferences and skills to the tasks they are asked to perform (Lee et al., 2004).

Indwelling through Embeddedness

One potential form of employment indwelling involves a sense of connection to the organization, people, and identifications associated with the career. Mitchell et al. (2001) developed the construct of job embeddedness, which involves attachment to colleagues, teams, and the company, the extent to which one sees themselves as a good fit for the employment community, and an appraisal of what would need to be sacrificed in order to leave. These factors have been shown to predict turnover intentions and voluntary separation from one's job. Mitchell et al. (2001) built this model from Kurt Lewin's[5] notion of field dependence and March and Simon's[6] review of the ease with which one can leave a position, as related to job attachment. In the embeddedness model, fit conveys the concept of compatibility with workplace values and community. It makes sense to consider how embeddedness may potentially interact with employee retention and promotion, as well as organizational citizenship behavior, which includes an array of extra-role activities, such as volunteering with non-mandatory job tasks, acting as an organizational ambassador, and helping others to succeed in their jobs (Lee et al., 2004).

Embeddedness may further be segregated into on-the-job versus off-the-job contexts, as shown by Lee et al. (2004). Building further on the work of March and Simon[7] and also Hulin's[8] work on the gradual forces that impact turnover decisions through withdrawal, these authors proposed that on-the-job embeddedness includes the perception that one's values and goals match the organization, that the cost-benefit analysis is favorable in terms of personal sacrifices, and that interpersonal attachments on the job are worthwhile. In contrast, off-the-job embeddedness examines the level of fit between the employee's life outside of work, including community participation, and the demands of the job. The impact of the job on interpersonal life and personal sacrifices at home are significant turnover considerations. Volitional absence and voluntary turnover were predicted by off-the-job embeddedness, while on-the-job embeddedness predicted organizational citizenship behavior and job performance. In general, the construct of embeddedness was predictive of absences and turnover.

When facing work-related stressors, the effects of social support on employee well-being are likely to be impacted by intervening variables, including personality traits, emotional closeness, and the type of support offered. For example, early studies on the effects of social support on anxiety found that the value of instrumental vs emotional support varied as a function of individual attachment style (Mikulincer & Florian, 1997). Those with avoidant attachment styles were more likely to benefit from instrumental support with problem-solving but were less responsive to emotional support and compensated through a self-reliance script, which may connect to difficulties with trusting the intentions of others. In contrast, those with anxious-ambivalent attachments benefited less from problem-solving and instrumental support, possibly due to the triggering of underlying schemas related to self-doubt.

Embeddedness may vary as a function of context, with team identification, conservation of resources, and community indwelling predicting organizational citizenship behavior, job performance, and turnover intentions (Fan et al., 2023). Part of embeddedness may include a nest-building response whereby workers seek to create a barracks around valued job-related resources and social capital. Building on the *Conservation of Resource Model* proposed by Hobfoll (1989), Fan et al. (2023) proposed that job newcomers may redeploy resources from one domain towards a deficient arena, with chosen strategies connecting to team identification and the ability to leverage community resources. The Conservation of Resource Model proposes that people seek to respond to threats to safety and wish to retain existing resources, building in protections against loss (Hobfoll, 1989). Various types of loss will result in different levels of potency, with loss spirals being possible as a function of evolving contexts (Hobfoll, 1989). Resources can include both subjective and objective features, and the response to loss may be mediated by personality features such as hardiness, locus of control, social support, and affective quality (Hobfoll, 1989).

Indwelling through Team Identification

Building on Self-Categorization Theory, which was proposed by Turner and colleagues,[9] Shemla and Wegge (2019) found that collective team identification moderated the quality of information brought to tasks. Collective team identification refers to the "psychological merging of self and team, which induces team members to perceive [themselves] as psychologically intertwined with the fate of the group" (Shemla & Wegge, 2019, p. 759).[10] Stronger levels of team identification have been shown to predict greater collaboration. While the effects of perceived versus objective team diversity may vary, as these constructs are not identical, the positive benefits of diverse perspectives are likely influenced by individual differences, team design, and leadership (Shemla & Wegge, 2019).

Team identification has been shown to partially mediate the relationship between organizational citizenship behavior and other variables, such as task mutuality, informational dissimilarity, and goal interdependence (Van Der Vegt et al., 2003). Important psychological goals may underlie the tendency to self-categorize, including factors identified by Turner et al. (1987, as cited in Van Der Vegt et al., 2003) such as reduction of uncertainty, creation of a positive and superior social identity, and maintenance of a self-view. Thus, individuals will tend to see themselves as either members of a particular social classification or not, which in turn affects prosocial behavior (Van Der Vegt et al., 2003).

Team identification as a form of embeddedness may help to curtail performance decline, although many additional variables are likely also at play. Derailment in the workplace, which is seen when career advancement plateaus or does not reach expected performance, can be costly to the maintenance of organizational innovation and worker retention

(Hezlett, 2023). As factors, career stallers and stoppers may help predict derailment in light of competencies that include the generation of vision, self-regulation, instilling trust, and problem-solving, among others. Career stallers comprise learning stagnation, political faux pas, decline in ability to inspire or maintain talent, poor regulation of effective staffing, excessive dependency on a perceived ally, and overreliance on a narrow skill set (Hezlett, 2023).

Bodily Indwelling in Merleau-Ponty

A workplace environment is experienced not only in consciousness but also internalized into the well-being and integrity of the body, being manifested through the senses within perceived time. In his chapter on emergence, Polanyi (1966) discusses how the body is involved in object perception (p. 29). This theme is also manifested in Simone De Beauvoir's discussion of subject-object, also considering the work of Merleau-Ponty. Polanyi's (1966) discussion of bodily indwelling as related to how the observer simulates movements in the performer predicts the later discovery of mirror neurons, potentially impactful for learning and empathy.

Learning is a social manifestation of workplace indwelling, expressed within a body that serves as observer and observed. The merging between the body as observer and the body as object of observation is shown in the work of Merleau-Ponty (1945), who explores the subjectivity of perception, for when I focus on an object, "I anchor myself in in" (p. 70). The intimate connection between the body, with its sensory capacities, and the external environment, is also implied by his statement that "…to see the object is to plunge into it…" (p. 70). Thought is viewed as integral to the essential qualities of the body (Merleau-Ponty, 1945, p. 74), and consciousness of the body, with attention to its multitude of parts in a system of relations, is unavoidable (pp. 75, 81). The synthesis of perceptions with the world is shown in Merleau-Ponty's (1945) view that the exterior cannot be legitimately separated from the body, for the schema of the body forms the basis of perception (pp. 211, 213). When the employee enters the workspace, there is no escape from this fundamental subjectivity of perception.

The capacity for objective analysis of the external world would only be possible if a "universal mind" could be derived from the place of never becoming a body, which would require a "transcendental I" (Merleau-Ponty, 1945, p. 216). The body is portrayed as the location that 'animates' concealed representations (Merleau-Ponty, 1945, p. 209). While perceptions are assumed to have real existence, they are encased in memory, which is at best a "probable synthesis" (Merleau-Ponty, 1945, p. 70). The intersection between self as observer and object of others' observations is a conundrum that points to the ambiguity of existing in a body that must interact with a mind, visual and emotional representations of the world, and nonconscious processes. If creativity is to be maximized in the workplace, it must appreciate the subjectivity and ambiguity of a perceptual world, for the organization is not an organism, even though it is comprised of living entities.

Interactions between features of the mind and body are significant for self-actualization and well-being in workplace settings and social life. Sigmund Freud's emphasis on the weight of unconscious fantasy for psychic life impacted the understanding of how self-determination functions in emotional and behavioral regulation and appraisals of the world and others. In his analysis of Freud's work, Jacques Lacan (1936, as cited in Roudinesco, 2003) responded in a lecture to questions about the relation between self, fantasy, will, impulse, and body, turning the notion of "subject" into a philosophical interpretation that incorporated the work of Hegel. Freud's usage of the term "subject" was often in a different sense than the philosophical usage, with some uncertainty as to his meaning; he seemed to emphasize an irrational and internalized world more than the external context or a reality principle. Roudinesco (2003) points out that it was commonly understood in Freud's work that "the subject is not fully contextualized" (p. 27). However, Lacan delivered expansion, noting the subject of desire, the subject as the unconscious, and the subject as the human being, a self with agency and knowledge, controlling internal cognitive spaces. The subject may also be prone to reactivity in response to intrusions and ruptures, mirroring internal and external realities within a developmental sequence. Flexible workplace environments may benefit from maximizing the creative potential and idiosyncratic lens of all employees, including those who are mentally ill or who present with autism spectrum disorders or other differences.

An inclusive workplace, esteemed for its openness to divergent thinking and rupture of conformity, will also recognize the distance between workers' internal mental worlds and their bodily manifestation of mind. In her analysis of the work of Merleau-Ponty, Simone de Beauvoir (1945) contrasts the spontaneous and lively experience of consciousness and subjectivity with the "frozen objects" of science (p. 159). She means to recognize the way that bodies are situated in time and space, with the body containing and revealing an entire history. Paradoxically, the revelation of the world and the minds of other people is opaque and unknowable, for the objects in the world evade us—they are "silence and mystery, and an Other who escapes us" (de Beauvoir, 1945, p. 162).

When considering the relationship between the body and the world, de Beauvoir's (1945) work offers a window into indwelling. Integrating components of Merleau-Ponty by both quoting his phrases and offering her own response, she states, "to perceive the blue sky…I must abandon myself to it, so that it "thinks itself within me"' (de Beauvoir, 1945, p. 162).[11] Indwelling includes more than incorporation, for it is also commitment rooted in sensory integration, for "perception…ties us to the world as to our homeland…"the taking back into ourselves of a foreign intention"' (de Beauvoir, 1945, p. 162). De Beauvoir (1945) intends to offer a non-coercive solution to the existence of the human being within a context; she reminds the reader of the integrity and subjectivity of one's conscious and lived experience. The affirmation is seen in her conclusion that, with awareness of both the reality of the world and the existence of our mind in temporality, "we embrace the very movement of life that is belief…in our own presence" (de Beauvoir, 1945, p. 164).

Symbiosis in Early Human Development, a Precursor and a Metaphor

Workplace creativity will be maximized in environments that foster attachment, manifested in relationships both inside and outside of the organization. Attachment proliferates towards identifications, teams, and symbiotic relationships within the system. While humans are interested in novel perceptions and complex designs from a young age, the orientation towards relationality is a cardinal feature of early development, for "the human face…in motion is the first meaningful percept…" (Mahler et al., 1975, pp. 45–46). The relationship with the mother is often emphasized in the object relations literature, for she is characterized as a "midwife of individuation" and the "symbiotic organizer of differentiation" (Mahler et al., 1975, p. 47). Early gaze patterns and eye-to-eye contact become "the organizer," triggering a social response in the releaser (Mahler et al., 1975, p. 46). Patterns of holding behavior are internalized into the psychological structure of the infant. What is it that will hold the adult in the organizational context? What experiences will subvert psychological safety?

The birth of the actualized employee will move beyond self-interest or preoccupation with safety into a sense of attachment to the community essential for flourishing. The psychological birth of a human being emerges from the forerunner of attachment, a sensory-egocentric phase (Mahler et al., 1975). Within this phase, which can be envisioned like the self-nourishing egg of a bird, the individual still lacks full awareness of the Other, being focused on perceptual, sensory, and recipient-oriented experiences that become more selective over time. As sensory awareness of the environment expands, the child develops a clinging response, described as anklammerung by Spitz (as cited in Mahler et al., 1975).

With workplace security and psychological safety, exploration and movement beyond fetal protectiveness become possible. Early development can serve as a motif for creative maturation within a series of workplace dyads: ideational splitting, omnipotent fantasies, and innovation rejection. As the self-containment phase transitions into the beginning of symbiosis, a primal entity materializes, paralleling as a novel idea. The dawning primal self orients towards psychophysiological events and expulsion from the body, a physical parallel of splitting the good from the bad and ridding the self of the bad introjection. The energy of drives is undifferentiated and potent, a main focus of the experience of pleasure and pain. A shield begins to form around the parent-child dyad, a unity that is referred to as a "symbiotic orbit" (Mahler et al., 1975). There is a sense of omnipotence that develops as the child's needs are gratified by the mother, producing the "boundlessness of the oceanic feelings" (Freud, 1930, as cited in Mahler et al., 1975). The fusion with the mother is an undifferentiated state where the self is not distinctive from the non-self in a space called the "symbiotic milieu interieur." Internal and external states are fused, and the ego begins to develop within a landscape of absolute dependence, which is both social and physical. With adaptive attachments in place in secure environments, the internal milieu of the mind can flourish, migrating into novel associations and forms of creative synthesis that would be impossible in an environment of threat or competition.

Reductionism, the Danger of Literalism

An appreciation of the limitless potential of creativity and the unknowability of the Other provides a corrective for the damaging effects of interpersonal and systemic reductionism. Polanyi (1966) warns about reductionism if one focuses too much on the particulars, stating, "Unbridged lucidity can destroy our understanding of complex matters" (p. 18). He adds that when one perceives the whole, the parts recover meaning—the comprehensive relationship among parts is restored. This recovery of meaning stands in contrast to workplace dehumanization, which simplifies the uncontainable Other into an 'it.'

Polanyi (1966) indicates that, when one diverts perception to atomistic elements, one loses the image of the entity, which holds relevance for the harmful nature of binaries in person-perception. Projections are extensions of internal states—beliefs, expectations, identities, and fears—which are then sent out as missiles towards the workplace Other (p. 34). Polanyi (1966) states that knowledge of the *laws* governing the particulars could never account for the organizing principles of the whole (p. 34); these are extended, potential, and dynamic. This stands as a reminder of a central thesis of the Gestalt branch of psychology, for Polanyi (1966) states that thinkers cannot represent the organizing states of the dominant level by the laws that determine or manage the parts (p. 36). A systemic view of the workplace and the people it contains will expand upon the dynamic and uncertain qualities of a non-coercive, creative space.

The argument for holism is an important contrast for neural identity theory, or the argument that mental states, representations, and other mental qualities will necessarily correspond to neural real estate. Neurochemicals cannot tell us what it is to have a mind. Yet, organisms must rely on laws of physics, as they govern inanimate matter (Polanyi, 1966, p. 37). There is genetic grounding that can be well connected to epigenetic processes and the norm of reaction, the wide range of possibilities where genes, biological factors, and environmental press interact. Polanyi (1966) points out that sentience cannot be explained by chemical processes (p. 37). The vast frontier of perspectives on human consciousness is a testament to uncertainty—the inability to contain minds with digital operating systems or economic formulas. Mechanism is a futile approach for the study of human beings (Polanyi, 1966, p. 38), yet logical positivism and its effects remain as signposts in the contemporary fusion between science and determinism.

Wholes and Parts

A model of wholes and components is useful for championing the complexity of dynamic minds pursuing creative impulse within the workplace system, considering the chemical reaction that exists when the individual interacts with the team and the employment hierarchy. In his analysis of the Berlin School of Gestalt Psychology, which was a primary academic seat for Kurt Koffka (1886–1941), Max Wertheimer (1880–1943), and Wolfgang Kohler (1887–1967), Greenwood (2020) examines two propositions regarding the relationship between wholes and parts. In the first viewpoint, termed *holism*, a whole is considered to be different from the parts that it contains. Greenwood (2020) indicates that this view was clearly endorsed by the Berlin Gestalt School. A holistic view would imply that workplace creativity cannot be deconstructed—it will emerge as a new product with qualities that expand outside of the expectancies of the individuals who design and envision it. The whole is grander than, beyond, and transcendent to, the elements that comprise it.

The second proposition about wholes and parts is explored in Greenwood's (2020) analysis of relativity, a concept that emphasizes how parts interact with other parts. Within this model, parts might be studied as entities that change in relation to one another, and the importance of viewing them next to, or inside of, the whole would be implied. This proposition articulates the view that parts can be understood only in relation to other parts and only when considering the whole; in fact, the identity of these parts is assumed to be actually *determined* by these relationships (Greenwood, 2020, p. 284). This proposition can be called the *principle of relational identity* (p. 289). When applied to a workplace context, one might assume that an atomistic study of particulars could provide a greater understanding of the ingredients of creativity and how these atoms form a lively and interactive entity.

Comparisons, measurements, distinctions, and the pursuit of underlying laws may be one approach to the science of creativity. Greenwood (2020) suggests that Wilhelm Wundt (1832–1920) was committed to the second principle of relativity of parts, based on his analysis of the *Outlines of Psychology, Völkerpsychologie, Logik*, and the work of Wundt scholar Arthur Blumenthal. In addition, Wundt's "principle of creative resultants" suggests that aggregates differ from their elements (Greenwood, 2020, p. 289). These creative outcomes are controlled by apperception, which can be described as a psychological law of consciousness that allows for the comparison and measurement of the intensity of sensations in relation to one another (Kim, 2022). Greenwood (2020) claims that Wundt did not see the whole as necessarily *distinct* from the parts but suggested rather that "configurations have a significance or properties that are not contained in their elements" (Greenwood, 2020, p. 290). The unique compositions of workplace creativity will necessarily be localized to context and culture, impacted by measures of intensity and distinctiveness.

Creativity configurations within organizational systems have emergent qualities, possibly with self-organizing features that resemble minds. Greenwood (2020) examines the idea of a "relational ontology" (p. 291), which posits that "all entities are constituted by their relation to other things" (p. 292). This notion lies in opposition to an atomistic understanding of psychological experience, perception, or sensation. Greenwood (2020) suggests that the Berlin Gestalt School believed that the dynamic and self-organizing features of wholes extended to social and natural contexts; however, he also concludes that there may be some elements that can be understood in an atomistic way (p. 291).

Cultural Entry and the Mind

Each workplace is a culture with ethical, normative, and social idiosyncrasies that may indwell the person. Kreppner (1999) asks the question of how culture may enter the mind, reviewing the work of Berveldt and Verheggen.[12] Kreppner adds an historical element, bringing in the work of Nicolas Malebranche in *The Search After Truth* (1678), which is said to move from Descartes' purely mental view of consciousness into a more holistic account that included emotional events, interacting with the external world in a reality that relies on ideas (Malebranche, 1678, p. 213).

A model of indwelling will consider the relation between mind and world, viewing a sense of co-regulation between the workplace system and the employee or creative. Gottfried Leibniz sought to construct a non-mechanistic model of the cosmos and human consciousness, considering the possibility of a microcosm within each mind, an entity within itself. Kreppner (1999) points out that Leibniz was influenced by Malebranche, and rejected the clockwork mechanism that was common in his era. Rather, according to Kreppner (1999), Leibniz proposed a sense of harmony between the mind and the material world, so that co-regulation is emphasized, rather than a closed system (p. 214). Likewise, the employee is not an individual in isolation but rather exists in a place where workplace signals and subtle communications are pulled into the self-system of the organism.

Kreppner (1999) critiques the idea of a self-regulating [autopoietic] system to explain human subjectivity; such a model would assume that consciousness produces itself while also generating its own conditions rather than assimilating and accommodating a world, as would be implied by the work of Jean Piaget.[13] Kreppner warns against a view of human beings where cultural and environmental forces are merely triggers and the individual is perpetually self-regulating, monitoring internal states with a stunning inattention to the external world. In contrast, Kreppner (1999) favors the open system suggested by a spiral interaction model, as described by Maturana and Varela.[14] Furthermore, he argues that cultural internalization relies on a subsumed shared meaning structure, building on the work of Cassirer.[15] Kreppner (1999) emphasizes the way that culture becomes embedded in an individual (p. 208), as the person constructs a reality through enactivism, or an active cognitive, emotional, and social exchange with the world and attachment figures (p. 209). This enculturation poses important challenges for the responsibilities of human resource management.

Leibniz, Monads, and Microcosms

A view of the workplace Other as a microcosm of potential and authentic substance could yield a humanistic ethic that would maximize a form of innovation with the potential to revolutionize not only the economic structure of individual organizations, but the well-being of societies. The turn towards some forms of idealism is likely more productive than yet another iteration of utilitarianism, pragmatism, and materialism. Although he did not describe himself as an idealist, philosophers often conclude that the theories of Gottfried Leibniz presented idealistic notions that seemed to originate in the study of Plato (Look, 2020). In his theory of monads, which can be thought of as a simple substance or essence that can be combined into more complex forms (Guyer & Horstmann, 2021), only the minds of beings, capable of perception and movement, could be considered to be authentic substances (Look, 2020). All other material substances were considered as derivatives of mind monads, which do not exist in space because the body has its existence only as an extension of the mind (Look, 2020). Each monad was representative of a universe, but from a unique perspective where the only infinite substance was divine (Guyer & Horstmann, 2021).

Polanyi emphasized the internalization of the cosmos, hinting at the notion of a microcosm. Building from this notion of monads as an analogy, we may consider the mind as an incorporation of substance from the world, internalizing from other minds and the world of appearances. Each mind, which constitutes a self, represents a vast expanse that cannot be fully known by other minds but can be viewed as an essential quality and an end. When we connect with the subjectivity of another person, we interiorize a universe.

The Principle of Marginal Control

The internalization of control and system justifications can be viewed as another form of indwelling. The organizing principles of a higher level (such as a mind) exercise control over the particulars (Polanyi, 1966, p. 40). This can be viewed in light of psychoneuroimmunology, where top-down processes of the mind interact with the matter of the body, changing epigenetic outcomes and ultimately, health. Yet the lower levels pose restrictions on this mind-body interactionism (hence the limits of a Platonic transcendence over the body). This could be extended as a metaphor to conceive of workplace hierarchies, where the supervisory mind controls the individual workers, with significant potential effects on well-being and upward mobility.

One mechanism of control could be viewed within the construct of workplace conditioning, which emanates from a view of reinforcement and association. With classical conditioning, associations are forged in response to external triggers and may occur in conscious or nonconscious processes (Razran, 1961). In contrast, interoceptive conditioning involves an interior milieu, which responds to the viscera by conveying a message to the periphery (Razran, 1961, p. 82). Proprioceptive feedback may alter the relationship between configurations of stimuli and their effects (Razran, 1961, p. 134). Various forms of conditioning may be subsumed as nonconscious learning, subject to contextual patterns of social control and dominance. Control represents a form of internalization that can be conditioned below the level of awareness in ways that instill slavish obedience or exit.

Mechanisms and Individual Differences, Workaholism, and Unrelenting Standards

Mechanistic views of personhood promote the form of prototype matching that interacts with decisions by administration about promotion. If the worker matches the projection—the prototype—he or she may be considered as a comprehensive entity with creative potential. When the worker/creator perceives (tacitly or explicitly) that he or she is not valued, this contributes to disengagement and disidentification. Disempowerment contributes to the spiral of despair and the resolve to withdraw effort and commitment.

In response to a dehumanizing work environment, there may exist forms of post-traumatic growth that can contribute to the enhancement of meaning and commitment to internalized ideals. Resilience is not the product of suffering, but can emerge despite suffering. Within Barbara Fredrickson's (2004) broaden-and-build theory of positive emotions, greater expressions of play, exploration, sensory integration, learning, intimacy, and savoring may develop within the context of emotions of joy, love, and curiosity. These experiences can strengthen connections between cognition and behavior, fostering movements towards social bonds and replenishing reserves to handle stress.

While a spiral of despair may emerge from the deflation of identity in a toxic workplace context, a broaden-and-build model (Fredrickson, 2004) may be used to consider a counter-movement. In an examination of a *Community Capitals Framework*, which takes a systems model to predict resilience factors, Emery and Flora (2006) look for evidence of an ascending "spiral of hope" (p. 19). One way to foster an ascending spiral can be through accessing social capital, which focuses on the resources of community attachments and positive interactions within networks. Other sources of capital can encompass: geographical resources, financial affordances, infrastructure and the built environment, the skills of people [human capital], cultural traditions, and political access (Emery & Flora, 2006). As individuals leverage these sources of capital, it is possible to gain the self-reinforcing mechanism of cumulative success, which expands into thriving.

Mechanistic views of personhood may support systems that oppress workers due to excessive emphasis on an unrelenting work ethic as a standard of success and social status. According to Oates (1971), workaholism includes a pressurized internal motivational system that is driven by a need to exceed expectations. However, this driven quality is not originating from passion for one's work or a sense of meaning; rather, it is obsessive and based on a sense that one ought to complete work to an uncontrollable quantity and quality. Constant rumination about work and superlative commitment to duty are often features of these unrelenting standards. In a study of academics during COVID in India, Krishnan et al. (2023) found that work-life balance suffered as individuals experienced lower levels of perceived control over their social lives as the boundaries between work and external life blurred. With excessive work came reduced recovery time, which contributed to physiological manifestations, chronic anxious ruminations, sleep disturbances, and feelings of being faint.

The Spiral of Despair: The Exit, Voice, Loyalty, and Neglect Model

A spiral of despair in a workplace environment can unfold when an employee attempts to communicate areas of frustration, but is met with punishment rather than appreciation; when managers fail to recognize emotions as powerful change agents and sources of information, employees can slide from optimism into anger or indifference as a product of neglect (J. Lowenstein, personal communication, January 28, 2024).

In Hirschman's (1970) *Exit, Voice, and Loyalty* model, a slack economy is posited as a location where "repairable lapses" can occur (p. 1). It is assumed that a utopian vision of a taut economy is unreachable due to human misbehaviors, and factors outside of the market can serve as recuperation, addressing reversible changes prior to customer or employee exit. Slack is presented as a feature of entropy and a source of reserve, and while voice is cumbersome for managers and risky for employees, it is also a sign of investment and loyalty, a "reasoned calculation" (Hirschman, 1970, p. 79). Companies that enact "severe initiation" policies and social or economic exit penalties will tend to decrease voice and exit, producing a form of unconscious loyalty that often includes self-deception but which tolerates organizational and product deterioration (p. 93).

Toxic Organizational Cultures

Creativity will naturally be thwarted in systems of marginal control that deny personhood, project limited human potential, and assume that workers will be unmotivated and deceptive unless they are carefully monitored and punished. Toxic organizational cultures thrive on fear-based motivation and mistrust, promoting and encouraging managers to cling proudly to their hierarchical status as decision-makers and persons of importance. The harmful effects of toxic organizational cultures assault basic needs for safety and survival, since economic deprivation or reward attaches the power hierarchy. Toxic organizational cultures communicate a value of sameness and conventionality, which is orthogonal to the creative impulse. This culture can be investigated at the local level, considering empirical models for components of the larger maladaptive context.

An example of the local level is the toxic work environment (TWE), which is defined as a context with decreasing employee engagement, followed by a downward spiral into burnout, anxiety, depression, poor health, and resource loss (Rasool et al., 2021). The TWE is likely to emerge in settings that tolerate workplace bullying, harassment, and aggression by co-workers and supervisors, while maintaining an interlocking threat of work pressure and job insecurity (Rasool et al., 2021). Narcissism in the workplace, a competitive and hostile peer environment, cruelty, and a culture that undermines physical or emotional health are prominent in a TWE. However, some of the harmful effects of a TWE may be reversed when the employee is able to invest in resources in ways that help to avert loss and if some members of the leadership can provide organizational support in the form of authentic and meaningful concern for the employee's well-being, offered while recognizing their individuality and humanity. Informal support may be the most helpful. It remains to be seen whether a resource-focused model may be more effective than a knowledge-oriented approach to support.

The TWE threatens basic needs, which is relevant to the work of Abraham Maslow (1954), as presented in his theory of human motivation. Maslow (1954) emphasizes the primacy of the need for safety, which can, when threatened, create urgency—a neurotic search for structure and familiarity. The intellectual, sensory, and societal structures are aimed at securing safety, and "we may...describe the whole organism as a safety-seeking mechanism" (Maslow, 1954, p. 39). Insecurity regarding potential job loss can connect to threats to both safety and physiological well-being, demonstrating the coercive power of employers and supervisors. When the work environment lacks psychological and social safety, this can yield insecurity regarding needs for self-esteem, belongingness and self-actualization. The resultant strategies to try to detour threats can include compulsive and regressive actions and an attempt to prepare for any contingency through "ceremonials, rules and formulas" (Maslow, 1954, p. 42).

Workplace bullying is often observed in a toxic organizational culture. The devaluing of one's contributions represents an important source of erosion on self-efficacy and motivation, especially when derogatory projections and communications occur either directly or through a process of third-person relational aggression (Laschinger & Nosko, 2015). The toll from workplace bullying can be substantial, with increased risks to mental and physical health and heightened turnover and sick-day over-utilization. Toxic workplace environments may also include harassment, work stress, social exclusion/rejection, and feelings of invisibility (Wang et al., 2020). Management and colleagues can ex-communicate marginalized members, with expulsion effectively silencing voices (Hirschman, 1970).

One way that indwelling affects employee outcomes is through internalized oppression, which alienates groups or persons who endure systemic discrimination (Nadal et al., 2021). People of color and other marginalized groups may experience a higher frequency of microaggressions in the workplace, which can be harmful to self-esteem, eliciting the salience of the imposter syndrome (Nadal et al., 2021). Internalized oppression can intersect with stereotype threat, causing individuals to devalue their own work, experience increased anxiety and self-doubt, and underachieve in the case of self-fulfilling prophecy effects.

Projections from supervisors and colleagues can reinforce discriminatory ideas, contributing to the maintenance of counterproductive work behaviors. The impact of negative expectations on work environments was explored in the mid-20th century by Douglas McGregor (1960), whose model of supervisory cognitions was impactful in terms of its focus on building trust and creativity. McGregor (1960) surmised that Theory X leaders assume that people dislike work and will want to avoid it; thus, coercive measures, punishment, and surveillance must be used. McGregor (1960) was influenced by Abraham Maslow's (1954) theory of motivation, and assumed that human beings would want to strive towards self-actualization and self-esteem in a growth-oriented environment. In McGregor's (1960) model, Theory Y leaders work from the foundational belief that human beings are naturally oriented towards creativity and problem-solving, thriving when given responsibility and supported in self-directed personal projects.

Numerous protective factors and strategies will interact with outcomes in toxic organizational cultures. Organizational support has been shown to moderate the relationship between workplace stress and a toxic workplace environment (Wang et al., 2020). Reallocation of duties, consolidation of tasks, and organizational attempts to more efficiently access human capital may be effective strategies to retain resources (Wang et al., 2020). Working to build a collaborative workplace culture is another important preventative measure.

Workplace bullying can be reduced through organizational structures that seek to monitor, educate or build social capital (Laschinger & Nosko, 2015). Hope can be leveraged to help the individual broaden and build into an upward spiral of self-motivation, contributing to the setting of achievable goals as one reframes obstacles as external to the self and time-limited. The employee who can separate their identity from the responses of others in the workplace will have a greater possibility of recovering from environments that are impoverished by support. The optimistic individual can learn to credit themselves for positive outcomes while externalizing failures and accepting the realities of stunted and constraining environments. Laschinger and Nosko (2015) have demonstrated a number of optimizing features that can assist the employee to maintain a sense of felt meaning, despite the sense of futility that can often accompany unhealthy workplaces.

Limitations

Ongoing research in industrial and organizational psychology continues to build in terms of the multi-trait and multi-method models originally suggested by Hobfoll (1989) and others. Increasing inclusion of behavioral and structural observations, clinician assessments (Hobfoll, 1989), and field studies (Lee et al., 2004) can support the internal validity and reliability of research. Some traits of interest are rarely present, which can make it challenging to study the unique variations that can modify outcomes (Lee et al., 2004). While some researchers suggest that it may be important to move beyond predictive research towards the uncovering of causal relationships (Lee et al., 2004), another option would be to move away from attempts to concretize psychological research in the same way that can be offered in organic chemistry or physics. While researchers who are deeply committed to the hypothetico-deductive model of science proposed by Karl Popper may seek to operationalize constructs with a high level of precision, it could also be argued that a sense of the whole can be sacrificed in the attempt to mechanize the study of human responses. Hobfoll (1989) suggests that models of stress have traditionally been too phenomenological and ambiguous; in contrast to that view, the current author proposes that a return to phenomenology could provide a welcome and needed change in a mechanistic workplace science that elevates moderator variables over persons.

A Spiritus Model of Workplace Creativity

The Spiritus Model is an extension of enactivism, where humans internalize a social and interpersonal world, not functioning as closed systems but rather as configurations that exceed their components. Indwelling can sabotage in cases of rumination, threats to safety, toxic organizational cultures, and internalized oppression. Maladaptive interiorization is likely in mechanistic workplace systems, which apply atomistic and formulaic approaches to an understanding of persons and creativity, legitimizing myths rooted in racism, sexism, and other forms of oppression. Workaholism may surface for the worker whose unrelenting standards represent an attempt to master that which can never be mastered. To receive a projection is to internalize a reduction, fusing self with other. To weaponize a projection is to commit violence against empathy, yielding slavish obedience and fear. Another alternative to a toxic organizational culture is a great resignation, an exit strategy that results from chronic rumination and conditioning within a hierarchy based on marginal control.

In contrast, a biophilous workplace will consider minds as monads, microcosms that are open systems connected to self-transcendence. Indwelling in the garden will expand the meaning-consciousness, creating a sense that the workplace environment is a living, dynamic, and not-fully-known entity. Transformational leadership can foster creativity through enhanced mindfulness and a thriving organizational culture (Srivastava et al., 2024). Protective factors will be planted to yield a harvest of creative produce, spiraling up to allow the individual to experience illumination, vitalism, attunement, and connection with archetypal sources of wisdom. Authentic encounters with others, a sense of safety regarding the conservation of effort, identity and resources, and mindful presence of the moment and one's body can be entertained in the biophilous space. This is a terrain of emanation—emergence for self, teams, identities, and creative unconscious inference rather than control. When physical realities are conceived and rooted in mental realities, top-down processing can serve to transfer knowledge, expand individual potentials, and enhance transcendent commitment as the individual recognizes both embeddedness and freedom within the uncertainty and relativity of the human condition.

Notes

1 This work was written over a period of time between 1914 and 1936, but the translation used by Polanyi was by H. A. Hodges, published in 1944 by Oxford University Press, pp. 213, 121–124.
2 Dilthey reports being influenced by Hermann Lotze's (1856) work, Microcosmus, volume I, p. 169 (175).
3 Dilthey refers to Brentano's (1874) work, *Psychology from an Empirical Standpoint.*
4 Dilthey refers to Kant's work, *First Introduction to the Critique of Judgment.* The source used by Dilthey's translator was published in 1965 (J. A. Haden Trans., p. 12) and *Anthropology from a Pragmatic Point of View* (Trans. M. Gregor, 1974), p. 119.
5 Mitchell et al. refer to Lewin's (1951) work *Field theory in social science*, published by Harper, which examines responses to embedded figures.

6 Mitchell et al. reference the work published in 1958, *Organizations*, which was published by Wiley. The authors describe the dominant paradigm of turnover intention research that was built from the March and Simon publication.
7 Also referencing the 1958 publication mentioned above, Lee et al. describe the way that March and Simon examined job performance in terms of motivational concepts related to expectations, level of social control, and personal goals. This was distinguished from decisions to participate at all, which related to ease of leaving.
8 Lee et al. accessed information from a presentation by Hulin at SIOP in 1998, but also Hulin, C. L. (1991). Adaptation, persistence and commitment in organizations. In M. D. Dunnette & L. M. Hough (Eds.), *Handbook of industrial and organizational psychology* (2nd ed., pp. 445–507). Consulting Psychologists Press; Hulin, C. L. (2002). Lessons from industrial and organizational psychology. In J. Brett & F. Drasgow (Eds.), *The psychology of work: Theoretically based empirical evidence*. Erlbaum, pp. 3–22.
9 This was noted in Shemla & Wegge's reference to Turner, J. C., Hogg, M. A., Oakes, P. J., Reicher, S. D., & Wetherell, M. S. (1987). *Rediscovering the social group: A self-categorization theory*. Blackwell.
10 Also note the references made by Shemla and Wegge to the work of Ashforth B. A., & Mael, F. (1989). Social identity theory and the organization. *Academy of Management Review, 14*(1), 20–39, who contributed to this definition.
11 De Beauvoir cites p. 248, in the French version of Merleau-Ponty's Phenomenology of Perception; see p. 214 in the English translation by Colin Smith, Routledge, 1962.
12 Kreppner refers to Baerveldt, C., & Verheggen, T. (1999). Enactivism and the experiential reality of culture: Rethinking the epistemological basis of cultural psychology. *Culture & Psychology, 5*(2), 183–206.
13 Kreppner builds this argument from Piaget, J. (1937/1954). *The construction of reality in the child*. Basic Books.
14 Kreppner refers to Maturana, H., & Varela, F. (1980). *Autopoiesis and cognition: The realization of the living*. Dordrecht: Reidel.
15 See Cassirer, E. (1944). *An essay on man. An introduction to a philosophy of human culture*. Yale University Press.

Works Cited

Batool, S., Ibrahim, H. I., & Adeel, A. (2024). How responsible leadership pays off: Role of organizational identification and organizational culture for creative idea sharing. *Sustainable Technology and Entrepreneurship, 3*(2), 1–9.
Brentano, F. (1874). *Psychology from an empirical standpoint*. O Kraus & L McAlister (Eds.), A. C. Rancurello et al. (Trans.). Routledge and Kegan Paul. Reprinted in 1973.
Conte, J., & Harmata, R. K. (2023, April 19–22). *Person-centered study of cognitive ability dimensions using latent profile analysis* [Poster presentation]. Society for Industrial and Organizational Psychology (SIOP), 38th Annual Conference, Boston, MA.
De Beauvoir, S. (1945). A review of the phenomenology of perception by Merleau-Ponty. In M. A. Simons, M. B. Timmermann, & M. B. Mader (Eds.), *Simone de Beauvoir, philosophical writings* (pp. 151–164). University of Illinois Press.
Dilthey, W. (1882). *Selected works, volume I, introduction to the human sciences*. R. A. Makkreel & F. Rodi (Eds.) & M. Neville (Trans.). Princeton University Press.

Emery, M., & Flora, C. (2006). Spiraling-up: Mapping community transformation with community capitals framework. *Community Development, 37*(1), 19–35.

Emery, M., & Flora, C. (2021). Spiraling-up: Mapping community transformation with community capitals framework. In N. Walzer, R. Phillips, & R. Blair (Eds.) *50 years of community development* (Vol. I, pp. 163–179). Routledge.

Fan, Q., Liu, Y., & Chen, J. (2023, April 19–22). *Retain or redeploy resources? Shared team identification and newcomer embeddedness* [Poster presentation]. Society for Industrial and Organizational Psychology (SIOP), 38th Annual Conference, Boston, MA.

Farrell, D., & Rusbult, C. (1985). Understanding the retention function: A model of the causes of exit, voice, loyalty and neglect behaviors. *Personnel Administrator, 30*(4), 129–140.

Farrell, D., & Rusbult, C. E. (1992). Exploring the exit, voice, loyalty, and neglect typology: The influence of job satisfaction, quality of alternatives, and investment size. *Employee Responsibilities and Rights Journal, 5*, 201–218.

Fredrickson, B. L. (2004). The broaden–and–build theory of positive emotions. *Philosophical Transactions of the Royal Society of London. Series B: Biological Sciences, 359*(1449), 1367–1377.

Goff, P., Seager, W., & Allen-Hermanson, S. (2022, June 21). Panpsychism. In E. N. Zalta (Ed.), *The Stanford encyclopedia of philosophy*. Retrieved from https://plato.stanford.edu/archives/sum2022/entries/panpsychism

Greenwood, J. D. (2020). On two foundational principles of the Berlin School of Gestalt Psychology. *Review of General Psychology, 24*(3), 284–294. doi: 10.1177/1089268019893972

Guyer, P., & Horstmann, R. P. (2021, March 21). *Idealism*. In E. N. Zalta & U. Nodelman (Eds.), *The Stanford encyclopedia of philosophy*. Retrieved from https://plato.stanford.edu/archives/spr2023/entries/idealism

Hezlett, S. (2023, April 19–22). *Predicting derailment risk: Looking beyond competencies* [Poster presentation]. Society for Industrial and Organizational Psychology (SIOP), 38th Annual Conference, Boston, MA.

Hirschman, A. O. (1970). *Exit, voice, and loyalty: Responses to decline in firms, organizations, and states*. Harvard University Press.

Hobfoll, S. E. (1989). Conservation of resources: A new attempt at conceptualizing stress. *American Psychologist, 44*(3), 513–524.

Hom, P. W., Lee, T. W., Shaw, J. D., & Hausknecht, J. P. (2017). One hundred years of employee turnover theory and research. *Journal of Applied Psychology, 102*(3), 530–55.

Islam, T., & Asad, M. (2024). Enhancing employees' creativity through entrepreneurial leadership: Can knowledge sharing and creative self-efficacy matter? *VINE Journal of Information and Knowledge Management Systems, 54*(1), 59–73.

Jones, B., & Miller, B. (2009). Mapping the tacit component: Getting away from knowledge conversion. *Manchester Business School Working Paper, 577*, 2–30.

Kim, A. (2022, December 21). Wilhelm Maximilian Wundt. In E. N. Zalta & U. Nodelman (Eds.), *The Stanford encyclopedia of philosophy*. Retrieved from https://plato.stanford.edu/archives/win2022/entries/wilhelm-wundt

Kodera, S. (2024). Translating renaissance neoplatonic panpsychism into seventeenth-century corpusclarism: The case of Sir Kenelm Digby (1603–1665). *Intellectual History Review, 34*(1), 145–163.

Kreppner, K. (1999). Enactivism and monadology: Where are Bearveldt and Verheggen taking the individual and cultural psychology? *Culture & Psychology, 5*(20), 207–216.

Krishnan, C., Singh, S., & Baba, M. M. (2023). Effect of work from home and employee mental health through mediating role of workaholism and work-family balance. *International Journal of Social Psychiatry, 70*(1) 144–156. doi: 10.1177/00207640231196741

Krohn, T., & Meinel, C. (Eds.). (2022). *Design thinking in education: innovation can be learned.* Springer Nature Switzerland AG.

Laschinger, H. K. S., & Nosko, A. (2015). Exposure to workplace bullying and post-traumatic stress disorder symptomology: The role of protective psychological resources. *Journal of Nursing Management, 23*(2), 252–262.

Lee, T. W., & Mitchell, T. R. (1994). An alternative approach: The unfolding model of voluntary employee turnover. *Academy of Management Review, 19*(1), 51–89.

Lee, T. W., Mitchell, T. R., Sablynski, C. J., Burton, J. P., & Holtom, B. C. (2004). The effects of job embeddedness on organizational citizenship, job performance, volitional absences, and voluntary turnover. *Academy of Management Journal, 47*(5), 711–722.

Lewin, K. (1951). *Field theory in social science: Selected theoretical papers.* D. Cartwright (Ed). Harpers.

Lipps, T. (1905). *Psychological studies.* Arno Press. Reprinted 1926, 1973.

Look, B. C. (2020, March 21). Gottfried Wilhelm Leibniz. In E. N. Zalta (Ed.), *The Stanford encyclopedia of philosophy.* Retrieved from https://plato.stanford.edu/archives/spr2020/entries/leibniz

Mahler, M. S., Pine, F., & Bergman, A. (1975). *The psychological birth of the human infant: Symbiosis and individuation.* Basic Books.

Maslow, A. H. (1954). *Motivation and personality* (2nd ed.). Harper & Row. Reprinted 1970.

McGinnis, D. (2018). Resilience, life events, and well-being during midlife: Examining resilience subgroups. *Journal of Adult Development, 25*(3), 198–221.

McGregor, D. M. (1960). *The human side of enterprise, annotated edition.* McGraw-Hill, 2006.

Mikulincer, M., & Florian, V. (1997). Are emotional and instrumental supportive interactions beneficial in times of stress? The impact of attachment style. *Anxiety, Stress, and Coping, 10*(2), 109–127.

Mitchell, T. R., Holtom, B. C., Lee, T. W., Sablynski, C. J., & Erez, M. (2001). Why people stay: Using job embeddedness to predict voluntary turnover. *Academy of Management Journal, 44*(6), 1102–1121.

Nadal, K. L., King, R., Sissoko, D. G., Floyd, N., & Hines, D. (2021). The legacies of systemic and internalized oppression: Experiences of microaggressions, imposter phenomenon, and stereotype threat on historically marginalized groups. *New Ideas in Psychology, 63*, 1–9. doi: 10.1016/j.newideapsych.2021.100895

Oates, W. E. (1971). *Confessions of a workaholic: The facts about work addiction.* World Publishing Company.

Pappas, N. (2020, September 21). Plato's aesthetics. In E. N. Zalta (Ed.), *The Stanford encyclopedia of philosophy.* Retrieved from https://plato.stanford.edu/archives/fall2020/entries/plato-aesthetics

Polanyi, M. (1966). *The tacit dimension*. The University of Chicago Press.

Rasool, S. F., Wang, M., Tang, M., Saeed, A., & Iqbal, J. (2021). How toxic workplace environment effects the employee engagement: The mediating role of organizational support and employee wellbeing. *International Journal of Environmental Research and Public Health, 18*(5), 2294.

Rattray, R. F. (1914). The philosophy of Samuel Butler. *Mind, 23*(91), 371–385.

Razran, G. (1961). The observable and the inferable conscious in current Soviet psychophysiology: Interoceptive conditioning, semantic conditioning, and the orienting reflex. *Psychological Review, 68*(2), 81–147. doi: 10.1037/h0039848

Reiter-Palmon, R., & Hunter, S. (Eds.). (2023). *Handbook of organizational creativity: leadership, interventions, and macro level issues* (2nd ed.). Academic Press.

Roudinesco, E. (2003). The mirror stage: An obliterated archive. In J. M. Rabaté (Ed.), *The Cambridge companion to Lacan* (pp. 25–34). Cambridge University Press.

Rogers, C. R. (1961). *On becoming a person: A therapist's view*. Houghton-Mifflin Co. Reprinted 1995.

Runco, M. A. (2023). *Creativity: research, development, and practice* (3rd ed.). Academic Press.

Saunders, D. M. (1992). Introduction to research on Hirschman's exit, voice, and loyalty model. *Employee Responsibilities and Rights Journal, 5*(3), 187–190.

Shemla, M., & Wegge, J. (2019). Managing diverse teams by enhancing team identification: The mediating role of perceived diversity. *Human Relations, 72*(4), 755–777.

Srivastava, S., Pathak, D., Soni, S., & Dixit, A. (2024). Does green transformational leadership reinforce green creativity? The mediating roles of green organizational culture and green mindfulness. *Journal of Organizational Change Management, 0953*(4814), 1–13. Retrieved from https://www.emerald.com/insight/0953-4814.htm

Van Der Vegt, G. S., Van De Vliert, E., & Oosterhof, A. (2003). Informational dissimilarity and organizational citizenship behavior: The role of intrateam interdependence and team identification. *Academy of Management Journal, 46*(6), 715–727.

Wang, Z., Zaman, S., Rasool, S. F., Zaman, Q. U., & Amin, A. (2020). Exploring the relationships between a toxic workplace environment, workplace stress, and project success with the moderating effect of organizational support: Empirical evidence from Pakistan. *Risk Management and Healthcare Policy, 13*, 1055–1067.

White, S. (2018). *An introduction to the psychodynamics of workplace bullying*. Routledge.

Withey, M. J., & Cooper, W. H. (1989). Predicting exit, voice, loyalty, and neglect. *Administrative Science Quarterly, 34*(4), 521–539.

Wu., Z., Ma., Y., & Lu, C. Q. (2023, April 19–22). *Another look at the performance-turnover link: A person-centered dynamic perspective* [Poster presentation]. Society for Industrial and Organizational Psychology (SIOP), 38th Annual Conference, Boston, MA.

6

TACIT KNOWLEDGE AND ITS CONTRIBUTION TO CREATIVITY IN THE ARTS AND SCIENCES

Nahanni Freeman

The Relevance of Tacit Knowledge for Innovation in the Workplace

Economic interest in intellectual property reveals awareness of the impact of the cognitive revolution on workplace innovation in a technological society (Bereiter, 2002). The value of "knowledge-creating companies" for expansion and success in business is established (Bereiter, 2002, p. 5), generating a call for a transmuted philosophy of science and creativity. However, a mechanized understanding of the function and development of expert knowledge limits the ability to maximize this resource, founded on an outdated epistemology. The science of studying workplace creativity reveals the self-organizing complexity of the systems that evolve and give rise to innovation. Although business literature may often thrive with the inclusion of aphorisms and case examples, a deepened theory of knowledge construction may guide revolutions in education, organizational research, and corporate training (Bereiter, 2002, p. 176).

Creative knowledge construction in groups can be envisioned as an emergent process that develops within the social context, irreducible to the atomistic ideas that preceded the illumination (Bereiter, 2002, p. 178). Idea generation may be expanded by incubation periods (Ellwood et al., 2009), which could imply subception. It is unclear whether the incubation periods work due to neural fatigue or whether nonconscious processing continues to occur during incubation (Ellwood et al., 2009). Functional fixedness is said to occur when problem solving is diminished due to a previous encounter with a phenomenon, which limits the scope of considered possibility (Birch & Rabinowitz, 1951).

DOI: 10.4324/9781003322894-7

As discussed by Merleau-Ponty (1945), the subjective state of the individual interacts with perceptions of figure and ground, for the individual's perceptions and sensations are fielded within an idiosyncratic environmental experience. The individual may perceive the self to be pre-objective yet remain adhered to context—the perception of indeterminacy is illusory (p. 12). The perceived properties of objects may shift in focus, bridged from prior experiences, in ways that reduce creative problem solving; this can propel adhesion to a particular solution (Yonge, 1966). Functional fixedness can sometimes be excised by giving space for incubation, rest, or alternative agency. Unconscious forerunners of incubation and their relation to tacit knowledge in the sciences are germane to the current discussion.

A narrow or mechanistic view of knowledge creation may attend closely to quantifiable elements of innovation (Nonaka, 2007). In contrast, the subjective, intuitive, and tacit elements of creativity may be the more significant drivers to evaluate (Nonaka, 2007). Attending to metaphors and symbols, as well as employee values and ideals, may facilitate knowledge construction, maintenance, and expansion. A model of organizational research will be most profitable when wrought from a sound epistemological base. Underlying assumptions about science will inevitably enhance or contaminate the research and development process. This chapter will seek to examine a philosophy of science and creativity that builds on the work of Michael Polanyi (1966), Francis Bacon, Kurt Lewin, and others, emphasizing the role of uncertainty, the unconscious, and tacit awareness in creativity, with relevance for scientific and artistic professions as well as businesses that rely on creative optimization.

Personhood and the Nature of Creativity

Polanyi (1966) states that perception bridges the creative mind with the body (p. 7). One impetus for scientific hypothesis construction may be Polanyi's idea of subception—expecting something to occur in the future but not knowing why (pp. 7–8). However, if mental operations are indivisible from sensations and matter, these forces may limit the mind's ability to understand itself, also constraining the opportunity to have direct knowledge of either physical objects or consciousness (Browne, 1728, as cited in Bettcher, 2007, p. 10).

When considering the interaction between personhood and scientific creativity, one may encounter the dynamic nature of the person within a field of influences, as described by social psychologist Kurt Lewin (1935, 1936, 1947, as cited in Burnes & Bargal, 2017). The life space in Lewin's theory signified the total context in which a person would exist, with social and organizational factors influencing behavioral probabilities. Lewin conceived of psychological phenomena as real but also subjective and influenced by constantly changing landscapes that sought equilibrium (Burnes & Bargal, 2017). Internal resistance to change promotes a freezing of action within convention; it would take an additional application of force to unfreeze the habitual response (Burnes & Bargal, 2017, p. 94). In Lewin's model, people construct mental realities in relational ways, but they use abstraction to arrive at classifications. Democratic and humanistic values are a natural byproduct of sensitive consideration of social forces and their impact.

Lewin's field of force, which was impacted by analogies derived from physics, can find broad applications in the study of industrial change (Lewin, 1951, as cited in Melin, 1987). In Lewin's model, a field of force is a form of interactionism and multiple causation, where "behavior is seen as a function of a multitude of co-existing, interacting and interdependent forces within the person and environment (both social and non-social)" (Papanek, 1973, pp. 318–319). The field-of-force metaphor is useful in considering how organizational changes can be influenced both by internal restraints, or barriers to change, and driving forces that prompt movement. Fields of influence within and between organizations and power contexts can yield change or resistance. People respond to the environment from an idiosyncratic perspective, reacting to the totality of simultaneous factors from a particular field position. The force is anything that produces change. Forces within the social and organizational fields can be indirect or direct, conscious or unconscious, and the understanding of the comprehensive whole is a closer approximation to reality than an analysis of parts. Forces can be internal, external, and strategic and are impacted by the deep structure of an organizational culture (Melin, 1987, p. 29). Givens within an organization are impacted by the desire for coherence and sense-making.

Associationism and Creativity

Polanyi (1966, pp. 9–10) describes the associationism between the first term (proximal, tacitly known cues) and the second term (distal, the specifically known event). He posits that we attend away from the parts in order to perceive the whole. When attempting to apprehend what cannot be perceived, truths are understood through analogy. This is highlighted when one encounters Browne's (1695, as cited in Bettcher, 2007, p. 14) view that faith arises from analogy rather than direct knowledge. Creative associations, taken as a form of faith, are often forged implicitly when memories, ideas, and sensations recombine in ways following unconscious operations. These ideas build on the work of John Stuart Mill, who contended that associations are a form of mental chemistry, developing in response to sensations, triggered when similarity, sequence, or contiguity is evoked, and producing some new form that cannot be reduced to its parts (Hergenhahn, 2009, p. 155).

While scientific creativity may be enhanced through an encounter with the unconscious, its faith is also grounded in a quest for unification, for "it is the faith of all science that an unlimited number of phenomena can be comprehended in terms of a limited number of concepts or ideal constructs. Without this faith no science could ever have any motivation" (Thurstone, 1947, p. 51). Scientific laws were confined to the attempt to comprehend nature, rather than a physical manifestation of nature, in the work of Thurstone (1947). Scientific laws are not viewed as objects with their own independent existence. Thurstone's recognition of the interaction between mind and science is shown by his statement that "to discover a scientific law is merely to discover that a man-made scheme serves to unify, and thereby to simplify, comprehension of a certain class of natural phenomena" (Thurstone, 1947, p. 51).

Associations have a paradoxical relationship with memories. While creativity requires one to draw flexible connections between recollected ideas, some associations can hinder the creative process, interfering with novelty, producing fixation, and yielding reliance on mentally accessible content (Lloyd-Cox et al., 2021). Following priming with common words, for example, participants show decreased creativity. While excessive thought regulation or suppression is likely to interfere with creativity, adaptive cognitive control may enhance it by facilitating access to less accessible ideas, which requires cognitive shifting, updating of information in working memory, and inhibitory control over distractions and salient thoughts (Lloyd-Cox et al., 2021). Greater functional connectivity between the default mode network of the brain and the frontal lobes has been observed in people with higher openness to experience, a trait that has been shown to correlate with higher creativity; this is not surprising in light of the fact that both regions are observed to be active during creative pursuits (Lloyd-Cox et al., 2021).

Francis Bacon and a Model of Creative Ambiguity and Flexible Associations

In the thought of Francis Bacon (1620a), observations can yield changes in mental habits in ways that forge new associations; he states, "I have decided to scatter the thoughts…and not connect them" (p. 263). This ability to accept the ambiguity of disconnection yields a springtime of novelty in the sciences. While the associations may be loose, there is also a unity, for "the whole sum of matter always stays the same" (Bacon, 1620a, p. 37).

Matter is described by Bacon as "clearly fundamental and catholic" (p. 39), implying coherence.

The ability to forge creative associations, and to freely reflect upon experience may be hindered in non-democratic workplace environments, which instigate threat and disempowerment. Prior investigations have demonstrated that cognitive flexibility is maximal in conditions of positive mood. This may be explained by hedonic contingency theory, which states that "happy individuals are interested in sustaining their positive mood state, whereas sad individuals are interested in mood repair" (Hirt et al., 2008, p. 216). Psychological safety and team sharing of information have been shown to predict greater workplace creativity (Hu et al., 2018). Furthermore, in low power-distance contexts, leader humility predicted greater team information sharing.

The relationship between organizational structure and creativity is culturally mediated. For example, Erez and Nouri (2010) found that greater creative novelty was observed in contexts of low uncertainty avoidance, low power distance, and low collectivism. In contrast, creative usefulness was greater in the converse settings. In cultural contexts with high power distance, greater supervisor-rated creativity has been observed when there is benevolent leadership and high social exchange between leaders and subordinates (Lin et al., 2018).

Creativity, Embodiment, and Incubation

Polanyi (1966) states that when we appreciate art, we indwell it, inhabiting the mind of the artist (p. 17). Furthermore, he goes on to claim that all observations include indwelling, which is a form of interiorization of morals. He states that an observer inhabits the mind of the artist. Both creativity and qualitative science require immersion; the role of constant interruption and distraction is significant and impairing. In contrast, deep, focused attention, followed by periods of inactivity for incubation, may precede an illuminating epiphany (Wallas, 1926). Prior to the epiphany, there may be an aura, or a sense of anticipatory expectation, that insight is near. This occurs following a prolonged period of preparatory activity and must be answered with a verification process.

Embodied views of creativity are less emphasized than cognitive perspectives, but they feature physical engagement with creative processes (Griffith, 2021). The body may reflect and be inhabited by social power structures (Griffith, 2021), as might be observed by an analysis of the impact of social dominance on nonverbal behavior. Embodied creativity could explore the interaction of internal sensations with the creative process, rooted in introspective self-examination. The notion that tacit knowledge can be acquired through attention to sensations is implied in Gestalt psychotherapy. The relation of thinking and insight to movement can be informative (Griffith, 2021).

In a critique of the lack of identity transformation and existential mission in higher education, Burwood (2007) discusses the indwelling of knowledge as a gradual process of acculturation that allows the body to become integrated with thought, stating, "the learning subject is essentially an embodied subject" (p. 130). This indwelling requires imitation, apprenticeship, assimilation, and modification of values and practices through tacit means.

Creativity is an act of immersion. Polanyi describes indwelling and knowledge through a consideration of the body (1965, p. 17). For example, humans rely on sensations to evaluate external realities, yet individuals are often unaware of the specifics of what is occurring within the body . We attend to something outside of the self while relying on the self for interpretation. Polanyi states that "when we rely on our awareness of some things for attending to other things, we have assimilated these things into our body…we arrive thus at the conception of *knowing by in-dwelling*" (p. 17). The experience of indwelling "involves a tacit reliance on our awareness of particulars not under observation" (Polanyi, 1965, p. 20).

While creative knowing may include an embodied form of knowledge—an incorporation—there is also a sense of focused detachment that is important for incubation. For example, Steindorf et al. (2021) found that participants whose incubation periods were interrupted, so that researchers could ask them about their mind wandering, reported experiencing fewer thoughts than non-interrupted subjects. However, a difference in divergent thinking was not observed between the interrupted mind-wandering incubation groups versus control. This was in contrast to some prior studies, which have demonstrated that incubation may promote increased creativity and innovation, especially in low cognitive contexts (Steindorf et al., 2021). Creative processes may thrive when unconscious associations can multiply during incubation periods, fostering preoccupation with unsolved mysteries, similar to the Zeigarnik effect. On the other hand, mind wandering may be associated with decreased performance in tasks that require academic output.

Swanger (1983) critiques Polanyi's (1966) concept of indwelling by pointing out that the closeness between the object and the observer is something other than empathy, a prerequisite for aesthetic appreciation. The empathic frame allows the individual to be aware of self and Other while experiencing or creating an artistic product. Swanger (1983) describes the unique function of art with the words,

> I contend that what art can do, through empathetic knowledge, is to enable the rower to become the water, the blind man to become the curb. We become something else, in this sense, by projecting ourselves

into it; and the way in which we know it is unlike any other way of knowing.

(p. 22)

For Swanger, the experience or creation of art is incomplete without empathic elements of indwelling, highlighting the distinction between deep and surface knowledge.

Reductionism: A Hindrance to Workplace Creativity

Polanyi (1966) discusses the dangers of reductionism for knowledge and exploration, stating that "unbridled lucidity can destroy our understanding of complex matters" (p. 18). The harmful effects of concrete literalism upon aesthetics in the arts and the reductive tendencies of scientific findings not linked to a greater and more meaningful theory suggest that innovation in the workplace requires capaciousness and regard for uncertainty. Yet, Polanyi (1966) states, "the meticulous dismembering of a text, which can kill its appreciation, can also supply material for a much deeper understanding of it" (p. 19). However, Polanyi states that the idea that particulars offer true conception is wrongheaded. When a percept is viewed from a distance, it can sometimes recover its meaning, previously obscured through surgical extraction. Reductionism can become a social process, embedded within the dominance hierarchies of an organization. The inclusion of democratic structures may curtail the reductionist model and its strangulating effects.

Reductionism assumes that certainty can be attained regarding truth; it overestimates what the biological and social sciences can provide. A reductionist view of science will also narrow the scope of science to existing paradigms where there is little controversy, which promotes an erosion of originality. Polanyi (1966, p. 70) points out that scientific pursuits can only be considered original when they inform a "still unrevealed reality."

The absolutistic and over-literalized approach to science can be considered erroneous, especially when inferences must be made from concepts like "force." Thurstone (1947) builds a pragmatic view of *science-as-agreement* for comprehension of phenomena, identifying the fact that "the laws of science are not immutable. They are only human efforts towards parsimony in the comprehension of nature" (Thurstone, 1947, p. 52).

By moving away from the reductionist account of knowledge, it becomes possible to recognize the distal and unconscious elements of truth that prepare aesthetic appreciation. Mitchell (2005) describes Polanyi's approach to the elusive by considering the idea that "knowing necessarily entails the integration of the focal and subsidiary elements by the active participation of the knower" (p. 86).

Reductionism can be considered as one example of the broader limitations of human reason, which are articulated by Francis Bacon (1620b) in his *Novum Organum*. Within this view, the idols of the tribe are innate to human nature, including the limits of sensation. The idols of the cave are individual discoloration, refractions, impressions, and prejudices. The obstructing force of economics and commerce on knowledge is seen in Bacon's idols of the market. The fourth limitation is the pervasive influence of dogma, termed the idols of the theater.

In contrast to the view that reductionism restricts and constrains creativity, there may be contexts where redaction can enhance convergent forms of creativity, also allowing dominant themes to better cohere. For example, in the area of design, clarity may emerge from reduction, as described by Inoue et al. (2015), who state,

> if reduced elements of an object describe the complete state of the object, element reduction might be utilised as a trigger for further creative imagination. In other words, designing the way to reduce elements of an object might be an opportunity to stimulate a design practitioner's imagination.
>
> *(p. 1)*

Possibly creative innovations that require a single correct response, such as those observed in some dimensions of math, chemistry, or physics, can benefit from reductionism.

In contrast, reductionism is likely harmful to creative activities requiring divergent thinking, or the production of many possible alternatives, especially in situations that do not call for a single "correct" response. The social context, if authoritarian, can thwart divergent thinking. On the other hand, individualism may also reduce the scope of creativity, limiting its practical application and self-scrutiny. Building on the work of Slater (1991), Montuori and Purser (1997) point out that "the "individual-versus-society myth" is deeply embedded in North-American culture (p. 4). This myth is closely related to the "lone genius myth"…which also sees culture and society—other people, in other words—as an obstacle to the self-realization and self-expression of individuals" (Montuori & Purser, 1997, p. 4). The form of reductionistic constraint, emerging from power hierarchies, may confine scientific paradigms, for "little attention has been paid on the societal pressures on creative individuals, and on creativity researchers themselves, to conform to certain socially sanctioned historical attitudes, behaviors, and research programs" (Montuori & Purser, 1997, p. 4).

Creativity may optimize within contexts that provide space for emergent qualities. Unlike reductionism and mechanistic accounts of reality, emergentism does not assume that the underlying causes of outcomes can necessarily be discovered or quantified (Sawyer, 1999). The complex inter-action of unknown forces may influence what is observed, with the out-come taking on unique features that cannot be fully contained by the sum of parts. While first applied to evolutionary biology, emergence has become a useful frame for understanding creativity. Building on the ideas of the psy-chologist who investigated flow states and creativity, Sawyer (1999) states,

> Csikszentmihalyi's influential *systems theory* (1988) is derived from Campbell's evolutionary model, and includes three analogous com-ponents: the creative individual, who generates a novel product; the *field*, a social system of individuals in a discipline, that evaluates novel products and selects some of them according to established criteria; and a *domain*, an external body of work whose stable physical traits allow it to serve the function of retention across time.
>
> *(p. 448)*

An emergentist perspective may also provide capaciousness to enfold the notion that creativity is extracted from unconscious processes (Sawyer, 1999). Additionally, greater complexity may develop over time, with new combinations of associations unpredictably clashing. According to Simon-ton's cognitive model (1988, as cited in Sawyer, 1999), "the individual first internalizes *mental elements*—facts, theories, images, and information from the creative domain...these are stored in the brain; during a subcon-scious creative process these mental elements combine into *chance con-figurations...*" (p. 449).

An emergentist account of creativity can extend the constellation of the possible. Emergentist and pluralist versions of science have largely sup-planted earlier views of logical positivism, which sought to create ency-clopedic accounts of phenomena, assumed linear progression, rejected metaphysics, and limited knowledge to the empirical realms (Cat, 2007). However, earlier models of the unity of science proposed the Kantian view, which suggested that "the unity of science is not the reflection of a unity found in nature; rather, it has its foundations in the unifying character or function of concepts and of reason itself" (Cat, 2007, p. 3). Immanuel Kant's formulation rejected attempts to apply mechanisms to biological organisms (Cat, 2007). Prior to Kant, Galileo's perspective articulated a vision of a unity of science derived from a divine source, with the natural world revealing the transcendent through the primary qualities of objective laws. One way to account for complexity within the social sciences is sug-gested by Enion Probability Analysis, which assumes that cycles contain somewhat independent systems with numerous, irreducible interacting components; within each micro-system are dynamic, probabilistic factors (Cat, 2007, p. 31).

Kauffman (2007) discusses the potential of emergence for scientific innovation in ways that build upon Polanyi's (1966) reference to a society of explorers. Kauffman concludes his article with a vision of an ethical civilization rooted in reverence for the reality of life, personal responsibility for human interaction with the earth, and dawning conscious awareness of humanitarian values. The optimism of Kauffman (2007) is shown by his contention that,

> ...we have the first glimmerings of a new scientific worldview, beyond reductionism. In our universe emergence is real, and there is ceaseless, stunning creativity that has given rise to our biosphere, our humanity, and our history. We are partial co-creators of this emergent creativity.
>
> *(p. 903)*

Authoritarianism and Creativity

Authoritarianism and disempowerment in the workplace are argued to be restraining forces that strangulate the creative potential of the individual. Authoritarianism is contrasted with adaptive models of self-regulation that occur among communities of experts. Interdisciplinary scientific interaction can unfold in a context of peer review, which requires mutual control within a circumscribed content arena (Polanyi, 1966, pp. 72–73). Each individual scientist is necessarily limited in scope, being able to only directly discover and evaluate the claims of other scientists within a fragment of potential counties. While science is rooted in the structure and authority of a tradition, it must also transcend paradigm conformity in order to truly innovate. Free science must disentangle itself from political and economic coercion (Polanyi, 1966, p. 81).

One perspective on creativity considers divergent thinking, which is often defined as the ability to generate a wide array of solutions or ideas; these notions are creative if they are purposeful and original (Storme et al., 2021). Individuals who are creative are often also unconventional, adhering less to social norms that require conformity, perspective-taking, empathy, or unselfish conduct (Storme et al., 2021). Organizations and societies that highly value centralized power, standardization, conventions, and branding for the purpose of consistency are likely to produce lower levels of creativity. Such environments are typically unappealing for original and independent thinkers.

Quantum physics can offer a useful stimulus for creative analogies. According to the interpretation of quantum physics provided by Born, which is described in Cross (1991), the wave function was not independent of mind, describing knowledge rather than the system itself. Wave functions provided only probabilities rather than precise solutions and were affected by human intervention, and uncertainty arose due to uncontrollable interactions that occurred during measurement. These notions, along with the idea that electrons could possess free will, produced a controversy for the Soviets that ultimately led to scientific retreat due to political pressure. Thus, the political field served as a barrier to open scientific dialogue.

As with quantum metaphors, one of the challenges in creativity research is to accurately and consistently measure the dependent variables, or to quantify the ineffable. Divergent thinking is often measured by evaluating the number and quality of ideas that are produced in response to a standardized prompt (Dumas et al., 2021). Open-ended responses are also used, which can be challenging to quantify because they rely on novel coding systems. The open-ended responses are coded according to originality, which is often evaluated by "associative distance," which represents the space traversed between a prompt and the response that has been given. Creativity is sometimes measured through latent semantic analysis, which applies mathematical principles in order to generate models that capture word meanings. However, a large number of words does not necessarily indicate originality.

Justification for Science

Experiments with light were deemed important to Bacon (1620a) on the basis of three domains. First, these experiments were felt to illuminate "the nature of bodies able to support life" (Bacon, 1620a, p. 229). Secondly, these experiments could produce evidence regarding "the principles of life" (p. 229). Third, luciferous experiments could provide information regarding vivification and its relation to putrefaction (p. 233). Bacon felt that raw observations of nature were of greater utility than blind allegiance to authority or tradition, and he also emphasized the changeable nature of science, indicating that he rejected a sense of obligation to his declarations. Bacon claimed that he did not assign natural laws for the sake of personal gratification but rather acted as a scribe, taking down what had been "proclaimed by the very voice of nature itself" (Bacon, 1620a, p. 261). Nature should be regarded with fresh inquiry, as the scientist sets aside the preconceived notions that convention produces, searching for ideas that serve to promote the Good.

In his review of the *Oxford Francis Bacon* by Graham Rees, Antsey (2003) argues that the Baconian approach has often focused excessively on inductive reasoning as a window for scientific discovery, showing inadequate attention to systematic studies of nature. Antsey (2003) also suggests that the legacy of luciferous experiments and fructiferous work, as well as crucial instances or experiments, was later taken up by Boyle (1671, as cited in Antsey, 2003), showing its longevity.

Tacit Knowledge in the Scientific Professions

Tacit knowledge (TK) is required for science, according to Polanyi (1966), because science begins with a problem. For Polanyi, science can best divulge originality when it informs a hidden reality (p. 70). The unrevealed features of problems justify the requirement of TK. Scientific problems and their solutions are often evoked through intuitive processes (pp. 20–21). Polanyi uses this context to address Plato's Meno's Paradox (p. 22). According to this paradox, if one already has knowledge, it is not really possible to truly *inquire* (Grgic, 1999). However, if a person does not yet know what something is or how to define it, there is a challenge in knowing what to study; the researcher may be unable to identify hypotheses or create a testable plan (Ebrey, 2014). This paradox, as described by Grgic (1999), connects to the eristic argument, which claims that a learner cannot investigate either what is known or what is hidden. One feature of this problem lies in the inability to craft relevant and meaningful research questions in the absence of knowledge.

Plato's solution, according to Polanyi (1966), is that the soul remembers, suggesting a priori knowledge (p. 22). The argument in favor of recollection implies that a scientific question may arise without knowledge, but Grgic (1999) suggests that there is a different solution for Meno's paradox than for the eristic argument. The possibility of recollection is supplemented by the need for a hypothesis, which can be corrected in light of the transient and unstable nature of opinion. Nevertheless, as Grgic (1999, p. 22) points out, "Socrates, by introducing the hypothetical method, does not abandon his principle that knowing what something is precedes knowing what something is *like*."

In his account of scientific requirements, Polanyi (1966) refers to Poe's purloined letter, a reference that may refer to the harmful effects of enforcement of uniformity in ways that undermine awareness of natural variation. This is seen in Poe's allusion to the authority of the Prefect in attempting to find a priceless, stolen letter; the magistrate's resistance to novelty is identified with the words, "a certain set of highly ingenious resources are, with the Prefect, a sort of Procrustean bed, to which he forcibly adapts his designs" (Poe, 1844/1910, p. 7). The inadequate search, directed by the Prefect, relies on the inability to consider a mind other than one's own. Poe (1844, p. 8) describes this mental rigidity when he critiques the unoriginal cohort, for "they consider only their own ideas of ingenuity; and, in searching for anything hidden, advert only to the modes in which they would have hidden it." Their minds are turned only towards extensions or exaggerations of their own ideas, producing a limited and selective attention that fails to see the obvious while diligently and microscopically reviewing the obscure.

Before scientific prospects can advance, there must have preexisted an indeterminate quality. Polanyi (1966) refers to the necessary incubation of discovery as the "solitary intimations of a problem" (p. 75). The person who is driven by the obsession for epistemic motivations will recognize clues and artifacts of a more coherent, yet clandestine, whole. Polanyi argues for the necessity of an intrepid article of imagination, which "crossed the uncharted seas of possible thought" (p. 76). The lackluster confinement to the conventional, the rigid adherence to authoritarian rules, will not champion innovation, for scientific discovery could not have been wrought by "persistence in applying explicit rules to given facts" (Polanyi, 1966, p. 76). The approach of truth is an anticipated aura. The truth-seeker will find a sense of personal responsibility in her epistemic endeavors, acting not according to individualism, raw volition, or conformity to authority figures but rather because she cannot do otherwise. Conclusions are ratified by Polanyi as commitments. That which is hidden is assumed to be imbued with some universal quality that awaits later verification. In legitimate science, which develops in a context of dissent, the scientist seeks to locate a country where "a superior life of the mind" can become a calling (Polanyi, 1966, p. 80).

The notion of the 'undiscovered,' within elements of scientific creativity, may prove relevant to Francis Bacon's (1620b) usage of the term 'ingenium,' found in his work Novum Organum, which has been translated from Latin in a large array of ways (as cited in Lewis, 2014). Ingenium has been variously interpreted as indicative of wit, ingenuity, inventiveness, forging connections between seemingly disparate ideas, and the imaginative talent that allows a poet or artist to transcend the created world, moving past imitation (Lewis, 2014, pp. 113, 122, 121). Many writers on ingenium would "privilege the display…above the claims of reason, philosophy, judgment, moderation, or externally determined ends of almost any kind" (Lewis, 2014, p. 123).

On the other hand, there are warnings against the abuses of ingenium provided in the work of Francis Bacon (Lewis, 2014). These include the error of arrogance "within the cells of human ingenium" (Bacon, 1620, as cited in Lewis, 2014, p. 124). In De Sapientia Veterum, Bacon refers to the mythological Daedalus as the exemplar of mechanistic industriousness, yet he did not employ restraint in the exercise of ingentium (Bacon, 1609, as cited in Lewis, 2014, 130). Lewis (2014) points out that three of Bacon's manuscripts reference the "clue to the labyrinth," a reference to Daedalus' creation of the labyrinth for King Minos of Crete, which could be suggestive of the potency that Bacon assigned to truth-seeking and scientific observation (p. 131). However, for Bacon, it was essential to avoid the corruption of philosophical motives, despite the journey into inscrutable worlds. While ingenuity is not equivocal to method, as pointed out by Thomas Hobbes (1661, as cited in Lewis, 2014, p. 152), it may be the illuminating force that allows a master craftsman to avoid the perilous and indiscriminate venture that is common to unrestrained ventures.

Intuitive Knowledge and the Verge of Discovery

Polanyi (1966) discusses how we cannot recognize the truth of a statement by its yet-undiscovered consequences (p. 23). This provides a gateway for the consideration of the significant role of unconscious thought and nonconscious processing in dislodging functional fixedness. This intuition is gained through many years of workplace preparation, with expertise that is gradually gained through exposure to a myriad of dynamic contexts. This gradual acquisition of expertise cannot be replaced by a younger or more energetic worker. Rather, there is the wisdom and judgment that accrue in middle age, which undergird the advanced ability of the creative work to show incisiveness.

Polanyi (1966) refers to how a scientist "senses" that she is approaching a solution (p. 24). This resembles the aura discussed by Graham Wallas (1926), which was hypothesized in response to the study of Poincaré's innovative work. Polanyi points out that the scientist feels a great sense of responsibility for the caretaking of this approaching epiphany (p. 25). The source of elucidation, traditionally described as the "muse" in Renaissance literature, remains elusive and open to the subjective vantage point of the creative. Some may envision this as grace, revelation, or transcendence. For the Greeks in the Sophist tradition, the soul's ability to recall the Forms as revelations of ideals was enhanced through education, dialogue, virtue and self-examination. Polanyi (1966) refers to the idea that there is a sense in the scientist of "valid anticipation of the yet indeterminate implications of the discovery" (p. 24). Polanyi states that all knowledge is equivalent to knowledge of a problem—it is intuited. Attention to the sensations of the body, emotions, and unconscious primes may facilitate intuitive movement. The scientist feels a great duty to pursue hidden truth (Polanyi, 1966, p. 25); this obligation is best maximized in a context where cooperation, collegiality, and uninterrupted autonomy are provided.

In support of the role of tacit knowledge for discovery, Polanyi (1966) claims that if we state that something is true, we are already claiming to know more than we can tell (p. 23). This sense of knowledge prior to knowledge implies a recollection of sorts, an encounter with something previously known. The inability to express this knowledge fully contributes to its power. In the same way, a ruthless dissection of a literary passage or work of art creates lifelessness. The profound is encountered within the ineffable features of knowledge. The risk of falsehood in science comes with awareness of a Type I error—the illusory. Such error is minimized through replication, re-analysis by external others, peer review, and longitudinal forays into competing explanations. Thus, a systematic process of verification is required.

However, an equally concerning issue is the Type II error, or the failure to detect a reality that is, in fact, there. Type II errors in the workplace may occur with the failure of introspection and in the context of superficial analyses. The manager who is excessively confident in his propositions and who does not seek evidence to the contrary will increase the probability of detection errors. In hierarchical organizations, the failure to consult with others, including those of lower status or power, can create blind spots that evoke functional fixedness. For the worker who is overly taxed with menial activities, distracted with unnecessary meetings, and overworked or exhausted, the still small voice of intuition becomes inaudible.

An Expanded and Redacted View of Science

Polanyi (1966) states that society requires a broader, emancipated view of science. There must be a role for personal knowledge (p. 20) and 'strict empiricism' leaves science in a state of vulnerability to political contamination (p. 81). In contrast, there may be a metaphysical ground for the exploration of natural revelation. In order for healthy science to emerge, Polanyi (1966, p. 81) argued that a society must "vindicate the freedom of science" from the sources of political corruption that lead to its misuse. The imposition of political ideologies upon science creates a form of subjugation that can obliterate the epistemic core of the discipline. Polanyi provides the model of scientists as explorers and emphasizes that expeditions cannot thrive in contexts where ideas are controlled by totalitarian leaders (pp. 83–83). Absolute submission to any political party is a thought commitment that will invariably undermine science, which thrives through dissent. A dogmatic society is in essence authoritarian, for the leaders in such regimes fear freedom of thought. Polanyi viewed the explorers as "in thought" (p. 83), aware of the social forces that seek to develop coteries of mutual admiration (p. 84). Historical determinism necessarily presents another force of contamination for science (Polanyi, 1966, p. 85). Determinism, "the demands of perfectionism," and the notion that self-determination is absolute, remain as "inordinate endeavors" in Polanyi's view (p. 85). He argues that the deconstruction of extremism requires an understanding that higher level principles in science rely on a substrate of supporting levels that undergird the process and its aims.

However, Polanyi seems to stray from the idealism that should support science when he points out that the "lower levels" in society rely on "power and profit" (Polanyi, 1966, p. 86). While this provides a warning against the conflicts of interest that are often observed with large corporate forays into science, it also commutes the quest for truth-seeking to a pragmatic course. Polanyi warns of the importance of protecting the mind against "critical and moral frenzy" (p. 86). In his explanation of the importance of self-doubt, Polanyi supports that kind of tentative integrity that must be an essential quality of science. A problem may only be known tacitly; the antecedents of solutions convey principles of emergence (p. 87). Polanyi appeals to the notion of reasonableness, asserting that solutions can be pursued through "an indeterminate process" (p. 87). The notion that indeterminate processes may have a place in psychological research supports forays into qualitative design and case studies, which yield high complexity and a plurality of themes and interpretive possibilities.

The expansion of science can be made possible when there is awareness of the impediments to truth-seeking, including bias, lack of moral courage, or predilection, which are described by Francis Bacon (1620, as cited in Lewis, 2010) as the idols of the cave. Learning was arguably inclusive, with an eye to history as well as towards the future, for "the present is like a seer with two faces" (Bacon, 1603, as cited in Lewis, 2010, p. 361). Bacon's account of human knowledge included imagination, narrative, represen- tational truth, memory, reason, and the allegorical (Lewis, 2010, p. 366). The symbolic doubling in allegory is expressed as a place where "we speak one thing and mean another" (Puttenham, 1589, as cited in Lewis, 2010, p. 366). For Bacon, learning was thought to include notions that were pro- bationary, subject to examination and testing (Lewis, 2010, p. 368).

Scientific Fruitfulness

In his 1620 publication of the Novum Organum, Francis Bacon distin- guished between experimenta lucifera, which intended to uncover causal relationships, and experimenta fructifera, which explored practical appli- cations of natural laws (Hergenhahn, 2009, p. 117). Bacon asserted that both experiments with light and fruit required the elimination of bias through systematic methods of observation. At the same time, one may not assume that an evaluation of scientific fruitfulness is necessarily linked to the "undiscovered consequences" of science, which are referenced by

Polanyi. Fruitfulness may be chronicled much after the fact, observing generations of research that have derived from a central question. Polanyi (1966) states, "since we have no explicit knowledge of…unknown things, there can be no explicit justification of scientific truth." (p. 23).

Scientific fruitfulness will occur within a social and organizational field. Within Lewin's theory, the life space includes the entire psychological field, a subjective experience that includes a topography of habits, paths, and regions (Wheeler, 2008). The visual representation of the topography of the social and organizational context would include vectors, which show directions of force, barriers, and positive and negative regions that intersect with expectations and ideas (Wheeler, 2008, p. 1640).

Occasionalism: A Root Word for the Unity of Science?

Although a popular mythology has arisen around conflicts between religion and faith, largely spurred by the intellectual degradation in 20th-century American thought and education, the anti-intellectualism of American Evangelicalism, and bolstered by the well-known abuses of the Catholic Church toward 16th-century scientists, historical roots also show the potential for a prolific engagement between metaphysical and scientific pursuits, both of which can appreciate the intuitive nature of creative imagination. Polanyi (1966) implies that a scientific paradigm is a form of tacit knowledge.

A common assumption until more recent scholarship has been that the movement towards occasionalism was motivated by a need to resolve the mind-body problem (Nadler, 2011). However, as noted by the extensive exploration of Nadler (2011), investigation of the works of notable occasionalists such as Nicholas Malebranche, Arnold Giulincx, and Geraud de Courdemoy has revealed that the motive for belief in divine causation was rooted in an understanding of human finiteness of will and power. Furthermore, the assertion that divine forces interact with physical and mental events was not circumscribed to full occasionalists but also included perspectives that understood the mind as an active agent, subject perhaps to metaphysical influences but not entirely controlled by an external source. This was the viewpoint of Descartes, which was also adopted by the later work of his protégé, Louis de la Forge. The latter eventually concluded that divine power sustained the movement of bodies but did not compel the activity of minds. In addition, de la Forge distinguished between effective causes and remote or occasional causes. A similarity is observed in Polanyi's (1966) distinction between distal and proximate cues, which bear upon unconscious and explicit cognitive processes.

Rene Descartes showed greater restraint than de la Forge in his orientation toward divine causation (Nadler, 2011). Discussing the awareness that one has no guarantee of the ongoing existence of consciousness and the lack of the sense of power to sustain a self, Descartes speaks in his Meditations about the necessity for divine sustenance for the ongoing existence of mind. Considering the intersection of natural philosophy, science, and mechanism, Nadler (2011) discusses the central questions that emerged in the 17th century, including the following: (1) How does physical change occur? (2) Can mind-related events directly or primarily cause physical events? (3) Do changes in bodily states influence the mind? and (4) Do causal relationships exist between mental states or activities? These questions, which clearly interact with the path of modern psychology, emerged within an understanding of causal variation. For example, a proximal or efficient cause was deemed to be the primary driver of an outcome, such that the event would not have transpired without this force. In contrast, a cause may be indirect, resulting from the combined effect of several forces. Immanent causes were understood to lead to internal change, while transeunt causes led to alteration in something external. Some forms of causation involve the transfer of energy or information from one source to another, while other forms could result without any loss from the causal agent. For Courdemoy, mind could effect change in the physical world, but only when mind was defined as that beyond the finite (Nadler, 2011).

Continuous Creation and Indeterminism

The idea of science merely uncovering hidden truths will naturally intersect with positions on cause, origins, and existence. Metaphysical questions will inevitably arise from the suggestion that scientific paradigms and scientific pursuits are a form of tacit knowledge, especially as one considers the personal or subjective qualities of perceiving and interpreting science.

Lee (2008) discusses English translations of the work of Nicholas Malebranche in his review of the latter's principal arguments used to understand the intersection between theism and natural causation. Principally, Lee refers to Malebranche's view that conservation (of what exists) relies on continuous creation processes. In addition, the author proposes that it was only in Malebranche's earlier works that he highlighted the notion of no necessary connections (NNC). The view of NNC offers the proposition that a cause can only be labeled as such when the mind perceives a *necessary connection* between an event and an outcome. Malebranche then argues that the only such necessary connection is between the will of divine perfection and outcomes. Citing other passages by Malebranche, Lee suggests that the notion of perception is not a prerequisite for necessary connections. While acknowledging some of the problematic features of NNC, Lee argues that there is an attractive element at the core of this principle, which is the notion that an understanding of cause presupposes an efficacious propulsion, for "all genuine causal relations are just necessary connections" (Lee, 2008, p. 564).

Schultz and D'Andrea-Winslow (2014) discuss divine compositionalism as an alternative to occasionalism; in this model, which is rooted in a medieval view of: (a) the existence and composition of the cosmos, and (b) the ongoing maintenance, dynamics, and constitution of the universe; the cosmos is rooted in a divine source. These authors posit that divine compositionalism may serve as a foundational principle for understanding the mechanisms of science, and suggest that this view is compatible with subatomic indeterminism. The indeterminate features are viewed not as random but as purposiveness anchored in divine freedom, with miracles or interventions resting in the transcendence of divine commitments to naturalistic laws.

While the notion of divine conservation, or the idea that God must continually sustain the existence of the universe and souls through action, has been common orthodoxy within Christianity, Nadler (1998) suggests that this view is incompatible with a strict reading of a Cartesian view. Furthermore, Nadler infers that La Forge, who was mentored by Descartes, assisted in the development of occasionalism in such a way that it was preparatory for Nicholas Malebranche. This development allowed for a deeper exploration of the idea that there was a divine origin for the continuous creation and conservation of conscious and nonconscious entities, as well as their modalities, motivations, and properties, which emerge within a context and impermanent place.

Innis (1996) presents the view that the philosopher Immanuel Kant's polemical argument against two forms of idealism, as leveled in *A Critique of Pure Reason*, offers a distinction between Kant's own form of transcendental idealism, versus those offered by Descartes and Berkeley. Cartesian (problematic) idealism is skeptical and asserts that only those things perceived by the mind can be absolutely known to exist because it is only the private world of the mind that is known. Objects outside of the mind are, therefore, seen as incapable of being demonstrated or may be considered unknown. Kant then opposes George Berkeley's ontological, or dogmatic, idealism on the claim that it recommends that objects outside of the mind are false or impossible. Thus, in Kant's reading of Berkeley, objects depend on the mind. It can be questioned whether Kant's understanding of Berkeley offers a complete formulation of the latter's view. Grave (1964) proposes that Berkeley viewed objects as collections of ideas, but that these ideas were not tied to any particular perceiver and merely suggested that physical entities do not exist in complete isolation from perception. Because objects are held in continuous perception by God, a permanent perceiver, the material world has ongoing existence. In contrast to these two perspectives on idealism, Kant's view proposes that appearances are representations rather than real objects (Innis, 1996, p. 60).

Astore (2018) compares the skeptical idealism of Descartes to that of Berkeley, privileging the position of ontological idealism. The author discusses Berkeley's claim that *to be is to be perceived*, rooting this in the idea that "if everything remains in the unceasingly watchful mind of a greater consciousness, or spirit, the observable universe will continue to endure" (p. 115). Thus, the representational aspects of reality are forged within the mind of God as sensory elements that ensure the conservation of existence. Astore's reading of Berkeley conveys that God is the "ultimate subjective spirit" (p. 116). Occasionalism, with its view of God as the permanent perceiver and ground of being, provides a metaphysical option to support some versions of the unity of science. This is ironic when contrasted with the post-enlightenment contention, championed in modernity, that metaphysical assumptions are necessarily false. Such assumptions could be considered non-empirical in the sense that the untestable assumptions of metaphysics cannot be disproven any more than they can be proven through scientific measurement. In many scientific models, the absence of data is not taken as falsification. If one asserts that the absence of findings does not falsify a hypothesis, but merely fails to support it, the outright claims of the Vienna Circle regarding metaphysics would be taken to extend beyond the standard model of scientific proof. For those who adopt a model that integrates faith with science, nature is a form of revelation. Its underlying consistencies and laws evoke a unity, but one that is also infinite, unknowable, and immeasurable.

Thought as Discovery

Quantum principles, such as uncaused causes, introduce principles of randomness and probability into the pursuit of truth-seeking (Polanyi, 1966, p. 88). There can be both animate and inanimate processes in discovery. Science will seek to uncover catalysts, the source of greater stability, and forces that serve to realize potentialities (Polanyi, 1966, p. 89). However, thought is also moved by an innate "imaginative thrust" that drives potentials, is moved by intentional effort, and serves as the uncaused cause. Problems that desire solutions function as something greater than stable configurations.

Although the Instauratio Magna (Bacon, 1620a) offers a useful lens into early scientific methods, it also illumines the reader with the view that scientific observation includes elements of intangible juxtapositions. In Bacon's section on topics of inquiry concerning light and lumen, the author considered the adversaries and kinsfolk of light, its attenuation, sources, and attributes. Some bodies only resemble light, reflect light, or produce an "aggregation of lucid bodies [which] multiples light" (Bacon, 1620a, p. 249). Light may be eclipsed if it is in close proximity to a light of greater intensity. While the light is short-lived, Bacon describes it as pleasing to the spirit as it generates and spreads out. Within the *New Abecedarium of Nature*, Bacon references Democritus, suggesting that, even within inanimate things, spirit can be found (Bacon, 1620a, p. 189). He states, "The quantum of nature or universal sum of matter admits neither increase nor decrease; for a force and resistance inhere in every particle of matter...and will not let itself be annihilated" (p. 191). The force found within matter is viewed as resistance in Bacon, and "bodies support each other by mutual connection and contact," being incapable of annihilation (p. 191). Motion involved in connection includes either locomotion or resistance to movement. Bodies were thought to move towards liberty rather than constraint but long to be rejoined by larger masses. Some bodies will seek placement in a particular context, while others seek to assimilate (p. 197), but the universe contains an orientation towards configuration, or wholeness (p. 221).

The Uncertainty Factor and Hope for Science in a Democratic Society

Beghetto (2021) suggests that creativity cannot thrive without uncertainty. Promoting the notion that uncertainty fuels genuine doubt and destabilization, eliciting questions about truth and reality, Beghetto (2021) describes this state as actionable. He offers the motto 'dubito ergo creo', or "I doubt, therefore I create" (p. 1). Building on the work of early American pragmatists, including Charles Sanders Peirce and John Dewey, Beghetto (2021) arrives at the conclusion that genuine doubt is evoked when a surprising event occurs, and the understanding of that event cannot be realized through standard modes of inductive or deductive reasoning. This requires the individual to access 'abductive' reasoning, or creativity, in response (Beghetto, 2021, p. 1).[1] The engagement with destabilizing forces is viewed as an opportunity in Beghetto's (2021) analysis, with particular implications for educational settings, which will be constrained by goals and criteria.

In a brief article that provides a haunting prophesy about the 21st century and the failures of social reform to liberate individuals from classism, Wallerstein (1998) points out that progress is by no means inevitable. Identifying the weakness in the assumption that theism accompanies epistemological certitude, Wallerstein (1998) states, "...the belief in certainties, a fundamental premise of modernity, is blinding and crippling. Modern science, that is, Cartesian-Newtonian science, has been based on the certainty of certainty" (p. 1). He offers a vision of a rational and ethically responsible society that is inexorably linked to both democracy and egalitarian pursuits. Noting the capacities, motivations, and responsible strivings that are unlocked by uncertainty, Wallerstein (1998) concludes, "if everything is uncertain, then the future is open to creativity, not merely human creativity but the creativity of all nature. It is open to possibility and, therefore, to a better world" (p. 2).

Creativity can be conceived of as a potential with an infinite array of permutations. The sense of infinitude is met with the constraining forces of the perceptual set of managers and the echo chambers that they seek to perpetuate. Research and development within organizations and governmental entities has benefited from the insight of Kurt Lewin, whose personal encounters with authoritarianism in Nazi Germany prior to his emigration in 1933 served to stimulate his interest in the harmful effects of autocracy on creativity, progress, collaboration, and human motivation. Building on a metaphor derived from physics, Lewin's notion of fields of force has been instrumental in research within industrial organizational psychology and human resource management.

Fields of Force, Action Research, and Constraining Forces in the Workplace

A field of force may find an analogy in the notion of the loadstone, which "attracts the powder of prepared steel" (Bacon, 1620a, p. 239). There is the possibility for different intensities of magnetism, for "one loadstone has much greater virtue than another" (Bacon, 1620a, p. 239). The activity of spirits, as seen through chemical compounds and dilations, is caused by the "liberation of spirits" (Bacon, 1620a, p. 239). The agitation of spirit and the "attenuation and emission of spirit" produced changes in structure, movement, and appearance, which are all influenced by an environmental context (p. 239). The idea of vivification revealed "the pre-existent spirit of the thing [as] inflamed" (Bacon, 1620a, p. 263). The reactions of agitation seem to be alchemical in the metaphoric sense; the recombination of ideas rests at the source of the creative impulse.

In a review of Kurt Lewin's earlier papers, which were not translated into English at the time of her article, Miriam Lewin Papanek (1973) identifies her father's early fascination with management, worker satisfaction, and finding a model to derail the 'drudgery' of work. In her own translation from the German, Papanek (1973) offers the following quote to demonstrate Lewin's remarkable foresight,

The worker wants his work to be rich, wide, and Protean, not crippling and narrow. Work should not limit personal potential but develop it.

Work can involve love, beauty, and the soaring joy of creating. Progress, in that case, does not mean shortening the work day, but an increase in the human value of the work.[2]

(p. 318)

Lewin's model rejected the determinism that was offered by radical behaviorism and traditional psychoanalysis, considering the interaction between personality structures and the social environment (Papanek, 1973). Field observations were used to examine the impact of contextual demands on the worker, including the ability to organize the work space and the impact of the environment on the psychological life space. Lewin labeled the research that he engaged in "action research"; it sought to connect field studies to applied questions pertinent to the matrix of work and the individual. In response to his experiences with fascism in Europe, Lewin became increasingly interested in social fields of force and how these repel or attract change, studying variations in outcome that arrive with autocratic versus democratic or laissez-faire leadership styles. If the primary restraining force is a person's commitment to uphold the group norm, then a shift in behavior and outcome is more likely when the restraining stimulus is removed.

Cronshaw and McCulloch (2008) provide a corrective to common misunderstandings about the application of Lewin's field of force model to organizational development and change. Based on their empirical study of 31 organizational professionals, Cronshaw and McCulloch (2008) observe that the diagnosis of factors that prevent organizational success may underestimate the role of blocking variables, despite the consideration of facilitating and constraining forces. This tendency to minimize blocking variables may represent a decision-making bias. Cronshaw and McCulloch (2008) also provide an analysis of Lewin's original works, published in 1929, 1935, 1936, and 1938, highlighting the fact that Lewin's model derived from an understanding of vectors and force in physics, and included the idea of dynamic change over time, including modifications in direction, strength, and point of application (p. 90). The authors conclude that Lewin's model never suggested that fields of force can be measured directly; rather, these intervening variables can only be inferred from observation. One might conclude that the causal vectors in the field of force operate by principles of emergence, taking on new qualities that cannot be reduced to the sets of parts that comprise the foundation.

Emergence, the Unconscious, and Reflections on a Society of Explorers

Polanyi (1966) describes emergence within a notion of stratification; he provides an evolutionary context for defining emergence as "the action which produces the next higher level" (p. 55). This is put forth as a movement from the inanimate state toward the living, and eventually evolves into the stratified layers of human reason. Polanyi (1966) offers a "rebuttal of exactitude as the ideal of science" (p. 56). This is the portal where he begins his discussion of a society of explorers, and he demarcates this as a foundation for a moral approach to empiricism. The evolution of life and reason occurs as a response; this response is evoked in the field of infinite potential meanings.

Within a society of explorers, the human being is "in thought" (Polanyi, 1966, p. 83). The imagination within a discipline is fully engaged, and collaborations across disciplines are systematically invented, remaining outside of tyranny, fanaticism, and cruelty. The vision of a society of explorers engaged in thought, is inconsistent with the notion of absolute self-determination, for the individual finds herself within a context, historical era, and societal demands and constraints. The finiteness of human capacity and the limitations of time truncate each explorer to a circumscribed area of expertise. A society of explorers cannot thrive within a "dogmatic society" (Polanyi, 1966, p. 83). Rather, the necessary controls for science are offered by peer review, through mutual consent to skepticism, correction, and reassessment. The vision offered by Polanyi for a self-renewable science is based on the tacit awareness of a yet-undiscovered potential.

However, even within his optimism regarding the creation of a society of explorers, Polanyi (1966) expresses skepticism about whether a self-renewable science of collaboration is possible. He recognizes the fragmentation to which humans are prone and their resistance to the organizing principles of scientific caution, academic humility, and peer review, stating,

> Must not such a fragmented society appear adrift, irresponsible, selfish, apparently chaotic? I have praised the freedom of a community where coherence is spontaneously established by self-coordination, authority is exercised by equals over each other, all tasks are set by each to himself. But where are they all going? Nobody knows; they are just piling up works soon to be forgotten.
>
> *(Polanyi, 1966, p. 92)*

The fragmentation of science into specialized camps may allow for referees within the systems of mutual control that are advocated by Polanyi (1966). However, specialization can also result in a fanaticism about minutia, which is critiqued by Hugo Munsterberg (1905) in his introduction to the journal for the International Congress of Arts and Sciences, an ambitious project with the goal of the unity of science,

> A reaction against the narrowness of mere fact-diggers has set in. A mere heaping up of disconnected, unshaped facts begins to disappoint the

world; it is felt too vividly that a mere dictionary of phenomena, of events and laws, makes our knowledge larger but not deeper, makes our life more complex but not more valuable, makes our science more difficult but not more harmonious. Our time longs for a new synthesis, and looks toward science no longer merely with a desire for technical prescriptions and new inventions in the interest of comfort and exchange. It waits for knowledge to fulfill its higher mission, to satisfy our ideal needs for a view of the world which shall give unity to our scattered experience.

(Munsterberg, 1905, p. 1)

While thoughts about the unity of science have often favored the direction of the quest for certitude, radical empiricism, and the rejection of metaphysics as false, another lens for this model looks back, *ad fontes*,[3] (Sweeting, 2016, personal communication) to earlier authors and their appreciation for the uncertainty when human finiteness encounters infinitude. Pluralism is thus encountered within a model of the unity of science, not as orthogonal but as an allegory of the cave. This quest to highlight the frailty of human reason in the encounter with infinite possibility is taken up in the work of George Berkeley and the occasionalists, with the recognition of the limits of human understanding and the resuscitation of intuitive knowledge for the arts and sciences.

Correctives in Science

Bacon (1620a) described experiments luciferous as those that illuminate cause. He identifies caveats to guide scientific processes, such as performing subtler versions of the original experiment and seeking to uncover weaknesses (p. 223). In addition, one may prompt other scientists to explore potential solutions. Bacon's work implies that, while it may be useful to create speculations, one must be cautious about fallacies and vigorously pursue error detection. Hypotheses can be generated regarding specific questions as well as rules, but interpretations must be circumspect, recognizing the research process as merely an initiation. Limitations in methods and measurements should be acknowledged, incentives provided should be provided for work, and abrupt inquiries or conclusions should be avoided. The scientist is warned not to overestimate the significance of his work, acknowledging areas of overlap between investigations while trying to diminish redundancies. Bacon's warnings about the idols of the cave, marketplace, tribe, and theater offer a useful framework for modern correctives of scientific bias (Hergenhahn, 2009).

Polanyi (1966) offers the corrective of circles of mutual control, accessed through peer review by a community of experts, which can serve a self-regulatory function by offering scientific correctives. Awareness of the creative potential that is present in unconscious thought, incubation, sleep, dreaming, and daydreaming does not undermine the importance of rigorous preparation and analysis by controlled cognitive processes (Ritter & Dijksterhuis, 2014). The necessity of verification within the creative process is observed in the case histories of great thinkers and creatives (Wallas, 1926). The preparation phase in the creative process involves self-discipline, formal and informal study, cognitive control, rejection and redaction, and conscientious self-correction.

Janusian reasoning includes the ability to consider two seemingly contradictory elements at the same time, pulling those together into investigations that can be applied to many disciplines (Rothenberg, 1971). Ambivalence can be a precursor to Janusian reasoning, for the individual may alternate between contradictory experiences, emotions, or impulses. The creative process is difficult to constrain because it is unpredictable and undetermined (Rothenberg, 1971, p. 203). Janusian reasoning may be particularly beneficial for science when it allows the individual to imagine the opposite of a current assumption or hypothesis, asking the question: If the opposite were true, what would be observed or known? This question can guide confirmatory research, which either falsifies or supports the dominant paradigm. Unfortunately, Janusian reasoning is underutilized in hierarchical workplace structures, which tend to value conformity, obedience, tradition, and compliance with norms established by power-holders.

Uncertainty also poses as a corrective in science. Without skepticism turned inward, lacking awareness of conflicts of interest, scientific endeavors can become lodged in the need for personal significance, power, wealth, and affiliation with dominant others. Without skepticism, one may become obsessed with the need to project an external image of virtue onto a conformist society. Uncertainty can facilitate the exploration of both the explicit and the implicit, highlighting the value of paradox and the simultaneous consideration of opposites. The underlying structure of tacit knowledge implies that there is a

Hidden interior, which we could explore; the sight of another person points at unlimited hidden workings of his mind and body. Perception has this inexhaustible profundity, because what we perceive is an aspect of reality, and aspects of reality are clues to boundless undisclosed, and perhaps yet unthinkable, experiences.

(Polanyi, 1966, p. 68)

Expeditions in the Hamlet

The metaphor of evolution may be fruitful for a topographical vision for a society of explorers, as outlined by the work of Polanyi (1966). This narrative suggests the contrast of life entering into an inanimate cosmos and concludes with the notion of the human individual, immersed in thought, within a system of mutual control that occurs within a context of peer review. The lifelessness of dogmatism, fanaticism, moral perfectionism, and authoritarianism is contrasted with the vital existence that is elicited when the unconscious operates on sensed possibility, subception, built on a structure of tacit knowledge. This creative work is inherently relational, emergent in dyads and parishes, precincts and counties, with explorers who encounter self, other, and the holy mysteries of the world, where ideas are "any sensible or imaginable thing" (Berkeley, 1784, p. 93).

If Berkeley's (1784) contentions are right that "people do not know what is meant by reality" (p. 94), ideas are produced by a will (p. 99), and cause is signified by ideas in succession (p. 101), then the preeminence of *mind-in-uncertainty* is emphatic. Berkeley (1784) wrote of a spirit that "acts, causes, wills, operates…is not knowable" (p. 99). The will was deemed to be "pure spirit, not imaginable, not sensible…no wise perceivable" (p. 99). This very unknowability of the Other casts a net of humanistic fervor, a valuation of the tacit within the employee. Imagination creates ex nihilo, for "ideas of sense are real things or archetypes. Ideas of imaginations, dreams…are copies, images of these" (Berkeley, 1784, p. 98). Moving from the idols of bias, materialism, and illusion into the luminosity of science that includes inductive and deductive approaches, the art of tacit creativity can inch towards mastery on a wide river of possibility.

Notes

1 Beghetto's discussion of abductive reasoning is derived from Peirce, C. S. (1958). *Collected papers of Charles Sanders Peirce*. Vols. 5–8 A. W. Burks (Ed.). Belknap Press of Harvard University Press.
2 Lewin, K. (1920). Die sozialisierung des taylorsystems: Eine grundsatzliche untersuchung zur arbeits- u. Berufs-Psychologie. *Praktischer Sozialismus, 4*, p. 12.
3 This reference towards a return to the source, was inspired by Sweeting, D. (2016, personal communication), as a vision for a university built from Christ as the headwaters of life, but was used in a different context.

Works Cited

Antsey, P. (2003). Bacon's last instalment. *Minerva, 41*(1), 89–92.

Astore, R. A. (2018). Doubting Descartes: How Berkeley's immaterialism outshines the Cartesian system. *Rupkatha Journal on Interdisciplinary Studies in Humanities, 10*(2), 111–117.

Bacon, F. (1620a). *The instauratio magna: Last writings*. In F. Rees (trans.), *The Oxford Francis Bacon XIII*. Oxford University Press.

Bacon, F. (1620b). *Novum Organum*. Retrieved from pages.uoregon.edu

Beghetto, R. A. (2021). There is no creativity without uncertainty: Dubito ergo creo. *Journal of Creativity, 31*(100005), 1–5.

Bereiter, C. (2002). *Education and mind in the knowledge age*. Lawrence Erlbaum.

Berkeley, G. (1784). The works of George Berekely, volume 1. In A. A. Luce & T. E. Jessup (Eds.), *Philosophical commentaries of George Berkeley, Bishop of Cloyne* (pp. 1–314). Thomas Nelson and Sons, 1948.

Bettcher, T. M. (2007). *Berkeley's philosophy of spirit: Consciousness, ontology, and the elusive*. Continuum International Publishing Group.

Birch, H. G., & Rabinowitz, H. S. (1951). The negative effect of previous experience on productive thinking. *Journal of Experimental Psychology, 41*(2), 121–125.

Burnes, B., & Bargal, D. (2017). Kurt Lewin: 70 years on. *Journal of Change Management, 17*(2), 91–100.

Burwood, S. (2007). Imitation, indwelling and the embodied self. *Educational Philosophy and Theory, 39*(2), 118–134.

Cat, J. (2007, Fall). The unity of science. In E. N. Zalta (Ed.), *The Stanford encyclopedia of philosophy* (pp. 1–41). Retrieved from https://plato.stanford.edu/archives/fall2007/entries/scientific-unity/

Cronshaw, S. F., & McCulloch, A. N. (2008). Reinstating the Lewinian vision: From force field analysis to organization field assessment. *Organization Development Journal, 26*(4), 89–103.

Cross, A. (1991). The crisis in physics: Dialectical materialism and quantum theory. *Social Studies of Science, 21*, 735–59.

Dumas, D., Organisciak, P., & Doherty, M. (2021). Measuring divergent thinking originality with human raters and text mining models: A psychometric comparison of models. *Psychology of Aesthetics, Creativity and the Arts, 15*(4), 645–663.

Ebrey, D. (2014). Meno's Paradox in context. *British Journal for the History of Philosophy, 22*(1), 4–24. doi: 10.1080/09608788.2013.869488

Ellwood, S., Pallier, G., Snyder, A., & Gallate, J. (2009). The incubation effect: Hatching a solution? *Creativity Research Journal, 21*(1), 6–14.

Erez, M., & Nouri, R. (2010). Creativity: The influence of cultural, social, and work contexts. *Management and Organization Review, 6*(3), 351–370.

Grave, S. A. (1964). The mind and its ideas: Some problems in the interpretation of Berkeley. *Australasian Journal of Philosophy, 42*(2), 199–210.

Griffith, A. (2021). Embodied creativity in the fine and performing arts. *Journal of Creativity, 31*, 100010.

Grgic, F. (1999). Plato's Meno and the possibility of inquiry in the absence of knowledge. *Bochumer Philosophisches Jahrbuch Fur Antike Und Mittelalter, 4*(1), 19–40.

Hergenhahn, B. R. (2009). *An introduction to the history of psychology*, (6th ed.). Wadsworth.

Hirt, E. R., Devers, E. E., & McCrea, S. M. (2008). I want to be creative: Exploring the role of hedonic contingency theory in the positive mood-cognitive flexibility link. *Journal of Personality and Social Psychology, 94*(2), 214–230. doi: 10.1037/0022-3514.94.2.94.2.214

Hu, J., Erdogan, B., Jiang, K., Bauer, T. N., & Liu, S. (2018). Leader humility and team creativity: The role of team information sharing, psychological safety, and power distance. *Journal of Applied Psychology, 103*(3), 1–11. Advance online publication.

Innis, W. B. (1996). The Refutation of the refutation. *Auslegung: A Journal of Philosophy, 21*(1), 51–63.

Inoue, S., Rodgers, P., Spencer, N., & Tennant, A. (2015). Reductionism as a tool for creative exploration. In *the 11th European Academy of Design Conference (EAD 11)*, 22–24th April 2015, Paris, France, pp. 1–16. Retrieved from https://ead.yasar.edu.tr/wp-content/uploads/2017/0

Kauffman, S. (2007). Beyond reductionism: Reinventing the sacred. *Zygon, 42*(4), 903–914.

Lee, S. (2008). Necessary connections and continuous creation: Malebranche's two arguments for occasionalism. *Journal of the History of Philosophy, 46*(4), 539–565. Retrieved from http://ezproxy.ccu.edu/login?url=https://www-proquest-com.ezproxy.ccu.edu/scholarly-journals/necessary-connections-continuous-creation/docview/210610243/se-2

Lewis, R. (2014). Francis Bacon and ingenuity. *Renaissance Quarterly, 67*(1), 113–163.

Lewis, R. (2010). Francis Bacon, allegory and the uses of myth. *The Review of English Studies, 61*(250), 360–389. Retrieved from http://www.jstor.org/stable/40783067

Lin, W., Ma, J., Zhang, Q., Li, J. C., & Jiang, F. (2018). How is benevolent leadership linked to employee creativity? The mediating role of leader–member exchange and the moderating role of power distance orientation. *Journal of Business Ethics, 152*(4), 1099–1115.

Lloyd-Cox, J., Christensen, A. P., Silvia, P. J., & Beaty, R. E. (2021). Seeing outside the box: Salient ideas disrupt idea generation. *Psychology of Aesthetics, Creativity and the Arts, 15*(4), 575–583.

Melin, L. (1987). The field-of-force metaphor: A study in industrial change. *International Studies of Management & Organization, 17*(1), 24–33. doi: 10.1080/00208825.1987.11656443

Merleau-Ponty, M. (1945). *Phenomenology of perception.* D. A. Landes (Trans.). Routledge, 2012.

Mitchell, M. T. (2005). Personal participation: Michael Polanyi, Eric Voegelin, and the indispensability of faith. *Journal of Religious Ethics, 33*(1), 65–89. doi: 10.1111/j.0384-9694.2005.00183.x

Montuori, A., & Purser, R. (1997). Social creativity: The challenge of complexity. *Le dimensioni sociali della creatività. Pluriverso, 1*(2), 78–88 [1–23 in preprint manuscript].

Munsterberg, H. (1905). The international congress of arts and sciences. In *Congress of Arts and Science: Universal Exhibition, St. Louis* (pp. 1–8). Houghton, Mifflin.

Nadler, S. (1998). Louis de la forge and the development of occasionalism: Continuous creation and the activity of the soul. *Journal of the History of Philosophy, 36*(2), 215–231. Retrieved from http://ezproxy.ccu.edu/login?url=https://www.proquest.com/scholarly-journals/louis-de-la-forge-development-occasionalism/docview/210615789/se-2

Nadler, S. (2011). *Occasionalism: Causation among the Cartesians.* Oxford University Press.

Nonaka, I. (2007). The knowledge-creating company. *Harvard Business Review, 85*(7/8), 162–171.

Papanek, M. L. (1973). Kurt Lewin and his contributions to modern management theory. *Academy of Management Proceedings (0065–0668),* 317–322. doi: 10.5465/AMBPP.1973.4981410

Poe, E. A. (1844/1910). The purloined letter. In *The works of Edgar Allan Poe.* Harper and Bros.

Polanyi, M. (1965). On the modern mind. *Encounter, 24*(5), 12–20.

Polanyi, M. (1966). *The tacit dimension.* University of Chicago Press.

Ritter, S. M., & Dijksterhuis, A. (2014). Creativity—the unconscious foundations of the incubation period. *Frontiers in Human Neuroscience, 215,* 1–10.

Rothenberg, A. (1971). The process of Janusian thinking in creativity. *Archives of General Psychiatry, 24*(3), 195–205.

Sawyer, R. K. (1999). The emergence of creativity. *Philosophical Psychology, 12*(4), 447–469.

Schultz, W. J. & D'Andrea-Winslow, A. (2014) Divine compositionalism: A form of occasionalism or a preferable alternative view of divine action? *Theology and Science, 12*(3), 216–235. doi: 10.1080/14746700.2014.927254

Slater, P. (1991). *A dream deferred. America's discontent and the search for a new democratic ideal.* Beacon.

Steindorf, L., Hammerton, H. A., & Rummel, J. (2021). Mind wandering outside the box: About the role of off-task thoughts and their assessment during creative incubation. *Psychology of Aesthetics, Creativity and the Arts, 15*(4), 504–595.

Storme, M., Celik, P., & Myszkowski, N. (2021). Creativity and unethicality: A systematic review and meta-analysis. *Psychology of Aesthetics, Creativity and the Arts, 15*(4), 664–672.

Swanger, D. (1983). The future of aesthetic education. *Journal of Aesthetic Education, 17*(1), 15–30.

Thurstone, L. L. (1947). *Multiple-factor analyses: The development and expansion of the vectors of mind.* University of Chicago Press.

Wallas, G. (1926). *The art of thought.* Harcourt Brace.

Wallerstein, I. (1998). Uncertainty and creativity. *American Behavioral Scientist, 42*(3), 320–321. Retrieved from https://link.gale.com/apps/doc/A53650289/BIC?u=christian&sid=bookmark-BIC&xid=424f0f85

Wheeler, L. (2008). Kurt Lewin. *Social and personality psychology compass, 2*(4), 1638–1650.

Yonge, G. D. (1966). Structure of experience and functional fixedness. *Journal of Educational Psychology, 57*(2), 115–120.

7

ONTOLOGICAL IDEALISM, THE PLATONIC REAL, AND OBJECT/ PERSON PERCEPTION IN THE WORKPLACE

Nahanni Freeman

Self as Subject and Object

Within a workplace environment, individuals evaluate themselves and others, forging comparisons against unseen ideals and internalized associations about the Good. These ideals are often conflated with particular examples, which are assumed to either contain or reject the ought. However, such *assumptions* about particulars are not equivalent to the real existence of an actual object, as shown in the work of Merleau-Ponty (1945) in his analysis of the *Phenomenology of Perception*. The self as a subject would also be the observer, relying on the apparatus of the body to draw conclusions. The self remains incarcerated in a body; therefore, the subject is also an object, for the inferences formed assume relations between parts of things and ideas, as if these were real (Merleau-Ponty, 1945, p. 69, 73). Influenced by the work of Gottfried Leibniz, Merleau-Ponty (1945) pointed out that the object in view "includes all possible perspectives" (p. 69). An individual who flounders in one workplace setting may thrive and be deeply valued in another. Retaining uncertainty in projections about the minds of others will recognize the colleague as an entity in constant change, becoming, and being. This prerequisite of potentiality can allow space for emergence, an essential feature of creativity.

Creative organizational work will be contextualized within a workplace system and culture, interacting with several layers of multidirectional influence between the individual and the external world, as described in Urie Bronfenbrenner's (1979) social ecological model. Bronfenbrenner's work has been adopted by the American Psychological Association

DOI: 10.4324/9781003322894-8

as a layered ecological model, which includes a series of nested eggs for domains of interaction between self-definition and relationships, including community, family, school, institution, domestic and international climate (Clauss-Ehlers et al., 2019). The multi-directional influences between domains are felt to represent both tension and fluidity. One extension of this model could include a concentric ring of interaction with external forms of knowledge, inspiration, and motivation, with the view that creative mimesis may be fostered by noetic and spiritual encounters, as well as cross-historical mentorship based on engagement with the written artifacts of philosophers, poets, playwrights, and scientists.

Within a workplace setting, the luminary quality of creativity is most ready to emerge when the relational environment fosters a sense of belonging. Learning environments within companies that seek to launch organizational belonging should emulate initiatives successful in securing nonjudgmental community in other spheres. Such projects strive to promote teams, address social inequalities, study perceptions of unfairness, enhance felt safety, reduce stress, and build socioemotional skills, absorbing these goals into existing structures (Allen et al., 2023). It is felt that the sense of organizational belonging can create a readiness for connectivity to the macrosystem of creative illumination, which emanates inward towards the self-defining person in a process that is fluid, paradoxical, and in tension with constraining forces and the limits of behavioral and cognitive latitude.

Examples from the literary and creative arts can yield information for an analysis of workplace innovation. In Renaissance literary works, it is not uncommon to hear the author invoke a muse, which implies a form of imitation and extension from a transcendent mind into the creative process. Keyser (2023) describes the way that Shakespeare calls forth the "muse of fire" as an invitation to the audience to transcend the physical space of the theater in a sensory way; Keyser also discusses the probable influence of poetry on Shakespeare's dramatic intentions (pp. 72–74). Burgess (1968) discusses a model of ontological poetics, which considers the muse in tension with human agency and identity, exploring the horizontal interactions between the poet, the poem as an object, and the reader as a poetic subject. Burgess advances the idea that early modernity attempted to essentialize the muse.

Attempts to concretize the notion of a creative muse are likely to develop within worldviews that emphasize materialism, mechanism, or reductionism. The assumption of creativity as rooted in unrelenting technologies of progress will tend towards the heuristic that *what-is-new-is-better*. One may ask whether innovation seeks to create that which is novel or that which is useful (Bol et al., 2024). In contrast, an immaterialist viewpoint can entertain time as a "train of ideas" (Berkeley, 1784, p. 9). From this lens, duration is not separated from existence, and time is a sensation that lacks the quality of being infinitely divisible. Within immaterialism, extended matter is a sensation that lacks existence without a mind (Berkeley, 1784, p. 10). In the view of Nicolas Malebranche (1674), union with truth is a communion with the divine object, a language oriented towards a Book of Wisdom that fosters illumination and transcendence beyond the illusory noise of sensory conversations within the mind.

Plato's Theory of the Forms: Creative Access and Remembrance

The notion that, external to the self and the constructions of society, there may exist concealed ideals of truth, creativity, beauty, or harmony can be extended from the work of Plato. Within a Socratic model of learning, an underlying principle is the notion that the soul remembers, for connection to the Forms is hidden within the mind. Thus, one would not teach creativity; rather, it would be through a process of inquisitive extraction that retrieval could be leveraged. The removal of hierarchical pursuits of creativity in favor of democratic discourse and inquiry is advocated for.

Creative fruition will be born in an ethical workplace. One way in which Plato's theories can be relevant to workplace environments is based on the notion of ethical ideals that arrive from a deontological investigative process. Derived from the Greek words for the science of duty, a deontological view of ethics examines what ought to be done based on the notion that certain guiding principles are morally required based on a contract, responsibility, or agency (Alexander & Moore, 2021). This perspective on workplace ethics suggests that there are some ideals that exist in reality that extend beyond subjective individualism or utilitarianism.

Another application of Plato's theory to the current discussion concerns the *origin* of creative ideas, which could be viewed as having some real existence in a realm beyond spatial, temporal, and material entities. Plato's work relates to tacit knowledge in the sense that intuitive understanding, extended beyond consciousness, may be envisioned as a form of recollection, exhumed through education, illumination, or retrieval via a cue or expansive context. In a society that values innovation as mere change, according to the heuristic that *what-is-new-is-better*, the stabilizing force of the constant, in relation to employee retention, is an important corrective that restores the life of the mind as inclusive of immutability and dynamism.

An energized model of creativity frames a process for change and disruption. Plato's work synthesized a philosophy of continual cosmic change expressed in Heraclitus, Parmenides' view of the mere appearance of change despite an underlying static reality, and the ethical philosophies of

Socrates (Silverman, 2022). In some interpretations, emphasizing immutability, Plato's work implies that the Forms are perfect, unchanging ideas that contain the essence of what really exists outside of time and the material. In contrast, the idea posited by Heraclitus that the only constant in the universe is change can be intuited from Plato's view of the physical world of appearances, where particular instances of things may reflect some essence of Form, but are in a state of flux with an ultimate demise. The philosophy of Forms is not directly expressed in Plato's work but has been interpreted through rational extraction from his *Dialogues* and *The Republic*, which make use of metaphor and often use the voice of Socrates (Silverman, 2022).

Models of creativity may subsidize attitudes towards creative synthesis, re-purposing, conservation of resources, and imitation with new representation. The creative usage of the bizarre, seemingly untenable, can prompt novelty if early-phase ideas are not handily dismissed before they have the opportunity to develop (Yang et al., 2023). Creative work often builds from some object of study, being an imitative extension that modifies, distorts, removes, or conjoins, even interacting with the illusory. Some interpretations of Plato's work imply that he viewed the physical world as an imitation or copy of the Forms, which are sets of ideas or abstract principles that convey the notion of unity, simplicity, and the Good (Silverman, 2022). Particular objects in the physical world may manifest some features of the Forms; in this sense, they partake in the Form, but they do not have any real essence (Silverman, 2022). Rather than viewing the Forms as an archaic leftover from a pre-scientific age, one may inquire about the possibility that consciousness, as a root of creative striving, has some real, irreducible, and immaterial existence.

The Visible and the Unseen: Representations of the Other

Literary and philosophical works can reveal, within the limits of the language of imagery, new vistas for a mission of creative flourishing. Ongoing study of literature, poetry, and art can allocate access to a creative epiphany that might otherwise remain latent and unrealized. Through her sensory and imagistic narratives, which are informed by a rich engagement with Greek philosophy, Virginia Woolf's writing illuminates the biospheres that can support creative growth, despite the entrapment of material and mechanistic views of self and other that pervade hierarchies. In response to Virginia Woolf's work, *A Room of One's Own,* and Simone de Beauvoir's analysis of embodiment and subjectivity, Freeman (2019) posits that creative work will best emerge in the capacious region expressed visibly in Woolf's notion of the incandescence of mind. The internalization of the unseen, which extends from de Beauvoir's (1945) analysis of Merleau-Ponty's phenomenology, implies that subjectivity is enlisted in perception due to the merging of one's position as both subject and object. Freeman (2019) explores the possibility of creative work as a sacred space, which is protected within a humanistic lens where indeterminism is applied to a view of the Other, and ideals are both valued and acknowledged in their elusiveness as the interior world of the mind interacts with the exterior world of appearances.

Sim (2005) suggested that Woolf's writing reflects the influence not only of Platonic Form but also of Pater's (1893) contention that Plato's view emphasized ways that the material world can provide a glimpse into the Real. Woolf's exploration of visual imagery in her writing implies a pursuit of Beauty—the mundane and transcendent qualities in nature (Dalgarno, 2001; Sim, 2005). The sanctuary of the visible world in Woolf's (1929) work is,

> Found in a dusty road, now in a scrap of newspaper in the street, now in a daffodil in the sun. It lights up a group in a room and stamps some casual saying. It overwhelms one walking home beneath the stars and makes the silent world more real than the world of speech…Sometimes, too, it seems to dwell in shapes too far away for us to discern what their nature is. But whatever it touches, it fixes and makes permanent.
>
> *(p. 165)*

Representation of the Other

The way that leaders, peers, and supervisors interact with projections about colleagues is encased within the limited vantage point of a body and a set of experiences, preventing the possibility of objective performance appraisals, which place the self as the subject and the judiciary against the Other as the object—the recipient of diagnosis. The view that performance appraisals represent the Real can enact a form of violence against the Other, limiting potential through an internalization process that results from gazing into the social mirror.

A position of self-organizing humility can be a starting point for workplace creativity. Developing from Merleau-Ponty's study of embodied existence, de Beauvoir (1945/2004) suggests that intersubjectivity may help to eliminate opposition between subject and object in power differentials in relationships. Mutuality will emerge within a context where empathy can co-exist with humility regarding the limitations of one's perceptual experiences. Views of self and other interact with bidirectional influence, as shown by de Beauvoir's (1945/2004, p. 160) perspective that, "It is impossible to define the object in cutting if off from the subject...and the subject reveals itself through the object in which it is engaged."

Platonic Realism, Tangibility, and Mental Events

Michael Polanyi (1966) argues that minds and mental events have an existence in ontology. His notions of representation and perception are influenced by his assumption that minds have a real existence. Minds are independent and comprehensive, empowered beyond objects, for the significance of an object trumps its tangible representation (Polanyi, 1966, p. 33). Considering variations of Berkeley's theory of immaterialism, Pater's view of Plato and Woolf's construction of the Real, innovation is annexed by mind-commandeering material. This would suggest a shift in organizational focus and the valuation of knowledge workers.

An encounter with workplace creativity will posit a proposition of the real. Realism includes arguments about existence and independence, with philosophers varying in how they approach categories of knowledge (Miller, 2021). The existence claim asserts that objects have real existence in the world; the independence claim offers that this existence is independent from the mind (Miller, 2021). The extent to which organizational objectives and systems are viewed as independent from the mind determines workplace methods of innovation.

For the Platonic realist, there are abstract ideas that exist outside of space, causality, and time; these are independent of the mind (Miller, 2021). The subpoint related to causation is somewhat ambiguous, however. For example, some approaches to the Platonic Forms imply that whatever exists in the physical world is caused by the Forms, for material objects are dependent on the Forms for their existence (Silverman, 2022). If one assumes that there is a spiritual or abstract set of ideals that exist outside of the mind, a creative process would seek to connect to these ideals. If these ideals are co-determined by the mind, then a process of remembrance could be used to activate them.

Models of workplace creativity and epistemology will settle on some vision of knowledge and ideational multiplication. Epistemology examines a theory of the methods and assumptions for how knowledge is secured. Arguments ventured include variation, such as the notion that the mind, despite its imperfection, can engage in some form of perceptual interaction with the abstract realm of ideas (Gödel, 1983, as cited in Miller, 2021). In Phaedrus, which is felt to be one of the principle examples of Plato's theory of the Forms, it is implied that tacit knowledge may be an extension of recollection, for Socrates states that "perhaps the mind itself has a kind of divining power" (Plato, 370 BC., p. 489). A sense of the transcendent quality of the mind is also intimated in the monologue by Socrates within Phaedrus, when he states,

> All soul has the care of all that is inanimate, and traverses the whole universe, though in ever-changing forms. Thus when it is perfect and winged it journeys on high and controls the whole world...The natural property of a wing is to raise that which is heavy and carry it aloft....
>
> *(Plato, 370 BC., p. 493)*

Forms of Idealism and Creative Cognition

Michael Polanyi (1966) underwrites mind-related things, stating that the *significance* of an object is more vital than its tangible qualities (p. 33). This valuation implies a focal emphasis on uncertainty orientation, ambiguity, and relativity. If there is an assumption that minds outvalue material objects, this will also suggest a way of ordering a set of workplace values. People would be emphasized more than products in this social ecology; inspiration would be championed more than material gain.

George Berkley's idealism, which he called immaterialism, sought to deconstruct a view of reality that emphasized matter in motion as the ultimate. This ontological idealism differed greatly from the modern usage of the term idealism in political and moral disputes, with its emphasis on the moral perfectionism that Polanyi (1966) critiques. Epistemological idealism campaigns for unknowability in light of finite human sensation, cognitive aptitude, and perception. This appreciation for uncertainty is also received in Carter and Narramore's (1979) model for the integration of science and religion, which emphasizes the possibility of error across domains. In contrast, certitude constrains an understanding of complexity, strangulating the creative process.

It can be useful to consider realism and idealism juxtaposed when it comes to questions of creative impulses, products, and the systems in organizations that might support them. Plato's work is both referred to as realist and idealist, an interesting conundrum that builds from the various elements of his theory. His notion of the Forms considers the perspective that perfect ideas have real existence outside of time and space, and thus this aspect of his theory can be viewed as a form of realism. This notion of independence of perfect ideas must be held in tension with the observation that humanity's attempts to access these Forms must always be limited; their clandestine appearance remains as a source of intrigue, motivating, and maintaining curiosity.

In contrast to the concept of Forms as real entities, Plato's viewpoint challenges the reality of the material world, which can be thought of as an imitation of the Forms (Guyer & Horstmann, 2021). In this idealist viewpoint, the physical world is a copy—like shadows on the wall of a cave, which are images based on imitations (Silverman, 2022). Plato's idealism can be considered as a forerunner to the immaterialism of George Berkeley (Guyer & Horstmann, 2021). While Plato is generally not thought of as a skeptic because he assumes that real knowledge exists (Silverman, 2022), his *Allegory of the Cave,* book VII within *The Republic,* describes an image of a world where "what he has seen before was all a cheat and an illusion" (Plato, 375 BC, p. 748). This world of appearances is contrasted with the dawning awareness of the *real* Real, which is unsettling, "as if he were compelled to look at the light itself" (Plato, 375 BC., p. 748). Plato envisioned a sublime real that transcends the perishable world, where unchanging archetypes have Being (Guyer & Horstmann, 2021).

A workplace reality is the location of minds and mind-related events, as well as purported tangible objects. Bringing idealism into salient view can elicit further questions about an underlying theory of creative responsibility. Two forms of idealism are commonly recognized by philosophers. In the first form, which is referred to as ontological idealism in Guyer and Horstmann (2021), mental events are assumed to give rise to and maintain reality. This form of idealism was supported by George Berkeley's immaterialism, which argued that things that exist emanate from the mind-- specifically emerging from the infinite mind of God (Guyer & Horstmann, 2021). Berkeley's works support the proposition that objects, which contribute to knowledge, cannot exist without a perceiver, and God was the immutable permanent perceiver who maintained the existence of reality. Ontological idealism would suggest that mental entities should have primacy in workplace objectives that are oriented towards creative products.

The second form of idealism is termed epistemological and suggests that reality exists independent of mind or mental events, but the ability to apprehend this external reality is limited by human subjectivity; thus, minds can only come to understand reality through a process of self-knowledge (Guyer & Horstmann, 2021). Immanuel Kant can be considered as a representative of this view, for with his transcendental idealism, he supposed that space and time do not have real substance of their own but are understood through the subjectivity of the mind (Guyer & Horstmann, 2021). The mind will impose a structure on experience if necessary, which gives rise to the sense of a priori knowledge or ideas that are not directly derivative from experience (Guyer & Horstmann, 2021). A viewpoint of epistemological idealism will support the study of heuristics and behavioral economics in recognition of the irrationality and peculiar logic of humankind (Freeman, 2022).

George Berkeley's Immaterialism and Emanations of Mind

A model of workplace creativity encircles a microcosm built on minds. Although the philosopher George Berkeley is often described as an idealist, he used the language of immaterialism to outline his theory. Berkeley's (1734) view suggests that existence is founded on ideas. His argument indicates that, behind ideas, are other ideas. The theory of immaterialism asserts that matter exists only in the presence of a divine permanent perceiver, who maintains the ongoing being of the cosmos and the world of ideas. There are also other perceivers, which Berkeley refers to as "mind, spirit, soul, or myself" and these observers are distinctive from the ideas in consciousness (Berkeley, 1734, p. 23). In his view, ideas emerge from attention, passions, and memory; the model seems to precede a view of top-down processing, whereby perceptions arrive from the mind rather than the senses. Berkeley was clearly indicating that the senses cannot be separated from perceptions and ideas, but he did not assume that sensations were causal, unlike William James (Berkeley, 1734, p. 24). A top-down processing view of workplace creativity will focus on the redemption and reformulation of dominant notions and paradigms of workers, consumers, and constituents rather than enlisting an overload of the senses wrought by the unrelenting captivity of worker time.

Concrete ideas originate from abstract ideas, the substrate of creativity. Berkeley's (1734) theory of immaterialism is grounded in his thesis of abstract ideas, which indicates that, while thoughts or images can be segmented, it is impossible to conceive of some phenomenon beyond previous perceptual forms. In his view, human abstraction is contradictory because no object can exist without a spirit to perceive, and the perception is connected to some former sensation, although not necessarily derived from it (Berkeley, 1734, p. 25). He concluded that the "furniture of the earth… [and] all those bodies which compose the mighty frame of the world, have not any subsistence without a mind" (Berkeley, 1734, p. 25). Furthermore, notions are not irrational or truly abstract, for they have existence because they are founded on other perceptions, which are attached to sensations. This showcases the unique way that Berkeley defines existence. To have existence, a creative idea will have some innate, rationalistic quality, rather than being derived from an empirical encounter with the senses.

Creative disruption requires a shift in frame of reference and a novel course of perspective-taking. Berkeley's (1734) conclusion regarding existence emanating from the permanent perceiver was also connected to epistemological idealism and a theory of relativity, for he recognized the impact of one's frame of reference on the perception of movement or size (p. 27). Ideas, brought together in arbitrary compounds, were felt to join in ways that gave the appearance of unity. However, Berkeley (1734) was skeptical of the possibility of knowledge, which relied on reason or sensations that were both assumed to be limited by relativity (p. 29). Ideas offered no real sense of agency (pp. 32–33), for while spirits could be active, ideas could not. In addition, ideas could represent copies or resemblances (p. 25) and could also be thought to "barely represent" the imprints of sensations, shown through memory, imagination, passions, and mechanical qualities of mind (p. 23). Moving away from certitude and towards an idea of imprints and imagination could foster greater openness to experiencing the minds and creative products of others.

Certitude is the foundational and egoistic impetus of the kind of authoritarian structure that derails both creativity and a humanistic workplace. The valuation of a humanitarian organization assumes some universal ethical appeal, in contrast to the uncertainty and subjectivity of human existence. This boundary is paradoxical, but not mutually exclusive. Primary qualities of objects, such as motion, rest, density, form, extension, and number, are assumed to be united with the mind, having no real existence outside of a spiritual view of reality, in Berkeley's (1734) view (p. 26). While it may at first seem paradoxical to think of Berkeley in terms of realism, we might claim that his notion of the real is connected to vital spiritual existence. This is seen in his statement that,

> The ideas imprinted on the senses by the Author of Nature are called *real things*: and those excited in the imagination being less regular, vivid and constant, are more properly termed *ideas*, or *images of things,* which they copy and represent.
>
> *(Berkeley, 1734, p. 35)*

Thus, it could be said that Berkeley's view emphasized the greater reality of the laws of nature, imparted by the permanent perceiver, rooted in an intelligence transcendent to the limited and error-prone imagination of the creaturely mind (p. 36). The chimera is seen in the ideas framed by human finiteness; the *Real* real is observed in those things beyond matter that exist in the mind of God.

Nicolas Malebranche, The Real, and Theories of Knowledge

Expression of the Other as ultimate reality will highlight the primacy of a workplace built on humanitarian values. The notion that the ultimate real is also indeterminate can foster awareness of the artificiality of limiting projections. The work of Malebranche refers to the "realissimum," which is contained in the indeterminate "being of beings...the universal being"

(Ginsberg, 1923, p. 43). The realissimum contains all possibilities, both mental and material, but also transcends these things, for "in the infinitely perfect being there is no non-being" (Ginsberg, 1923, p. 43). Ginsberg (1923) argues that Malebranche envisioned a fusion between religion and metaphysical philosophy, seeing no ultimate conflict between the two systems, for truth-seeking pursuits were a "means of communication with Eternal Reason, the Divine Logos, a means of sharing in that vision which is salvation" (p. 62). In his theory of occasionalism, Malebranche viewed the Divine Logos as acting within certain natural laws, non-arbitrary, and within the best possible world (Ginsberg, 1923, p. 64). However, unlike Leibniz, Malebranche did not express the hope of a universe with "infinite perfectibility" (Ginsberg, 1923, p. 64). In the view of Leibniz, the mind emanates from Divinity in a moment-by-moment act of will, with a pre-established harmony that allowed each monad to mirror some feature of the cosmos from a relative vantage point (Ginsberg, 1923, p. 65).

The attempt to move towards some Form of infinite wisdom, a headwater of creativity, may be implied by the pursuit of Malebranche, Leibniz, and Berkeley. In the perspective of Malebranche, there is some vague intuition about the soul, which remains unknown, but all ideas, immaterial and finite realities exist in the mind of Infinite Reason, including an archetype for the existence of each spirit (Ginsberg, 1923, p. 31). While his theory supposes a supreme designer of minds, the archetypes of these minds remain unavailable to human consumption (p. 32). The finite psyche is incapable of containing any representation of the Infinite Mind, who has no archetype (p. 33) and whose mind is an internal system of ideas (p. 34).

Theories of Knowledge and Creative Discovery in the Work of Gottfried Leibniz

Intuition, and how one may tap into it, remains an intriguing prospect in the theory of creative initiation. In Leibniz's (1684) work, *Meditations on Knowledge, Truth, and Ideas,* ideal knowledge includes intuitive elements as well as that which is accurate, distinct, and revealed in clarity (p. 291). Most thought, in his view, was symbolic and constructed in order to allow for simplification and consideration of several simultaneous elements (p. 292). Real definitions are based on possibility, and perceptions focus on the synthesis of the whole, lacking awareness of the minute elements that comprise it (p. 294). The elemental structures are elusive for the human perceiver. Thus, creativity might be at its zenith in non-concretized form, with the exercise of symbolism rather than the operational management of ideas.

The constraining force of atomism on creativity can be considered. In his publication on *Universal Synthesis,* Leibniz (1679) suggests that, while a mathematical classification of knowledge may be useful, it is often the case that concepts are confused, definitions are merely nominal, contradictory features in ideas exist, or paradox gives rise to doubt (pp. 229, 230). He critiques the argument, given by Descartes and the Scholastics that the existence of a being can be founded on the demonstration of a clear definition, for ideas presuppose being (Leibniz, 1679, p. 231). Leibniz (1679) argues that most knowledge is derived from experience, verified by replication, observation, or consensus (p. 232). He describes the necessity of organizing principles and sequences of logic to inventory the resources of existing ideas. The creativity of discovery arrives through analysis, which is a "higher art" than synthesis when based on original problem solving; nevertheless, Leibniz (1679) claims that synthesis is preeminent due to its longevity (p. 233). Analysis is more productive for uncovering mechanisms, yet it is also prone to repeating discoveries already made. Synthesis is useful for application, and represents a form of creativity where similarity and dissimilarity are used to contrast and evaluate ideas, favoring particular rules for combination. Analysis can be a mechanism of creative translation from the atoms of parts into the configuration of the greater good.

The Mind: Active, Passive, Mechanical, or Intuitive?

Polanyi (1966) advised that the mind is active in shaping experience (p. 6). This conclusion relates to Wilhelm Wundt's voluntarism, which emphasizes the force of will to perceive a motivational element. Contemporary and 20th-century views of social neurocognition tend to support these notions of motivated cognition (Freeman, 2022). Awareness of the motivational and heuristic features of the human perceptual apparatus has implications for a behavioral economic model that accounts for randomness, change, and cognition in context. The volitional aspects of thought are relevant not only for the consideration of consumers but also modify an understanding of how creatives in an organization may come to deliver a wider sea of innovations.

Voluntarism is a viewpoint that emphasizes the leading edge of volition on mental operations; it is also referred to as "effort consciousness" (Lindsay, 1918, p. 435). While earlier philosophers had also conceived of the impact of will on mechanical and intuitive features of the mind, Wundt delivered voluntarism to the new school of thought found within empirical psychology. The work of Wundt, often considered for his pioneering contributions to empirical psychology, has largely been subsumed and misrepresented in English empirical scholarship (Blumenthal, 1975). This is partly due to issues of translation; it is evident, for example, that all of the original sources consulted by Blumenthal were printed in German. Many scholars have noted the distortions about Wundt seen in textbooks, which may represent Wundt's work as structuralist rather than voluntarist, partly due to the misrepresentations of his British student Edward D. Titchener. Within Wundt's voluntarism, emphasis was placed on the selectivity of attention, which was volitional and rooted in motivation (Blumenthal, 1975, p. 1082). The emphasis on volition was also found in the work of Josiah Royce, whose Absolute Voluntarism argued that individuals orient themselves towards a world, shifting the will to express attitudes towards theories of reality (Brunson, 2018, p. 2).

Industrial-organizational psychology has long valued careful empirical pursuits of workplace systems, outcomes, and antecedents. This empirical focus has also pervaded the approach towards an understanding of creativity and finds historical analogues in the work of Wundt's lab in Leipzig. Wundt's contributions include a discipline-specific philosophy of science. While he could see the public agreement and replicability of findings from the natural sciences, Wundt argued that psychology studies the experiences of the *individual*, who perceives the world and sensations in ways that can be examined only through tests and explanations (Blumenthal, 1975, p. 1081). Psychological science sought to find objective means to measure phenomenology, or the subjective experience of the individual.

Wundt was not a mind-body dualist; rather, he believed that the mind was not a viable organ of scientific study, being unified with the brain and body (Blumenthal, 1975, p. 1082). Likewise, he deemed language and reasoning as outside of the scope of true experiments, being subject instead to other methods such as naturalistic observation or historical analysis. A return to phenomenology in the science of workplace relationships and creative cognition would be consistent with some of Wundt's original intentions.

As an addition to the emphasis on the primacy of ideas and Forms within this chapter, volition raises a pragmatic set of questions and offers a more complete understanding of creative cognition. Rationalism posits that thought is that which initiates a world, but Lindsay (1918) critiques this notion as incomplete, adding the essential reference to volition and pointing to the inadequate focus on sensation as a source of knowledge (pp. 433, 434). Nevertheless, he argues that "reason is the organ for the supreme discovery of truth" (Lindsay, 1918, p. 435). The limitations of voluntarism are outlined by its failure to recognize that early stages of impulse and feeling may be associated with a preceding thought, albeit in seedling form (Lindsay, 1918, p. 435). Reason is the illumination of will, following an internal structure that serves to guide volition as the ground of all things (Lindsay, 1918, p. 436). By following reason as a manifestation of divine things, Lindsay (1918) concludes with "spiritual monism, in which spiritual reason is...the ultimate principle" (p. 455).

Organizational Humility and a Frame of Reference

Awareness of the limits of agency would be an unpopular position in many business-oriented training models that emphasize personal empowerment, optimism, and confidence. In contrast to material monism, Malebranche suggested that even mind-related and physiological states arrive only by "intelligible extension" from an omnipotent being who maintains the existence of the cosmos (Schmaltz, 2022). In this model, ideas exist through an unchangeable and essential reason, which enlightens the mind through union with the source of life (Schmaltz, 2022). A form of spiritual monism will elevate reason, finding unity in the diversity of consciousness, for,

> One finds a correlation of subject and object, of "I" and "not-I," or soul and body, of consciousness and existence, of nature and spirit, of God and the world, but we cannot rest in the end without...some principle or power that embraces them all, and inwardly binds them all together.
>
> *(Lindsay, 1918, p. 455)*

Humility acknowledges the relativity of a frame of reference, essential for encountering the workplace Other as an entity not fully known. Consciousness cannot be thought of as the simple compound of an array of parts but as an emergent entity that exerts effects on both material and immaterial realities. Josiah Royce argues against an atomistic or reductive view of the mind, stating that consciousness is continual, volitional, and transcendent to a mere addition of parts; it synthesizes innumerable elements into a perceived unity (Brunson, 2018, p. 3). The sense of reality is subject to a projective process that is based on a synthesis of present and past, with anticipations of what is to come and references to a "Universe of Truth" that imagines the mental worlds of others (Brunson, 2018, p. 3).

Limitations

An attempt to bring historical philosophy into conversation with modern views of workplace creativity is no easy endeavor. The contemporary preference for pragmatic and tangible applications is powerful. It is also limiting. By trying to concretize the infinite, which is mind, consciousness, and Being, we run the risk of trivializing it. The notions put forth in this chapter cannot easily be mapped onto a four-part, alliterated plan or acronym. The concepts of immaterialism, Platonic Forms, and dynamic processes are not amenable to a set of strategic priorities that can be easily operationalized and measured. Indeed, the very concepts of mechanism are in tension with the themes of the chapter.

As alluded to in Allen et al. (2023), there can be challenges in clarifying and framing research questions. Effect sizes in psychology are often notably small, with many studies being based on survey and self-report data that may not dig down into hidden biases, social desirability, revelation of personal weaknesses, and avoidance of interpersonal conflicts (Allen et al., 2023). Philosophical ideas can serve as a substrate for future empirical investigation, but the linkages are covert and murky, for there is difficulty in reducing the configuration to the parts.

An Immaterial-Volitional Model of Creative Cognition

An immaterialist view will emphasize the primacy of minds and the power of mental events to change physiological and social outcomes. The notion that the most important objects are minds will support a *consciousness-first* view of the creative process. This view implies that there is a realissimus, founded in a Form of infinite Truth, Ethics, and Love, which is external to the mind but also accessible to some degree. The access can be rendered through the symbolic language of intuition, imagination, and change, but it is recognized in embodied form.

An immaterialist view of creativity will also include recognition of the inherent relational quality of creative synthesis. This emerges within a world of appearances, where projective processes cause representations of the workplace Other. These representations, while difficult to dislodge, can be released in ways that facilitate the potential for both the person and the organization. When representations lose their power, knowledge sharing has a greater chance to take root. The tacit qualities of workplace knowledge and their value for creativity are best encountered within a setting that favors both the solitude and time needed for creation and the *free-yet-connected* space of workplace belonging and social identification that fosters an authentic team.

The immaterialist view will also capitalize on human relativity. Human observers remain subject to a relative position in the universe. Consciousness is only a simulation of other people's minds, providing an inkling or intuition of the real, the object of pursuit. The volitional features of this model emphasize human attention, motivation, and subjectivity. Being rooted in epistemological idealism, there is acknowledgement of human error and randomness, with the limited perceptual apparatus of a single point in time and location in space. Thus, reliance on the sense of belongingness to a community of fellow investigators will prove beneficial while acknowledging the ultimate unknowability of these others. The reality of mental events and the potency of language are seen as formative for the construction of a humanistic workplace that will maximize creative potential. The muse, arriving like the fire of the kings, chooses a symbolic, rational, and disruptive language, moving from the outward concentric ring of influence into the core of the layers, the *person-in-self-definition*.

Works Cited

Alexander, L., & Moore, M. (2021, December 21). Deontological ethics. In E. N. Zalta (Ed.), *The Stanford encyclopedia of philosophy*. Retrieved from https://plato.stanford.edu/archives/win2021/entries/ethics-deontological

Allen, K. A., Gallo Cordoba, B., Ryan, T., Arslan, G., Slaten, C. D., Ferguson, J. K., … & Vella-Brodrick, D. (2023). Examining predictors of school belonging using a socio-ecological perspective. *Journal of Child and Family Studies, 32*(9), 2804–2819.

Berkeley, G. (1734). Of the principles of human knowledge, part I. In K. Winkler (Ed.), *A treatise concerning the principles of human knowledge* (pp. 1–148). Hackett Publishing Company, 1982.

Berkeley, G. (1784). *Philosophical commentaries*. In A. A. Luce & T. E. Jessup (Eds.), *The works of George Berkeley, Bishop of Cloyne* (vol. 1). Thomas Nelson and Sons, 1948/1964.

Blumenthal, A. L. (1975). A reappraisal of Wilhelm Wundt. *American Psychologist, 30*(11), 1081–1038.

Bol, J., LaViers, L., & Sandvik, J. (2024). The trouble with your innovation contests. *MIT Sloan Management Review,* 1–5.

Bronfenbrenner, U. (1979). *The ecology of human development.* Harvard University Press.

Brunson, D. J. (2018). Voluntarism. A difference that makes the difference between German Idealism and American Pragmatism? *European Journal of Pragmatism and American Philosophy, 10*(X-2), 1–21.

Burgess, A. (1968). The muse. *The Hudson Review, 21*(1), 109–126.

Carroll, B. (2014). *The early-modernization of the classical muse* [Dissertation]. University of New Mexico, Department of English Language and Literature. Retrieved from https://digitalrepository.unm.edu/engl_etds/29

Carter, J. D., & Narramore, B. (1979). *The integration of psychology and theology.* Rosemead psychology series. Academie Books.

Clauss-Ehlers, C. S., Chiriboga, D. A., Hunter, S. J., Roysircar, G., & Tummala-Narra, P. (2019). APA multicultural guidelines executive summary: Ecological approach to context, identity, and intersectionality. *American Psychologist, 74*(2), 232–244. doi: 10.1037/amp0000382

Dalgarno, E. (2001). *Virginia Woolf and the visible world.* Cambridge University Press.

De Beauvoir, S. (1945). A review of the phenomenology of perception by Maurice Merleau-Ponty (M. B. Timmermann, Trans.). In M. A. Simons, M. Timmermann, & M. B. Mader (Eds.), *Philosophical writings* (pp. 151–164). University of Illinois Press, 2004.

Freeman, N. (2019, October). *Artifacts of power and the quest for a sacred space for art, humane sexuality and scholarship: A consideration of de Beauvoir and Woolf* [Paper presented], Psychology and the Other, Boston College, MA.

Freeman, N. (2022). *Social neurocognition, heuristics, and the psychology of attitudes*. Kendall-Hunt Publishers.

Ginsberg, M. (1923). Part III, Malebranche's metaphysic. In N. Malebranche (1688), M. Ginsberg (Trans.), *Dialogues on metaphysics and religion* (pp. 43–68). George Allen & Linwin, Ltd.

Guyer, P., & Horstmann, R. P. (2021, March 21). *Idealism*. In E. N. Zalta & U. Nodelman (Eds.), *The Stanford encyclopedia of philosophy*. Retrieved from https://plato.stanford.edu/archives/spr2023/entries/idealism

Keyser, E. (2023). Shakespeare's muse of fire. In L.G. Black, C. Connors, A. Orchard, D. Wu, & E.G. Stanley (Eds.). *Notes and queries* (pp. 72–74). Oxford University Press.

Leibniz, G. (1684). *Meditations on knowledge, truth, and ideas*. In L. E. Loemker (Trans. And Ed.), *Philosophical papers and letters* (pp. 291–295). D. Reidel Publishing Company, 1956.

Leibniz, G. (1679). On universal synthesis and analysis, or the art of discovery and judgment. In L. E. Loemker (Trans. and Ed.), *Philosophical papers and letters* (pp. 229–234). D. Reidel Publishing Company, 1956.

Lindsay, J. (1918). Rationalism and voluntarism. *The Monist, 28,* 433 455.

Malebranche, N. (1674). The search after truth. In T. M. Lennon & P. J. Olscamp (Trans.) and S.Nadler (Ed), *Nicholas Malebranche, philosophical selections*. Hackett Publishing Company (pp. 3–7), 1992.

Merleau-Ponty, M. (1945). *Phenomenology of perception*. D. A. Landes (Trans.). Routledge, 2012.

Miller, A. (2021, December 21). Realism. In E. N. Zalta (Ed.), *The Stanford encyclopedia of philosophy*. Retrieved from https://plato.stanford.edu/archives/win2021/entries/realism/

Pater, W. (1893). *Plato and platonism: A series of lectures by Walter Pater*. MacMillan and Company.

Plato. (370 BC). Phaedrus. In R. Hackforth (Trans.) & E. Hamilton & H. Cairns (Eds.), *Plato: Collected dialogues*. Bollingen Series LXXI. Princeton University Press, 1989.

Plato. (375 BC). The republic. In P. Shorey (Trans.) & E. Hamilton & H. Cairns (Eds.), *Plato: Collected dialogues*. Bollingen Series LXXI. Princeton University Press, 1989.

Polanyi, M. (1966). *The tacit dimension*. University of Chicago Press.

Schmaltz, T. (2022, March 21). Nicolas Malebranche. In E. N. Zalta (Ed.), *The Stanford encyclopedia of philosophy*. Retrieved from https://plato.stanford.edu/archives/spr2022/entries/malebranche

Silverman, A. (2022, September 21). Plato's middle period metaphysics and epistemology. In E. N. Zalta & U. Nodelman (Eds.), *The Stanford encyclopedia of philosophy*. Retrieved from https://plato.stanford.edu/archives/fall2022/entries/plato-metaphysics

Sim, L. (2005). Virginia Woolf tracing patterns through Plato's forms. *Journal of Modern Literature, 28*(2), 38–48. Retrieved from https://www.muse.jhu.edu/article/184567.

Woolf, V. (1929). *A room of one's own*. Harcourt Inc. 1981.

Yang, S., Loewenstein, J., & Mueller, J. (2023). Finding creativity by changing perspectives: How the evaluation process contributes to creative idea recognition. *Creativity Research Journal, 35*(3), 481–498.

8

COMPREHENSIVE ENTITIES, POSSIBILITY, AND WORKPLACE INNOVATION

Nahanni Freeman

Ecological Contributions to Comprehensive Entities

A construct of comprehensive entities will afford the individual the ability to become rather than freeze. This dynamic view of Others is pertinent to workplace creativity because it suggests that others can surprise, move, grow, regress, or actualize. Moving from the anesthetized view of persons, which rests on trait theories and determinism, a model of comprehensive entities will seek not to delimit the boundaries of the Other but rather to celebrate and explore their infinitude of Being over a developmental sequence. In this way, a model of comprehensive entities will seek to reverse hegemonic power structures that prevent access to creative contribution, even reaching into concepts of self-knowledge that incarcerate Being. One portal into a comprehensive entity perspective of creativity can be derived from a systems theory of social ecology, which sees the person as surrounded by an interactive series of nested eggs; each ring of influence is fluid, interactive, multi-directional, and self-organizing, adding to the rich complexity of an understanding of personhood.

Well-known for his contributions to potentiality theories that continue to influence multi-cultural models in psychology, Urie Bronfenbrenner (1979) developed a theory regarding systems that surround the individual in his work, *The Ecology of Human Development*. In this text, he considers the dyad nearest the individual, engaged in reciprocal relations and joint activity, where there exists a mutuality of change. The balance of power may be unequal, but the activity of this dyad is considered molar, underscoring its foundational significance and continual fluidity (Bronfenbrenner, 1979,

DOI: 10.4324/9781003322894-9

p. 45). Moving outward from family relations and close attachments, one finds the mesosystem, which secures direct or indirect interactions across settings (Bronfenbrenner, 1979, p. 209). Varying levels of power and reciprocity can be expressed, with knowledge shared across settings by third parties and systemic, boundary-crossing mechanisms (p. 210). Micro- and mesosystems motivate work-family conflict or enrichment, while non-work factors intervene with creativity processes.

The exosystem, external to direct participation by the individual, is potently impacting the molar activities nearest to intimate life (Bronfenbrenner, 1979, p. 237). Empowerment is creedal, for wellbeing may be affected by the quantity and type of intermediate links to power (p. 256). In the orbit outside of the exosystem is the macrosystem, which Bronfenbrenner (1979) refers to as consistency in the cultural content, which traverses boundaries, creating "continuities of form" (p. 258). The macrosystem can contribute to patterns of motivation and momentum, with expectations that crossover from one setting or system to another (p. 284). These microcosms of impact propel energy back towards the person at the core, influencing cognition, affect, attachments, and the sense of a bodily self.

A comprehensive entity model will appreciate the complexity of layers that extend from, and emanate towards, the self. Multiple layers of interaction influence the person within a workplace context, including co-worker and supervisor relationships, political alignment with the firm, which is denoted through signal interpretations (Song & Sojourner, 2023), social categorizations based on informational and demographic diversity (van Knippenberg et al., 2004), and team trust and task cohesion (Zhang et al., 2023).[1] At the team level, a social-cognitive and informational map is derived that details who-knows-what, creating a transactive memory of the system hierarchy (Wegner, 1987). External and familial factors also interact with the employee's overall functioning, including chronic worry about debt, which can prompt increased errors, lower productivity, and lead to emotional and cognitive depletion, which can be partially mitigated through optimism (Graham et al., 2023).

A comprehensive entity model is concerned with the individual, seeing the functioning person through empathy and support for actualization, with awareness of meta-cognitive events. Attributional processes have the potential to recruit cognitive resources, burdening memory and attentional load in ways that deplete creativity. Employee perceptions of workplace unfairness can detour progress, with supervisors' use of procedural justice being fundamental to worker satisfaction and engagement (Carroll, 2023). Procedural justice includes the belief that one's supervisor is unbiased, ethical, and consistent, able to suppress stereotypes while showing representation for various groups, and being open to correction (Leventhal,

1980). The procedural justice model proposes that employees form cognitive maps related to how rewards are distributed, observing the antecedents to such reinforcers through an evaluative lens based on a perception of equity (Leventhal, 1980). Carroll (2023) argues that supervisory usage of procedural justice can tax managers' emotional and cognitive resources, leading to depletion, which is known to be a risk factor for reductions in organizational citizenship behavior. However, the depleting effects of procedural justice efforts may be mitigated through the use of self-affirmation, a self-enhancement strategy that can increase self-regulation (Steele, 1988; Carroll, 2023).

A comprehensive entity model will be concerned with the intersectionality of the person with time, power, and technology. Contemporary concerns about "quiet quitters" raise interest in the question of employee engagement, which may be enhanced with an increased sense of perceived time control; this is particularly relevant in light of the perishable and non-renewable features of time (Cho, 2023). Technology creates an additional concentric ring around the person, impacting work seepage into non-work hours, which can increase both voluntary and involuntary work connectivity (Yuan et al., 2023). The extension of technology into one's personal time can become deeply habitual, collectively mediated, viewed across multiple digital platforms, and offers alternative forms of presence and witness (Yuan et al., 2023). While this technological ring around the person can be provisional and unplanned, it has the potential to foster either competition or meaningful collaboration (Yuan et al., 2023).

Surrounding the individual creative is a ring of relationships that hold bi-directional influence over cognitive illumination. The matrix of leader-follower interactions retains the potential to influence creativity by strengthening dialectical thinking, or the integration of disparate elements and contradictions into a comprehensive understanding, sometimes accompanied by meta-cognitive processes regarding the fluid and impermanent nature of thought (Chong et al., 2023).[2] The person experiences crossover effects in relation to others' emotional expressions, which are often internalized into the self-system. In addition, spillover effects can occur, whereby emotions are transferred into cognitive processes (Chong et al., 2023). Creative products and outcomes are often perceived as risky by employees, because they can potentially change boundaries; a constructive approach to managing errors can be a protective element (Chong et al., 2023).

Interactionist models consider the relationship between persons and context, including cybernetic loops and dynamic processes. One such model includes the perceived level of fit between employees and their organizations, which includes perceptions of value alignment; this form of compatibility has been shown to explain a large percentage of variance in motivations to lead (Woods, 2023). Perceptions of fit between individuals and their job role and duties are also connected to turnover intentions, satisfaction, organizational commitment, and co-worker support (Woods, 2023). Trait and interactionist models both contribute to an understanding of persons in the workplace context. For example, Kanfer (1990) seeks to unify disparate theories that have included a focus on: need satiation, equity and justice, cognitive expectations, self-regulation, cybernetics, and social learning perspectives. A view of leaders as comprehensive entities will consider their felt responsibility to adhere to social norms, their affective identification with a leadership role, and non-calculative elements, which are leadership costs not initially considered when the position was accepted (Woods, 2023).

Ontology and Tacit Knowledge

A model of persons as comprehensive entities will include varying levels of awareness of particular and holistic configurations of personhood, which include at least four levels of tacit knowledge. Michael Polanyi (1966) discusses the ontological features of tacit knowledge, asking the reader about the type of knowledge that is contained within the tacit, for "all meaning tends to be displaced away from ourselves" (p. 13). He considers functional, phenomenal, and semantic features of tacit knowledge, with the understanding that ineffable wisdom "establishes a meaningful relation between two terms" (Polanyi, 1966, p. 13). Functional tacit knowledge facilitates goal completion by attending to the whole instead of parts. Phenomenal structures of tacit knowledge are about awareness, and semantic forms include signification and meaning. An ontological understanding includes awareness of a comprehensive entity, which includes both the particulars and the whole. The *proximal* term in Polanyi's model is tacitly known, while the *distal* or second term is specifically known and attended to.

A comprehensive model of personhood will include feedback loops between various processes activated in the person. In her work on motivational theories, Ruth Kanfer (1990) presents a range of cognitive, systemic, and self-regulation theories. Presenting the *Kanfer and Ackerman Integrative Resource Model,* she examines attentional allocations as related to *distal* and *proximal* terms, assuming that attentional resources will adjust based on motivational factors. In her model, proximal processes include self-regulation, feedback, and task-orientation, while distal processes influence effort and the allocation of cognitive resources, limited by capacity range.

Polanyi (1966) discusses how people are more profound than cobble-stones because they are not fully known (p. 32). This acknowledgement of the elusiveness of the Other is relevant to workplace person perception, representation, and prototype-matching. Rather than seeking to support the creative work of the few while suppressing the potential of the many, a comprehensive entity perspective will see each individual as creatively capable, given a growth-oriented context. Rather than attempting to match leaders to prototypes, seeking to confirm a representativeness heuristic, a comprehensive entity model acknowledges the breadth of possibility—the expansiveness of a galaxy of ideas and persons. Polanyi (1966) states that scientists will view something as profound if it prompts ongoing discovery. Persons elude us because they are not fully known. As with Apophatic theology, an anthropology of persons might invoke the assumption that we best define others by what they are not.

Self-Understanding

The significance of meta-cognition for intellectual and creative life is revealed in the work of Abraham Heschel, who argues that innovation is emergent from a deeply personal phenomenology (Heschel, 1955, p. 5). Distinguishing between vital and inert cognition, considering the dead thoughts that arrive from pure reason detached from that which profoundly alters the soul, Heschel states that "a living thought is like a seed" (Heschel, 1955, p. 3).

Awareness of one's calling is a form of attunement to self-understanding, which may connect more to the concrete than the ideal for those who are highly sensitive to human suffering and injustice, iconoclastic, and con-cerned with human experience (Heschel, 1962, pp. 3–10). The sense of responsibility to exhort others towards change and the creative and meta-phorical vision of a potential future that could be realized or averted is part of the nature of the concept of prophecy, which can be viewed as a model for innovation; however, such a divergence from the mainstream tends to also portend loneliness and distress (Heschel, 1962, pp. 14, 17).

Self-understanding can be considered as a form of consciousness expressed as evidence of existence, which can be presented within the models of Descartes, Berkeley, and Varisco, yet this remains in contrast with English Neo-Hegelianism (Sabine, 1915). Sabine (1915, p. 650) argues that Varisco's model of self-knowledge diverges from English idealism in its refusal of the notion that finite selves are caught up in an absolute, also rejecting the idea that phenomena are illusory appearances. The model of self-knowledge espoused by Varisco is described as a form of monadology and includes the idea that self-understanding is possible due to the unity of the unconscious, the priority placed on the subjective, the possibility of non-determined associations at the micro level, and the spontaneous emergence of psychological structures from recombination of multiple factors that are co-essential (Sabine, 1915, pp. 652–654).

Varisco (1915) considered the universe to contain a sense of unity among many diverse things. He did not take a monist view, but observed objects in relation to other objects. Stating that "since one thing exists only in so far as others exist—since therefore each thing is an essential constituent of every other, we can and must say that all things together constitute one thing: the universe" (Varisco, 1915, p. 174). He also highlights that the One is reliant on the many, and the whole will exist only with a particular set of elements. He also viewed consciousness as a unification of multiplicity; the whole continuum of possibilities is contained within the single act of a conscious mind. Varisco (1915) viewed consciousness as inclusive of the primitive subconscious, as well as forgotten memories that potentiated into awareness. The majority of mental events were deemed to reside in the nebulous space of the subconscious rather than within the explicit clarity of logic. The elements of the individual are inclusive of the universe, and seem to exist through the experience of a mind (Varisco, 1915, p. 180). The multiple constituents of consciousness include spontaneous matter and are not merely additive but systemic (Varisco, 1915, p. 188). All of the elements are essential for unity, which in the universe relies on Being (Varisco, 1915, p. 189).

Idealism and Uncertainty

The impossibility of perceiving the comprehensive entity of the Other is defended. An epistemological form of idealism will tend to focus on unknowability in light of incomplete pathways and receptors for knowledge. Rescher (1987) points out that Plato's model of ideals implied the existence of Forms of knowledge in some reality, discoverable by human subjectivity (p. 118). Nevertheless, ideals as guideposts are described by Rescher (1987) as unattainable and borne from imagination. Some forms of idealism focus on moral exemplars, while other expressions denote the mind's power to alter the world (pp. 122, 119). In Kant's philosophy, ideals could regulate the mind (p. 118).

Perceptions of self and other symbolize assertions, acting as volitional participants in consciousness. The vision of the creative *ideal* is inherently connected to a metaphysical set of commitments. Heschel contends that divine thought transcends object and tangible content in Aristotle's metaphysics, while the ultimate good in Plato implied a certain self-sufficiency, or a notion of the irrelevance of the world (Heschel, 1962, pp. 12, 14). This contrasts with the ideal of the Tao, which is "eternal silence," tranquility, the absence of desire, and harmonious order (Heschel, 1962, p. 15).

Martin Buber, Representativeness Heuristics, and Non-Reductive Observing

Martin Buber's work on "I-it" vs "I-Thou" relationships reveals the harmful effects of the representativeness heuristic and prototype matching. As a simplification strategy, humans in workplace settings are likely to generate internal prototypes for the ideal supervisor, employee, or administrator. The level of match between this implicit image and the candidate who seeks promotion can influence decision-making, steering employment decisions away from objectivity and justice and towards the recirculation of stereotypes, discrimination, and dominant paradigms. People assumed to match the stereotype will be rewarded; those who differ are dismissed, their work undermined and invisible. Such an employment setting treats the human as an 'It' rather than a comprehensive entity.

Martin Buber's (1937) work implies the significance of language in establishing the existence of an entity (p. 53); this underscores the importance of language that is generative and speaks into the construction of a perceptual world. Communication that is rooted in the enrichment of life recognizes the Other person as a "you" rather than an "it" and nourishes a world of relations over tasks, transcendent above museums of information, or experience-seeking. The knowledge of the infinite possibility that is another Being is suggested by Buber's claim that "through everything that becomes present to us, we gaze toward the train of the eternal you; in each we perceive a breath of it, in every You we address the eternal you" (Buber, 1937, p. 57).

The Concealed Representation

In his work, *The Hidden Human Image*, Maurice Friedman (1974) presents the notion that the human quest for authenticity involves awareness of an internalized vision of possibility. This is a tacit understanding of what the person is moving towards, "an image that helps him discover his humanity" (p. 4). This representation can include internalized features of humanity's great examples, such as sacrificial others who stood for peace and personal obligation to the community. Responsivity to the present must enlist the person in moving beyond cultural conformity; the root of a creative response is found in genuine communication, where the comprehensiveness of a person is beyond essentializing references, for the human is "imageless" (Friedman, 1974, p. 4).

Emmanuel Levinas and Non-Representation of the Other: The Importance of the Ineffable

One way to reject the dehumanization of workplace stereotypes and the constraining expectations of others is to see beyond the representations of peers, administrators, and subordinates, transcending a concretized perspective of language and image. Being open to not knowing the Other, and expressing the humility of one's own subjectivity, can coalesce in administrative practice. Allowing the image of the workplace Other to expand and change recognizes the individual's capacity for growth, reflection, atonement, and redirection. The philosophy of Emmanuel Levinas, rooted in the experience of profound suffering, provides an ethic that goes beyond a humanistic workplace environment.

In his work, *The Servant and her Master,* Emmanuel Levinas (1966) examines the work of his former classmate and French literary critic, Maurice Blanchot. Although they had often disagreed in school, Blanchot, a member of the resistance against the Nazi occupation, saved Levinas' wife Raïssa, and daughter Simone, who were hidden by nuns in a monastery in Orléans (Bergo, 2019). Levinas and Blanchot began a lifelong friendship. Other members of the Levinas family were murdered in the Holocaust, and he was detained in a German prisoner of war camp during WWII. As expressed in the analysis of Levinas, Blanchot's work explores ineffable themes related to paradox, with death as absence and impossibility and being untethered from the cosmos (Levinas, 1966). The detachment from the Astron (Greek star) is noted as a Dis-Aster, a location beyond consciousness and language where words are metamorphized in substance into an infinity of signs. The sense of illumination beyond the bland simplification of a material worldview is suggested by the statement that, "Not so long ago, we still distinguished…the role of the intellect as master of its intentions…and on the other hand… the better role…the muse, the unconscious" (Levinas, 1966, p. 151).

Levinas (1966) discusses the circular and swollen language of tedium, contrasting this with the transcendent language that goes beyond poetry, which meets with the logos and represents a form of freedom from the constraints of memory. In a remote location, beyond these confines, one may encounter a form of forgetting and patience that releases movement beyond the self. The *forgetting of self* permits an extended view beyond time, outside of logical contamination of that which should conserve the enigmatic. Levinas describes the poetic language that exists outside of circles of praise and acculturation, offering the idea that this language is a disruption—an abrupt change from the known and expressed into a prophetic zone.

Like these expressions of liberated language that are rooted in Levinas and his account of Blanchot, Heschel (1951) examines connections between the unspoken and the movement of light. Abraham Heschel's work explores the grandeur of the ineffable, recognizing the omissions that are embedded in human perceptions and knowledge, which are built from reminiscence (Heschel, 1951, p. 6). He admits that, while people feel compelled to represent the sublime, there is an inability to capture "the hidden vitality of the earth" (Heschel, 1951, p. 4).

Levinas (1968) describes the limits of freedom in light of responsibility to the Other. This is an absolute responsibility, a form of substitution of self for Other, which is the great calling. In thinking of the election to this call, Levinas also recognizes that we work on projects for which we are not the authors. The justification for this absolute responsibility is connected to the matchless quality of human life—it cannot be reduced, expressed, represented, or replicated. Levinas provides this justification for the substitutionary offering of self by grounding his work in awareness of our own subjectivity, stating, "the responsibility for another, an unlimited responsibility...requires subjectivity as an irreplaceable hostage" (Levinas, 1968, p. 113). In his work, the vital spirit and source of creative energy is rooted in voluntary subjugation of self to other, proximate to suffering and trauma, for "I approach the neighbor for whom, without having wished it, I have to answer, the irreplaceable one is brought out" (Levinas, 1968, p. 113).

The sense of the Other being incorporated into the self is contained in Levinas (1968, p. 114). The presence of the Other is intertwined with one's own identity, and movement from the tautology of one's identity and the imperialism of the ego is a form of freedom. The self is a sort of hostage to another person, and there is a multiplicity of selves introjected. Being is not considered as the end, but rather the acceptance of the subjectivity of the self and the relinquishment of the reification of the ego.

Erich Fromm (1955) discusses creativity in terms of the pursuit of transcendence in his work, *The Sane Society*. Here he includes the idea that transcendence comes from planning, developing ideas and art, indwelling religion and myth, loving, and generating new life through birth (Fromm, 1955, p. 37). His model of the human situation and needs also emphasizes rootedness, which is founded in the enveloping unconditional love of the mother and a desire to regress towards a state of dependent passivity. The need to feel safe, protected, and fully loved is part of the recollection of the maternal complex, which offers non-contingent full acceptance. Adults need this still, and will pursue it through various forms of "refusal to leave the all-enveloping orbit of the mother" (Fromm, 1955, p. 39) or a pseudo-attempt expressed through destructiveness. The search for rootedness can be seen in attachment to social identities, including tribe, family, religious group, sexuality, romantic love or nation. Satisfied authentic root-edness inclines creative reconnaissance.

In Fromm's (1955) analysis of the Promised Land within Jewish thought, he discusses the Old Testament prophets. These writings confer a notion of an ideal of brotherly love, shared reason, moral conscience, intellectual vibrancy, equality, and a new spiritual awareness. In contrast to this vision of the enlightened homeland, there is the critique of fixation with blood and soil, representing a form of idolatry. Fromm goes on to explore his theory of rootedness through an historical evaluation of various governmental and social structures around the world and over time. These serve as examples of destructiveness or a sane society—a "truly human home" (Fromm, 1955, p. 60).

Projective Process and the Tao of Constant Change

Polanyi (1966) discusses how things change their appearance when one directs attention away from something towards another object (p. 16). This alteration in appearance urges a projective process, a destructive impulse that causes the dehumanized Other to freeze. The recognition of the world of appearances emancipates colleagues from representation as static entities.

Research by Wenzel et al. (2003) explores manifestations of the projective process in group behavior. This research shows that people in groups are likely to see their group as the prototype to which other groups should aspire. Projection is more likely in cases where social identification with the ingroup is pronounced. The belief that one's group is the primary prototype or norm evokes outgroup prejudice. Citing the work of Mummenday and colleagues,[3] Wenzel et al. (2003) state that discrimination is more likely when categorization is combined with an endorsement of the legitimacy of hierarchical power inequities.

Self-categorization theory (SCT) can animate an understanding of internalized oppression within the workplace. According to SCT, people come to view themselves in ways that align with socially projected expectations and social classifications or group statuses; these self-views are impacted by salience and awareness of norms and values (Wenzel et al., 2003).[4] A more inclusive social categorization would include a larger array of subgroups. Projection regarding the attributes of one's finite ingroup and the perceived prototypicality of one's group relative to the larger social category being considered can maintain social identification, leading to greater contentment with one's privileged status and less concern over discrimination (Wenzel et al., 2003).

The workplace environment that can allow the individual to grow and change will acknowledge and celebrate shifts in being, rather than clinging to outdated views of others' work, character, habits, or ideas. Martin Buber's work employs the metaphor of the natural world to support the vision of plants that can grow even in dark places, with the idea of edges showing contrasts between what *is* and what *could be*. Like a regal garment that presents as an aura to the wearer, he discusses "the train of the eternal you" in recognition of the sense of possibility in the Other person and the notion that the hem of the Other's garment is only a perceptible delimiter, a margin that moves beyond the person. This recognition of the possibility of the Other extends from the shift that occurred with death or change, contrasted with transcendence. Each death is an extinction of a former mode of being and signifies the release of the non-creative. Buber references Isaiah in this discussion, which reveals the edges between death as a marker of a season of absence and personal lack[5] verses Isaiah's commission and his atonement, for "in the year that King Uzziah died, I saw the Lord seated on a throne, high and exalted, and the train of his robe filled the temple" (Isaiah 6:1, NIV). The connection to a transcendent Other is in line with Buber's metaphysical vision of the beyond, the country of creative relation where growth occurs in "the life with spiritual beings" (Buber, 1937, p. 57). The non-representational quality of this country, which also includes an illumination of the Other's potential, is shown in his description of place, for "here the relation is wrapped in a cloud but reveals itself" (Buber, 1937, p. 57). The relational world arrives with a responsibility for action, which can be seen in the Isaiah account of a prophet's commencement, for "[6] Then I heard the voice of the Lord saying, 'Whom shall I send? And who will go for us?'" And I said, "Here am I. Send me!" (Isaiah 6: 8, NIV).

Self-as-Microcosm and Leibniz, Monadology

When considering the self within the context of an employment universe, one may imagine a membrane between self and other, self and world. Is this membrane semi-permeable, like a cell's encasement? Or is the person a self-sustaining whole, which cannot be added to or deleted from, regardless of the machinations, abuses, or ruptures that ensue in the world of appearances? Does the individual employee connect to a creative divine force who illuminates and sustains existence? Is the energy of innovation emergent from the collective of a beloved community? Might creativity be a dynamic cybernetic with spiritual, linguistic, imagistic, and communitarian engines? A human body, like ecological and cosmological systems, is more than a composite of parts; it contains a dominant unity, expressed in continuity of mind. Likewise, an employment environment might be conceived as a self-contained microcosm, a biosphere with ponds and gardens inside of other conservatories and pools—a series of microsystems within cycles, producing recursive interactions.

In his work, *The Principles of Philosophy, or Monadology*, Gottfried Leibniz (1714) discusses his theory of souls as essential substances rather than composites. The monads, or simple substances, are not presumed to be lacking complexity but are elemental rather than compounded. Thus, souls cannot self-create, nor can they perish naturally through a dissolution of parts. These monads, which are distinguished from physical bodies, are said to be windowless, from which nothing can exit or enter, which assumes that there is an internal unity that drives gradual change. While the monads have a plurality within, and these diverse aspects are in relation—there are not parts that could be lost or gained—the soul is complete and possesses consciousness and perception. Consistent with an ethic that esteems life as an end rather than a means, the soul monads are all distinctive and irreplaceable. Each monad is also an imitation of the Supreme Being, imperfectly reflecting some dimensions of the only Necessary Being, who was uncreated and maintains the existence of all that is.

While a humanistic model of workplace ethics does not require such a model, there is value in considering the implications of the view of Leibniz for creative energy, employee-as-end rather than means, and the indestructibility of the interior of a human being, who is irreplaceably unique. Such a view could elevate conduct towards the Other, connecting awareness of the plurality and inexpressible unity of selves.

In Leibniz (1714), there is the concept that soul monads can internalize some features of the environment through the sensory organs, which capture light, wind, heat, sound waves, and other events. Nevertheless, this harnessing does not change the essential unity or *diversity-in-relation*, which is expressed in the soul. The unity of a soul also includes a form of self-sufficiency; within itself and its systems, there is the discovery of a form of perfection. Nevertheless, sufficiency is contingent on the will of the Supreme Being. The sense of the soul as a microcosm is expressed in Leibniz (1714) when he recounts the way that each monad "represents the entire universe," and the impression also extends to the body, which belongs to the soul and follows an order reflective of that in the cosmos (p. 77). The organized body is thus a "divine machine" (Leibniz, 1714, p. 77). The interconnectedness of the cosmos is seen not only in these reflective qualities, but also within the notion that everything that occurs in the universe influences the body.

Souls in monadology are indestructible, while bodies can experience diminution (Leibniz, 1714, p. 79). Souls are final causes, and bodies are efficient causes impacted by fitness for an environment, but Leibniz supposes a unity of soul and body rather than detachment at death. Both body and soul are representations of a universe with a preestablished harmony, which allows them to work in consort. Leibniz sees the unfolding of life in generations as seeds that hold the preformation—the beginning of a thing yet to come. He speaks to the soul's existence in nascent forms, awaiting transformation, and yet he does not support the transmigration of souls.

One can conceive of the Leibniz view of soul monads as nested eggs, for within each section is another tiny world, inside of a world (1714, p. 78). Any chaos lies only in the world of appearances, for Leibniz emphasizes order, the sequences of reason, and memory as representation. The souls are described as "living mirrors or images of the universe of creatures," and minds are "images of the divine" (Leibniz, 1714, p. 80). Leibniz seems to envision a beloved community, for "the collection of all minds must make up the city of God, that is, the most perfect possible state" (Leibniz, 1714, p. 80). This city of God would be a perfect "moral world" (p. 80), a "moral kingdom of grace" (p. 81), with the revelation of the wisdom, power, and goodness of the divine in a benevolent monarchy in the "divine city of minds" (Leibniz, 1714, p. 81). In this divine city, the architect of nature offers unlimited concern for the beloved.

Limitations

The translation of philosophical positions into the empirical objectives of industrial-organizational psychology will remain challenging. But operationalized constructs often originate in a world of ideas. Research within psychology often suffers from limitations in the ability to manipulate psychological factors in a laboratory setting, which can result in a reduction of experimental control and increased potential for confounding variables to exert an effect (Chong et al., 2023). Another challenge with psychological research is assessing outcomes over time, which involves a complex methodology that looks at both contextual drivers and target individuals (Woods, 2023). Research methods in psychology can be enhanced through the identification of critical incidents, which may suggest moments of transition and change (Woods, 2023). This model is sometimes observed in microgenetic research in developmental psychology and could be adopted to a greater degree in the field of industrial-organizational psychology. In addition, movement towards a greater inclusion of developmental models could benefit an understanding of workplace outcomes, offering comparisons across the stages of career and leadership (Woods, 2023). Research on perceptions of the workplace Other as a comprehensive entity may involve the analysis of teams. It would be important to monitor team attributions at initial and later stages of development, introducing a range of contextual modifiers (Zhang et al., 2023).

A Comprehensive Entity Model of Creative Personhood

Within the social-ecology of the Other lies a microcosm of worlds. These soul atoms represent proximal terms, things that we know and do not know, the non-explicit sense of an Other. The memories of work teams, the social classifications, and the phenomenal awareness of motives to create, lead, or destroy are subsumed under distal terms, known within the symbolism of language and metaphor, and outwardly expressed. Spilling over into cognition is emotion, intuition, and the internalization of oppression. Crossing over into emotions is the relational space—the dyadic and group mind that provides a nest for the individual, seeking safety and esteem. The person will cling to rootedness, suppressing risky prophetic urges, unless the sense of social responsibility is great. Memory is a transaction between self, other, and system, an attentional awareness of self within context.

A model of comprehensive entities will represent the Other as ultimately unknowable, extended beyond projections, and residing within constant becoming. Self-knowledge is limited by the close proximity of the observer to the object. A recognition of the potentiality and complexity of the Other also allows for a deeper valuation of the long-term retention of workers and a pervasive eagerness to facilitate the thriving of the individual, seeing tacit knowledge transfer as fundamental to the communication of ideals and Forms. Workplace artistry relies on representations, simulations, and phenomenal awareness of a thing yet to be called into existence. A sense of the possibility of an ideal beyond the uncertainty can motivate creative urges, as the hatchling struggles against the containment of a categorical shell, seeking freedom with all of its danger.

Notes

1 This work builds from Deutsch's (1949) model of Interdependence Theory.
2 Chong et al. (2023) refer to the work of Paletz, S. B., & Peng, K. (2009). Problem finding and contradiction: Examining the relationship between naïve dialectical thinking, ethnicity, and creativity. *Creativity Research Journal, 21*(2–3), 139–151.
3 Wenzel et al. refer to Mummendey et al. (1992); Otten et al. (1996); Mummendey & Otten (1998).
4 Wenzel et al. build their own theory from the work of Oakes et al. (1994) and Turner et al. (1987), and Turner (1987) regarding Self-categorization theory.
5 Later in the passage, there is the movement from a sense of personal inadequacy towards restoration, as shown by the verses, [5] "Woe to me!" I cried. "I am ruined! For I am a man of unclean lips, and I live among a people of unclean lips, and my eyes have seen the King, the Lord Almighty."
6 Then one of the seraphim flew to me with a live coal in his hand, which he had taken with tongs from the altar.[7] With it he touched my mouth and said, "See, this has touched your lips; your guilt is taken away and your sin atoned for" (Isaiah 6: 5–7, NIV).

Works Cited

Bergo, B. (2019, September 21). Emmanuel Levinas. In E. N. Zalta (ed.), *The Stanford encyclopedia of philosophy*. Retrieved from https://plato.stanford.edu/archives/fall2019/entries/levinas/

Bronfenbrenner, U. (1979). *The ecology of human development: Experiments by nature and design.* Harvard University Press.

Buber, M. (1937/1923). *I and Thou.* In W. E. Kaufmann (Trans), *I and Thou, Martin Buber, A new translation, with a prologue and notes* (pp. 1–185). Simon and Schuster. 1970.

Carroll, T. (2023, April 19–22). *Mitigating depletion-driven change in managers' procedural justice behaviors* [Poster presentation]. Society for Industrial and Organizational Psychology (SIOP), 38th Annual Conference, Boston, MA.

Cho, A. (2023, April 19–22). *Leader's daily time plan sharing and its effects on daily subordinate outcomes* [Poster presentation]. Society for Industrial and Organizational Psychology (SIOP), 38th Annual Conference, Boston, MA.

Chong, S., Banu, S., Wu, T., & Gao, R. (2023, April 19–22). *Leader emotional complexity and follower creativity: A dialecticism perspective* [Poster presentation]. Society for Industrial and Organizational Psychology (SIOP), 38th Annual Conference, Boston, MA.

Deutsch, M. (1949). A theory of co-operation and competition. *Human Relations, 2*(2), 129-152. https://doi.org/10.1177/001872674900200204

Friedman, M. (1974). *The hidden human image.* Delacorte Press.

Fromm, E. (1955). *The sane society.* Henry Holt & Company.

Graham, B. A., Sinclair, R. R., Black, K. J., Siddiqui, D. A., & Bergman, M. E. (2023, April 19–22). *Better days ahead: The role of positive expectations and debt in worker health* [Poster presentation]. Society for Industrial and Organizational Psychology (SIOP), 38th Annual Conference, Boston, MA.

Heschel, A. J. (1951). The sense of the ineffable. In A. Heschel (Ed.) *Man is not alone: A philosophy of religion* (pp. 3–10). Farar, Straus & Giroux.

Heschel, A. J. (1955). Self-understanding of Judaism. In A. J. Heschel (Ed.) *God in search of man: A philosophy of Judaism* (pp. 3–23). The Noonsday Press.

Heschel, A. J. (1962a). What manner of man is the prophet? In A. J. Heschel (Ed.) *The prophets, An introduction* (Vol. 1, pp. 3–26). Harper & Row Publishers.

Heschel, A. J. (1962b). Comparisons and contrasts. In A. J. Heschel (Ed.) *The prophets* (Vol. II, pp. 12–26). Harper & Row Publishers.

Kanfer, R. (1990). Motivation theory and industrial and organizational psychology. In M. D. Dunnette, L. M. Hough, & M. Leaetta (Eds.), *Handbook of Industrial and Organizational Psychology*, second edition (pp. 75–130). Consulting Psychologists Press.

Leibniz, G. W. (1714). The principles of philosophy, or the monadology. In D. Garber & R. Ariew (Ed. and Trans.), *Discourse on metaphysics and other essays* (pp. 1–96). Hackett Publishing Company.

Leventhal, G. S. (1980). What should be done with equity theory? New approaches to the study of fairness in social relationships. In K.J. Gergen, M.S. Greenberg, & R.H. Willis (Eds.) *Social exchange: Advances in theory and research* (pp. 27–55). Springer US.

Levinas, E. (1966). The servant and her master. In S. Hand (Ed.), *The Levinas Reader* (pp. 150–159). Blackwell Publishers Inc.

Levinas, E. (1968). Substitution. In A. Lingus (Trans.) and S. Hand (Ed.), *The Levinas Reader* (pp. 88–126). Blackwell Publishers Inc.

New International Version. (2011). BibleGateway.com. http://www.biblegateway.com/versions/New-International-Version-NIV-Bible/#booklist

Polanyi, M. (1966). *The tacit dimension*. University of Chicago Press.

Rescher, N. (1987). *Ethical idealism: An inquiry into the nature and function of ideals*. University of California Press.

Sabine, G. H. (1915). A new monadology. *The Journal of Philosophy, Psychology and Scientific Methods, 12*(24), 650–657.

Song, Y., & Sojourner, A. (2023, April 19–22). *Now it's a matter of taste: Effects of firm's political ideology on human capital inflow* [Poster presentation]. Society for Industrial and Organizational Psychology (SIOP), 38th Annual Conference, Boston, MA.

Steele, C. M. (1988). The psychology of self-affirmation: Sustaining the integrity of the self. In *Advances in experimental social psychology* (Vol. 21, pp. 261–302). Academic Press.

Van Knippenberg, D., De Dreu, C. K., & Homan, A. C. (2004). Work group diversity and group performance: an integrative model and research agenda. *Journal of Applied Psychology, 89*(6), 1008–1022.

Varisco, B. (1915). *Know thyself*. G. Salvadori (Trans.). George Allen and Unwin, Limited.

Wegner, D. M. (1987). Transactive memory: A contemporary analysis of the group mind. In B. Mullen & G.R. Goethals (Eds.). *Theories of group behavior* (pp. 185–208). Springer.

Wenzel, M., Mummendey, A., Weber, U., & Waldzus, S. (2003). The ingroup as pars pro toto: Projection from the ingroup onto the inclusive category as a precursor to social discrimination. *Personality and Social Psychology Bulletin, 29*(4), 461–473.

Woods, J. (2023, April 19–22). *The influence of fit on motivations to lead* [Poster presentation]. Society for Industrial and Organizational Psychology (SIOP), 38th Annual Conference, Boston, MA.

Yuan, S., Inness, M., & Jia, J. (2023, April 19–22). *Rethinking work connectivity after hours: A conceptual and operationalized framework* [Poster presentation]. Society for Industrial and Organizational Psychology (SIOP), 38th Annual Conference, Boston, MA.

Zhang, L., Seong, J. Y., & Hong, D. S. (2023, April 19–22). *How does diversity lead to team performance? Redefining and extending the Categorization Elaboration Model (CEM)* [Poster presentation]. Society for Industrial and Organizational Psychology (SIOP), 38th Annual Conference, Boston, MA.

9

ARCHETYPES OF POWER, SOCIAL DOMINANCE, AND CONSTRAINING FORCES ON WORKPLACE CREATIVITY

Nahanni Freeman

Internalized Oppression, Fear, Criticism, and Creativity

Internalized oppression survives when an individual assimilates harmful stereotypes and expectations about one's own group, experiencing the effects of covert shame; this can emerge through a process of modeling (David & Derthick, 2018). Concealment of social identifications, masking evidence of affiliation, believing that one's group must change to accommodate the dominant assembly, and discriminating against one's own group can develop within a context of internalized oppression, which fuels an engine that negates one's subjectivity (David & Derthick, 2018). Internalized oppression can also take place at the institutional level, interacting with policies, norms, and conventions.

Internalization can include the acceptance of legitimizing myths, which are "attitudes, values, beliefs, stereotypes, and ideologies that provide moral and intellectual justification for the social practices that distribute social value within the social system" (Sidanius & Pratto, 1999, p. 45). Legitimizing myths will tend to justify systemic homeostasis, empowered when strong consensus persists about representations of others, forged in a context of high embeddedness, certitude, and ideological attachment to aesthetic symbols (Sidanius & Pratto, 1999). Dominant groups and individuals in the workplace will be likely to support myths and policies that enhance existing hegemonies (Freeman, 2019).

DOI: 10.4324/9781003322894-10

Authoritarianism

The harmful effects of authoritarianism on individuals and social groups have been well studied, with several measurement tools emerging from that work (Adorno et al., 1950; Altemeyer, 1981; Altemeyer, 1988), but some authors suggest a parity between the instruments (Meloen et al., 1996). Authoritarianism reproduces in heuristic-valuing ecologies (Freeman, 2022). While Erich Fromm (1976) is well-known for his evaluation of the social contagion that occurs in authoritarian societies, he also cautions against a form of anti-authoritarianism that leads to attempts to escape from reality through trance, dreams, self-indulgence, arbitrary substitutes for freedom, or delusion (p. 29). Fromm (1976) cautions against corporate authoritarianism, which persuades the worker that he/she/they are free while still decreasing emancipation through an advancing system justifying myths and unlimited consumerism, redefining happiness as acquisition (p. 27).

Fromm (1955) describes the problem of an inauthentic society as one that produces the alienated person, who "experiences himself as a thing, an investment, to be manipulated..." (p. 204). The sense of impending urgency of the loss of possibility and the squandering of unused talents can create a motivation to seek security through automaton conformity. In this state of mind, conscience is dimmed, humiliation and guilt are repressed, and the individual avoids despair by seeking security, which often arrives through a powerful Other.

The relationship between authoritarianism and creativity is complex, with some research suggesting that decreased creativity within authoritarian environments may be mediated by psychological capital, defensive silence, and fear (Guo et al., 2018), as well as employee voice (Dedahanov et al., 2016). The effects of authoritarian leadership on employee creativity may vary across cultural contexts. For example, in a Chinese sample, these effects were mediated by discipline-specific orientation, and the authors describe former research on leader benevolence and moral orientation in relation to follower self-efficacy (Zhao et al., 2022). Nevertheless, the authors caution about the use of supervisor evaluation to quantify creativity. In a comprehensive literature review, Mehraein et al. (2023) point out that the main effects from over 100 studies tend to support the suppression of creativity via authoritarianism, despite the moderator variables that surface in some cultures.

Fear, Negative Feedback, and Workplace Bullying

One manifestation of organizational morbidity is workplace bullying, which can include covert actions such as relational aggression and rumor proliferation, a strategy that is often successful (White, 2013). Abusive supervision also predicts counterproductive work behaviors and decreased work performance (Sheng et al., 2023). Other covert forms of bullying include: creating untenable workloads or deadlines, withholding training, restricting the target's access to success-dependent information or tools, denying promotion, and lying (White, 2013). Knowledge sabotage occurs when an employee or supervisor intentionally provides false or misleading information geared towards harm or engages in material concealment (Rhee, 2023). Social ostracism of victims is a strategy that contributes to scapegoating, often eroding victim self-efficacy. When the target's belongingness needs are thwarted and felt competence is undermined, depression, obsessiveness about work, and intrusive paranoid ideas may surface. Some victims tend to be agreeable and under-socialized for assertive behaviors, which can expand vulnerability.

In cases of abusive supervision, shame and threats to identity may conversely trigger a desire for repair; when coupled with danger avoidance and survival, the ironic effect can include increased organizational citizenship behavior (Sheng et al., 2023). Other adverse working environments may cause employees to perceive that organizational politics are based on self-interest and manipulation, which can lead to knowledge sabotage, mediated through the moral disengagement and diminished remorse that accrues due to the mechanisms of social learning and emotion appraisal (Sheng et al., 2023). Structurally oppressive workplaces may foster counterproductive work behaviors by failing to enforce policies that protect employee psychological safety; cultures of fear tend to evoke aggressive behaviors across departments (Priest et al., 2023). When ethical violations become systemic and legitimized, employees may feel pressured to tolerate corrupt behaviors and policies, developing internalized justifications that perpetuate toxicity (Gluman et al., 2023).

Projective Processes, Gender, and Racial Oppression

Building her theory from client interactions, Klein (1955) claimed that projection emerges from the interiorization of an excessive, punitive super-ego, rooted in envy and hatred, which perpetuates internal persecution, paranoid ideation, depression, and anxiety (p. 17). Klein's (1955) object relations structure emphasizes the idea that the infantile mind, which develops during the primary attachment stage, experiences primitive expressions of splitting and idealization, fortifying defenses and fantasies aimed to restrain the experience of the good and bad as separate entities (pp. 21–22).

Within a negative social environment, suppression, blaming and ostracism of the victims of gender or sexual harassment may reduce reporting, creating a toxic culture (Tay et al., 2023). When psychological safety is threatened and interpersonal trust is low, victims are likely to become hypervigilant and sensitized to cues of punishment, orienting towards self-preservation (Tay et al., 2023), which recruits cognitive resources and potentially shuttles attention away from creative insight. Gender differences in pay remain significant, with women also being assigned less-important roles, consistent with gendered-task segregation perspectives (McHugh et al., 2023). Attention to peripheral details remains problematic in gendered reactions to source credibility (Jones et al., 2023), with likely impacts on collective representations of workplace power. Females are more likely to detect subtle gender microaggressions, which reveal derogatory, indifferent, or demeaning attitudes or behaviors (Basford et al., 2014).

Racial microaggressions are everyday indignities experienced by people of color, which can include invalidation, insult, and verbal or nonverbal assault, sometimes accompanied by avoidant or discriminatory behavior (Sue et al., 2007). Internalized prejudice, which can truncate leader self-development, can alter self-relevant cognition and motivation (Hogue et al., 2023). The interaction between culture and the mind suggests a reciprocal, recursive network of cognitive and social change, but new status phenomenology in an organization may help to dislodge self-limiting beliefs and actions (Hogue et al., 2023). Racial inequality in the workplace may also be driven by projective identifications in dominant groups, where devalued parts of the self are externalized onto scapegoats in ways that seek to induce shame in the recipient (Mobasseri et al., 2023). Organizational holding environments can work to dismantle oppressive policies and structures, prompting non-defensive inter-group contact and safe spaces for intrapsychic wrestling with threats (Mobasseri et al., 2023).

Archetypes of power employ: bureaucracy, systems, technological expertise, information control, deprivation threats, heroic leadership, deception power, rhetoric, emotional manipulation, survival needs, and conformity drives in ways that secure and maintain power (Kenrick et al., 2005; Brey, 2008). The built environment, seduction power, and persuasive statistical and data distortion can be leveraged to maintain status hierarchies, often conjoined with nonverbal expressions of dominance and power-based threats (Kenrick et al., 2005; Brey, 2008). Trappings of competence wield the props and habits that seek to convey expertise, social capital, status, and managerial persona (Kenrick et al., 2005) in ways that can neglect, undermine, and invalidate the Other.

Limitations

Inferences derived from psychological studies can sometimes be extended beyond their evidence. Many studies of workplace scenarios rely on critical incident sampling, which narrows the field of study and may exclude a range of other contextual and systematic forces (Barron et al., 2023). Increased reliance on diaries, journals, and multi-sourced data can increase the scope of understanding for critical theories (Wessels & Perez, 2023). Measures of workplace perceptions and attitudes are challenging in light of the reliance on brief screening tools. When revisions to instruments create greater brevity, content validity can be compromised (Priest et al., 2023). It is often beneficial to include an interrupted time series design in order to derive clearer conclusions regarding the impact of time (Priest et al., 2023), as well as maturation and history effects. Bridging between the particular and the molar remains challenging.

A Preservation of Self and Other Model

Tacit knowledge sharing, nurturing towards complexity, job security, embedded structures for intrapsychic work, expansive psychological safety, and incubation of the Beloved Community may facilitate creativity by reducing the strangulating effects of racial and gender oppression, authoritarianism, internalized prejudice, and bullying. Michael Polanyi (1958) posits that the knower, as a responsible agent, must personally participate in the enterprise of enlightenment. Personal knowledge attempts to fuse self-relevant and external realities, for "we must inevitably see the universe from a center lying within ourselves" (Polanyi, 1958, p. 3). A commitment to ethics can assert that principles, like a map, are "extended over space and time" (Polanyi, 1958, p. 4). Workplace ethics that support human rights, democratic procedures, and equality can move beyond mechanisms into transcendent relativity.

A psychodynamic model of interpersonal aggression and exclusion can yield a blueprint that maps hypotheses for the social transformation of archetypes of power. Deficient self-care and self-interest motives may underlie many counterproductive work behaviors, being instigated by attempts at social competence and belonging, strategies to manage stress, reactions to perceived unfairness, and goal pursuit (Gu & Converse, 2023). Mentoring, coaching, modeling, and subordinate goals can strengthen teams in a holding environment. Cochran (1977) describes Polanyi's approach to tacit knowledge transmission as an affiliation of the self towards a community; the tacit features are essential for validation within a community of explorers who seek creative discovery (Cochran, 1977).

A preservation of Other model will protect non-mechanistic construal of self and other, rooted in a theory of knowledge that extends from self towards a community. Cochran (1977) describes Polanyi's opposition to authoritarian limitations on knowledge, rather than recruiting the integration of focal and distal perceptions in the artistic pursuit of authentic knowledge. Cochran (1977) argues that Polanyi's view of authority is hospitable to scientific consensus, interconnected mutuality, and genuine contact with what exists (pp. 555–556).

Preservation of self and other ecology must be a just real estate. Interactional justice emphasizes how employees are treated when decisions are made in the workplace (Barron et al., 2023). Studies of interactional justice emphasize the importance of interpersonal and informational strategies that provide a logical, timely, and dignified experience of bad news, despite the apparent tendency to either be compassionate but dishonest or cold and misleading (Barron et al., 2023). It may be important to expand concepts of interactional justice towards broader contexts and definitions, which may support movement from abstract to more practical goals.

A just workplace will also be a location where self-esteem and organizational identification are supported through the elimination of illegitimate tasks, given the tendency of these tasks to communicate "disrespect, lack of appreciation, or negative evaluation" (Wessels & Perez, 2023, p. 5). The presence of tasks that seem to undervalue an employee's skills, job description, or time can increase turnover intentions (Wessels & Perez, 2023), with longevity being advantageous for tacit knowledge sharing. Despite exposure to adverse work experiences, some individuals will respond with empathy, prosocial behavior (Tay et al., 2023), and a desire to respond proactively to unethical climates (Gluman et al., 2023). Ultimately, a theory of preservation will not be one that "disregards our terrestrial location" (p. 4), but will embrace "the vision of a reality beyond the impressions of our senses" (Polanyi, 1958, p. 5).

Works Cited

Adorno, T. W., Frenkel-Brunswik, E., Levinson, D. J., & Sanford, R. N. (1950). *The authoritarian personality.* Harper.

Altemeyer, B. (1981). *Right wing authoritarianism.* University of Manitoba Press.

Altemeyer, B. (1988). *Enemies of freedom.* Jossey-Bass.

Barron, A. H., Bobocel, D. R., & Shen, W. (2023, April 19–22). *Strategies underlying interactional justice enactment: A latent profile analysis* [Poster presentation]. Society for Industrial and Organizational Psychology (SIOP), 38th Annual Conference, Boston, MA.

Basford, T. E., Offermann, L. R., & Behrend, T. S. (2014). Do you see what I see? Perceptions of gender microaggressions in the workplace. *Psychology of Women Quarterly, 38*(3), 340–349.

Brey, P. (2008). The technological construction of social power. *Social Epistemology, 22*(1), 7195.

Cochran, C. E. (1977). Authority and community: The contributions of Carl Friedrich, Yves R. Simon, and Michael Polanyi. *American Political Science Review, 71*(2), 546–558.

David, E. J. R, & Derthick, O. (2018). *The psychology of oppression*. Springer.

Dedahanov, A. T., Lee, D. H., Rhee, J., & Yoon, J. (2016). Entrepreneur's paternalistic leadership style and creativity: The mediating role of employee voice. *Management Decision, 54*(9), 2310–2324.

Freeman, N. (2019). American cultural symbolism of rage and resistance in collective trauma: Racially-influenced political Myths, counter-myths, projective identification, and the evocation of transcendent humanity. In D. M. Goodman, E. Severson, & H. Macdonald (Eds.), *Race, rage, and resistance: Philosophy, psychology, and the perils of individualism*. Routledge, Taylor and Francis Group.

Freeman, N. (2022). *Social neurocognition, heuristics, and the psychology of attitudes*. Kendall-Hunt.

Fromm, E. (1955). *The sane society*. Rinehart & Company. Owl Books Edition 1990.

Fromm, E. (1976). *The art of being*. Continuum. Reprinted 1992.

Gluman, S., Nguyen, H. H., & Gluck, D. (2023, April 19–22). *Should I blow the whistle? Antecedents of perceiving and reporting ethical violations* [Poster presentation]. Society for Industrial and Organizational Psychology (SIOP), 38th Annual Conference, Boston, MA.

Gu, S., & Converse, P. D. (2023, April 19–22). *Counterproductive work behavior motives: Conceptualization and measurement* [Poster presentation]. Society for Industrial and Organizational Psychology (SIOP), 38th Annual Conference, Boston, MA.

Guo, L., Decoster, S., Babalola, M. T., De Schutter, L., Garba, O. A., & Riisla, K. (2018). Authoritarian leadership and employee creativity: The moderating role of psychological capital and the mediating role of fear and defensive silence. *Journal of Business Research, 92*, 219–230.

Hogue, M., Knapp, D. E., Peck, J. A., & Weems-Landingham, V. (2023). The status of internalized prejudice in leader self-development. *Management Decision, 61*(4), 944–958.

Jones, A. C., Repke, A., Batastini, A. B., Sacco, D., Dahlen, E. R., & Mohn, R. S. (2023). The power of presentation: How attire, cosmetics, and posture impact the source credibility of women expert witnesses. *Journal of Forensic Sciences, 68*, 962–971.

Kenrick, D. T., Neuberg, S. L., & Cialdini, R. B. (2005). *Social psychology: Unraveling the mystery* (3rd ed.). Pearson Education New Zealand.

Klein, M. (1955). The psychoanalytic play technique and its history. In M. Klein, P. Heimann, & R. E. Money-Kyrle (Eds.), *New directions in psychoanalysis* (pp. 3–23). Karnac Books. Reprinted 1977.

McHugh, B., Glerum, D. R., & Berenbon, R. F. (2023, April 19–22). *It's women's work: Gender-based task segregation evidence in job analysis survey data* [Poster presentation]. Society for Industrial and Organizational Psychology (SIOP), 38th Annual Conference, Boston, MA.

Mehraein, V., Visintin, F., & Pittino, D. (2023). The dark side of leadership: A systematic review of creativity and innovation. *International Journal of Management Reviews, 42*, 25308–25330.

Meloen, J. D., Van der Linden, G., & De Witte, H. (1996). A test of the approaches of Adorno et al., Lederer and Altemeyer of authoritarianism in Belgian Flanders: A research note. *Political Psychology, 17*, 643–656.

Mobasseri, S., Kahn, W. A., & Ely, R. J. (2023). Racial inequality in organizations: A systems psychodynamic perspective. *Academy of Management Review, 17*, 1–28. doi: 10.5465/amr.2021.0446

Polanyi, M. (1958). *Personal knowledge: Towards a post-critical philosophy.* University of Chicago Press.

Priest, R., Sackett, P. R., & Schmidt, A. M. (2023, April 19–22). *Clarifying correlates of oppressive work situations* [Poster presentation]. Society for Industrial and Organizational Psychology (SIOP), 38th Annual Conference, Boston, MA.

Rhee, J. (2023, April 19–22). *The effect of perceived organizational politics on knowledge sabotage* [Poster presentation]. Society for Industrial and Organizational Psychology (SIOP), 38th Annual Conference, Boston, MA.

Sheng, Z., Fiscus, J., He, Y., Yao, X., & Zhu, G. (2023, April 19–22). *How abusive supervision can lead to OCBs and CWBs through discrete emotions* [Poster presentation]. Society for Industrial and Organizational Psychology (SIOP), 38th Annual Conference, Boston, MA.

Sidanius, J., & Pratto, F. (1999). *Social dominance: An intergroup theory of social hierarchy and oppression.* Cambridge University Press.

Sue, D. W., Capodilupo, C. M., Torino, G. C., Bucceri, J. M., Holder, A., Nadal, K. L., & Esquilin, M. (2007). Racial microaggressions in everyday life: implications for clinical practice. *American Psychologist, 62*(4), 271–286.

Tay, E., Wang, Y., & Lim, S. (2023, April 19–22). *From survivors to saviors: Sexual harassment victimization and helping behaviors* [Poster presentation]. Society for Industrial and Organizational Psychology (SIOP), 38th Annual Conference, Boston, MA.

Wessels, J., & Perez, L. M. (2023, April 19–22). *Linking illegitimate tasks and organizational identification with turnover intentions* [Poster presentation]. Society for Industrial and Organizational Psychology (SIOP), 38th Annual Conference, Boston, MA.

White, S. (2013). *An introduction to the psychodynamics of workplace bullying.* Karnac Books.

Zhao, H., Su, Q., Lou, M., Hang, C., & Zhang, L. (2022). Does authoritarianism necessarily stifle creativity? The role of discipline-focused authoritarian leadership. *Frontiers in Psychology, 13*, 1–12, 1037102.

PART 2

Applications in a Human Resource Management Context

10

CREATIVITY, CULTURE, AND HUMAN RESOURCE MANAGEMENT

Bren Slusser

What Is Tacit Knowledge?

Every organization would like to have a diverse workforce where knowledge is shared and transferred freely. However, it is easier said than done, particularly when you are discussing different languages, cultures, skills, and experiences. As organizations diversify their workforce, creativity and innovation will be more prominent if the leaders of the organization are in full support and provide the right atmosphere for transferring the knowledge of the team members to one another. The knowledge that is shared amongst team members is known as "tacit knowledge." The sharing of tacit knowledge not only helps with creativity and innovation but also impacts an organization's performance. As we journey through part two of the book, we will explore how tacit knowledge affects creativity and innovation, along with the impact on an organization's performance, as well as how ethical leadership and HR activities facilitate the transfer of this tacit knowledge.

As has been discussed in the first section of the book, tacit knowledge is knowledge that you gain by doing the job, obtained through experience, and communicated through the natural socialization of individuals within an organization (Polanyi, 2009 [1966]). Basically, we know more than we can tell a person, which is very insightful when we are thinking about how much a person knows in general, such as in their job or just in different experiences we all have throughout life. Furthermore, if tacit knowledge is a "central part of knowledge in general, then we can both (1) know what to look for and (2) have some idea about what else we may want to

DOI: 10.4324/9781003322894-12

know" (Polanyi, 2009 [1966], p. xi). Knowing "what" and knowing "how" go together when discussing tacit knowledge. Tacit knowledge is rooted in an individual's experiences allowing the individual to perform proficiently within a certain social context (Hatch & Cunliffe, 2006). More specifically, when learning and performing the job, a person will develop adaptations to the way in which different functions are performed, making it their own. This makes tacit knowledge incredibly difficult to capture in a manual or develop into a process, as people tend to rely on what they know, and trying to explain the how and why to another person can prove to be difficult, although not impossible. Nonaka and Takeuchi (1995) confirm these contentions by deducing that tacit knowledge is not easily explainable or visible and that it is "highly personal and hard to formalize, making it difficult to communicate or to share with others" (p. 8). Furthermore, as knowledge moves up the ontological levels, there is knowledge conversion that occurs, where tacit knowledge and explicit knowledge become larger in scale. More specifically, knowledge starts at the individual level and is transferred throughout a team, department, division, and then the organization (Nonaka & Takeuchi, 1995). This is magnified as these individuals get together, creating and innovating within the organization, expanding their knowledge, and growing the organization. Organizations have realized the importance of attaining and retaining the tacit knowledge that employees possess.

From an epistemological perspective, both explicit and tacit knowledge that is new and useful is important; however, tacit knowledge is more difficult to identify and transfer (Fliaster & Spiess, 2008). More specifically, tacit knowledge is described as knowledge that exists within an individual and is acquired through experiences that occur through learning and doing (Nonaka & Takeuchi, 1995). Polanyi (2009 [1966]) describes tacit knowledge in four different aspects, one of which is an ontological aspect, where "tacit knowing is a knowledge of [establishing a] meaningful relationship between two terms" (p. 13), and in this case it is the knowledge an individual will gain through experience. However, differences exist between explicit and tacit knowledge. More specifically, tacit knowledge is subjective knowledge that is gained through experiences in the here and now through simultaneous personal interactions, while explicit knowledge is objective based on rationality through sequential knowledge of past events or objects and gained through digital activities (Nonaka & Takeuchi, 1995). Thus, having those simultaneous interactions for sharing and transferring tacit knowledge is crucial within teams. Tacit knowledge is not easy to transfer between people, and it becomes even more complicated when discussing low and high context cultures and how these cultures send and receive communication.

Tacit Knowledge in Low and High Context Cultures

When discussing high and low context cultures, it is important to understand what this means and how it could affect creativity and innovation in the workplace. The differences between the cultures can create a barrier for the successful transfer of tacit knowledge between high context cultures and low context cultures (Gudykunst, 1983). First, high context cultures are cultures where body language is the main source of communication versus using words (Mujtaba & Balboa, 2009). Whereas low context cultures rely more on verbal communication (words) than body language and have a harder time identifying what a high context culture individual is trying to convey due to this communication disparity (Mujtaba & Balboa, 2009). These differences create challenges and barriers between cultures in effectively communicating between team members. These challenges are not necessarily seen in homogenous cultures but are seen in cross-cultural teams due to cultural differences (Inkpen & Tsang, 2005).

These challenges and barriers may be particularly noticeable when transferring tacit knowledge, which again is information that is learned and shared through experiences working within the organization (Gupta & Govindarajan, 2000). It is important to acknowledge these barriers due to the significantly slower rate at which relationships are developed within high context cultures with other cultures. Thus, the barriers could impact the performance of the teams and ultimately the organization, impacting the overall performance of the organization (Chow, 2009). Cultural distance, as discussed by van Wijk et al. (2008), can stifle the process of tacit knowledge transfers. This is not because team members are not wanting to share their knowledge or are being uncooperative; it is because of a lack of understanding of the values and norms that reside between the cultures. You may be asking yourself why this even matters for transferring tacit knowledge. Just given the distinction between high and low context cultures, one can see where problems would arise in the workplace, particularly as our world continues to become more blended, providing a ripe opportunity for increasing creativity and innovation, but more challenging as language barriers and cultures may not necessarily be understood. Transferring knowledge across diverse sources can be difficult, particularly where there are language, social, and cognitive barriers; however, it is within the ability of the knowledge recipients to recognize, incorporate, and utilize the external knowledge (Murray & Chao, 2005).

It is important to identify some of the countries that may be identified as either high context or low context cultures, as this helps to give a perspective and better understanding of the differences in the cultures when forming working relationships. Specifically, the different cultures that are considered high context cultures include Japan, China, and Arab countries, which are more of a collectivist culture. Whereas the United States, Australia, and Western European countries are considered low context cultures and have more of an individualistic culture. While this is not an exhaustive list of the different countries and cultures, it does help to get an idea of the high and low context cultures, particularly as they are prominent in the workplace. Once both types of cultures understand how each other communicates, this will pave the way for more effective communication whereby tacit knowledge can be transferred.

As discussed by Mujtaba and Balboa (2009), "cultures tend to regularize human behavior or make them more predictable for each group in their own unique ways, and effective communication becomes extremely critical in a diverse environment where different cultures are present" (p. 82). Cultural diversity is important within an organization and will ultimately help to raise its performance as diversified thoughts and ideas are shared and implemented. These differences will be more visible when low context and high context cultures are brought together (Cox et al., 1991). Through the establishment of social networks (natural working relationships) in the organization, where trust and tacit knowledge are shared amongst the team members, the barriers that have prohibited creativity and innovation in the workplace will be reduced (Inkpen & Tsang, 2005). Culture is the software of the mind and is not taught the same way in which language is taught, which adds to the curiosity of culture and how it works, not to mention the differences that exist between cultures and how culture controls behavior (Hall, 1959). Knowledge of the differences between high and low context cultures will help organizations understand the diverse cultural communication barriers that may exist. Thus, when there is diversity of thought within an organization, this allows for greater innovation and creativity to thrive. If there is a reduction or elimination of cultural and communication barriers so that social networks can be formed for tacit knowledge to be transferred freely, the teams as well as the organization will benefit.

Further discussing the differences between cultures, the collective society is much different than the individual society, which is dominant in the Western world. In a collective society, the interests of the collective are more important than those of the individual, whereas in an individual society, the person is more important than the team or group, i.e., people will look out for themselves first, then what's best for the team (Hofstede et al., 2010). This distinction will become even more apparent as the world's boundaries seemingly continue to blur, where individualistic and collective societies engage in more and more business together. American organizations have tried to implement some form of collectivistic pattern of behavior by instituting projects that require cross-functional teamwork. However, because of the individualistic nature of Americans, individuals tend to ensure they are taken care of first before the team, causing conflict within the collectivist culture (Slusser, 2012). Further distinctions between these two as they pertain to the workplace include the following:

- Individualism: This is where personal time is very important; allowed to have the freedom to adapt tasks to however the person feels is best; and given the opportunity to have more challenging work to feel a sense of accomplishment (Hofstede et al., 2010).
- Collectivism: This is where priorities are established that are best for the team; cohesiveness and harmony within the group are important over individual needs; and individuals are identified through group allegiance and role (Hofstede et al., 2010).

The biggest difference between these two examples discussed above is that the individualist way of thinking has a more independent view of self and the organization, whereas the collectivist view has a more dependent view of the organization and less on self (Hofstede et al., 2010). Neither is right nor wrong, but it is important to be able to clearly identify some of the differences because these barriers could prohibit the transfer of tacit knowledge, thus hindering creativity and innovation from naturally flourishing.

Whether the person is receiving or sending the information, it is important for both high and low context cultures to understand how the other sends and receives information and to understand the differences in communication to share information, do business, or just communicate effectively. Specifically, when working with individuals from a high context culture, non-verbal body language is most prominent when communicating, and it is expected for the low context culture sending or receiving the information to know and understand this type of communication. On the other hand, when discussing low context cultures, this is more verbal in nature, and when a low-context culture person is communicating with a high-context culture person, there could be some miscommunication that occurs due to these differences. For example, a co-worker from a high context culture nods when a co-worker from a low context culture is speaking; however, this does not necessarily mean that they agree or understand completely with what is being said. It simply means that they are listening. In discussing the high context culture co-worker sending information, the low context culture co-worker will need to slow down and watch the non-verbal cues given by their high context co-worker. The high context culture co-worker needs to know and understand how the low context culture co-worker communicates, be cognizant of their own culture and try to be more verbal when communicating. Again, it is critical for the sender of the information to ensure that the receiver understands what is being said so that there is no miscommunication, creating problems that do not need to exist regardless of culture. Basically, both cultures should be willing to meet each other in the middle so that there is effective communication for effectively transferring tacit knowledge.

Tacit Knowledge Transfer, Ethical Leadership, and the Impact on Creativity and Innovation

Tacit knowledge and how it is transferred between high and low context cultures within an organization can have a profound impact on the creativity and innovation of the organization. For example, in research conducted within a Japanese organization with a subsidiary in the United States, it was not the differences in culture or the differences of the high and low cultures, but the language barrier that created most of the challenges the workforce faced with one another. This was a significant discovery since someone outside of the department, who was a Japanese national, was the one who was the "liaison" between the home country (headquarters) and the subsidiary staff. This could have also posed some challenges due to the language barrier and the translation of information (Slusser, 2012). The fact that the liaison was outside of the department could have also impacted the flow of tacit knowledge between the team, inadvertently creating a barrier. However, this did not occur, and the teams had no problem communicating amongst each other, sharing ideas and information, thus lending themselves to a naturally creative and innovative environment. A reason that this was not a problem could have been due to the ethical leadership that was apparent within the leadership team. While leaders are important to teams, this can also hinder the transfer of tacit knowledge due to the power distance between the team members and the leader. Specifically, Hofstede et al. (2010) bring up the good point that power distance in the workplace is important to remember as there is a hierarchy of power between the leaders and employees. This power distance is seen even more in larger organizations, where the smaller organizations are more apt to see each other as equals, which can provide for a riper atmosphere for knowledge to be transferred. It is important to note that in larger organizations, the power distance naturally creates an existential difference (Hofstede et al., 2010); however, with a willingness and opportunity to develop a positive and transparent working environment, the transfer of knowledge, either explicit or tacit, becomes much more manageable, whereby creativity and innovation can flourish. Leaders affect innovation through their involvement within the organization, nurturing a positive working atmosphere to help stimulate creativity and innovation (Lei et al., 2019). Of course, in an environment that is considered more competitive where collaboration is not nurtured, these same leaders can also hinder creativity and innovation, which impacts the opportunity to share tacit knowledge. Ethical leadership greatly impacts the opportunity for the transfer of knowledge, both explicit and tacit, and a willingness to do so. Furthermore, in this environment, the leaders create an atmosphere where employees feel psychologically safe to share their knowledge to challenge the status quo (Lei et al., 2019). With ethical leadership in place, this is perceived as a "key force" (Lei et al., 2019, p. 851) for implementing a creative and innovative culture, which then translates into more of a competitive advantage for organizations. Ethical leadership has a profound impact on innovation within an organization, which includes the firm's operations as well as the transfer of knowledge, both explicit and tacit, which impacts the stimulus of creativity (Lei et al., 2019). When employees know that they work for an ethical employer, the morale climate is apparent, establishing a strong collective culture as well (Lei et al., 2019). Being ethical must accompany being trustworthy. Productivity, job satisfaction, and commitment are all dependent on a leader's trustworthiness. Without it, then the organization suffers, not only by losing great people but also by sacrificing performance, affecting the organization's market share. Being a trustworthy leader creates an atmosphere of commitment and higher job satisfaction, whereby employees are more willing to transfer their tacit knowledge.

Tacit knowledge is a competitive advantage for an organization (Lopez-Cabarcos et al., 2019). Nurturing the natural flow of tacit knowledge among the team is critical for sustaining creativity and innovation. Since tacit knowledge cannot be codified in any form other than repeating the behaviors and teaching others, the knowledge that is being transferred between team members increases the competitive advantage for the organization, along with the importance of the leaders continuing to create an atmosphere for transferring tacit knowledge. Moreover, sharing knowledge allows employees to learn and synthesize information to help them become more adept at translating new ideas, which leads to greater innovation (Yang et al., 2018). Organizational leaders that are successful in motivating employees to contribute both their explicit and tacit knowledge within groups is more likely to create new ideas and business opportunities, facilitating innovation to occur within the organization and increasing their market share and competitive advantage.

Creativity and innovation are not only for product development but also for the creation of new ideas, processes, or any other task where creativity and innovation increase the competitive advantage of an organization. Leadership is generally associated with or perceived to influence a creative culture within an organization (Lei et al., 2019). The power that leaders have will ultimately encourage or discourage the behaviors of their employees, thus inspiring the employees to exhibit acceptable behaviors. Specifically, ethical leadership provides clear direction and motivation for fostering creativity and innovation (Lei et al., 2019). In research conducted by Lei et al. (2019), through positive, ethical leadership, the opportunity and commitment in sharing knowledge was more apt to occur as employees felt safe enough to share knowledge and ideas. Employees who share ideas, information, skills, and feedback allow the organizational goals to be achieved as well as individual goals and duties to be achieved. As the transference of knowledge occurs, this new information adds to the knowledge the employee already has; synthesizing this new knowledge expands the creativity and innovation opportunities within the workplace (Lei et al., 2019). In essence, ethical leadership tremendously impacts employees' behavior when sharing valuable information, expertise, insights, and experiences with colleagues (Lei et al., 2019). Thus, leadership, particularly ethical leadership, is instrumental in fostering an atmosphere to transfer tacit knowledge between individuals within an organization resulting in creativity and innovation.

Social Network Theory and Low and High Context Cultures

Social network theory is not a discussion about social media. Instead, social network theory is the social networks that are developed within an organization, where social relationships are fostered for individuals to access information, resources, and opportunities (Cross & Parker, 2004). Some believe that these networks are hard to manage. However, according to Cross and Parker (2004), these "social" networks with "appropriate connectivity in well-managed networks within organizations can have a substantial impact on performance, learning, and innovation" (p. vii). The challenge has been why these networks have not been well supported, believing that better communication, increased team-building, and off-site meetings will help to promote collaboration, which will result in transferring knowledge. However, this is not the answer. Instead, the answer is to provide a more targeted way in which to promote collaboration and network connectivity, tapping into these social networks and the power that lies within them (Cross & Parker, 2004).

Another theory that plays a significant role in the establishment of these relationships within the high and low context cultures is social context theory, as this also affects the transfer of tacit knowledge. More specifically, social network theory is based on individuals in a network of social relationships where information, resources, and opportunities are obtained and shared. Individuals will be nurtured through the complex establishment of these social relationships, allowing the members of the team to learn from and use the information held by the members of these social networks. Additionally, one of the most important key ingredients in these relationships is trust, which allows access to a social network or for a network to be established (Chow, 2009). It is important to note that trust takes time, so this process cannot be sped up or artificially developed. The challenge for organizations is allowing these social networks to naturally be established where knowledge can flow between them. Another challenge will be for the social networks to not become so siloed that the members will quit trying to seek knowledge from outside of the network. Additionally, the biggest violators of siloed teams are the leaders within the networks, which may result in the networks becoming less effective and stagnant in expanding their knowledge (Cross & Parker, 2004). Therefore, it is important to identify how social networks are established and the role of managers in these social networks for the effective transfer of tacit knowledge.

A challenge that organizations face is the blending of cultures with the global nature of business today. More specifically, low, and high context cultures are working side by side in organizations through all the language and communication barriers that exist. As has been discussed, high context cultures establish their social networks through the development of trust, which, according to Rousseau et al. (1998), occurs through "deep dependence and identity formation" (p. 396). While the low context cultures use more verbal communication, allowing the social networks to have the appearance of developing more quickly but not necessarily establishing a truly cohesive and trust-dependent social network, as this takes time, experience, learning, and growing together. Nevertheless, as the two cultures are brought together, there can be tension and barriers that will exist due to these differences and ultimately how they develop social networks (Slusser, 2012); thus, it is important for the leaders to understand that it will take time for these social networks to be established where tacit knowledge can freely flow between all team members.

The ability to effectively communicate between cultures is vital to the success of transferring knowledge (Kalling, 2003). This also expressly relies on the motivation of the participants in the network to transfer tacit knowledge and work hard to learn this knowledge. The motivation will also come from the encouragement of the leaders and an atmosphere for sharing information. Regardless, the norms of these social networks do take time to develop as cooperation, trust, and reciprocity are driven by the cultures; thus, the establishment and acceptance of the social networks impact how and when tacit knowledge is transferred (Slusser, 2012). Once these social networks are established and accepted, the flow of tacit knowledge will occur, provided it is reciprocal. More specifically, members are more likely to share information if it is viewed as reciprocal rather than exploiting it (Lin, 2007).

As has been discussed, social network theory plays a critical role in the building of relationships between high and low context cultures. Social network theory is grounded in how the establishment of social relationships includes the gaining and sharing of information, resources, and opportunities (Chow, 2009). This is accomplished by the development of trust, which is a foundational component in the establishment of these social networks, which also impact the working environment. When they are safe and supported by leadership, then these networks thrive, allowing for the exchange of tacit knowledge (Slusser, 2012). Furthermore, it is important for leaders to acknowledge and recognize that these social networks have unique features as they are made up of employee networks, not only within the team but throughout the organization (Cross & Parker, 2004). Specifically, these networks are dynamic and driven by strategy, infrastructure, and the work that is occurring in the organization. If there is a disturbance in these networks, such as leadership behaviors or organizational design, however unintentional it may be, this could fragment the networks. As Cross and Parker (2004) contend, "incentives and work management practices frequently preclude collaboration between colleagues in different departments" (p. ix). This generally results in certain people within the organization being sought after because of their specific job skills or knowledge, which can slow down progress. Another important point about social networks is that they cannot be captured on an organizational chart, but they are intricately intertwined within the organization and its performance, how strategy is developed, and ultimately its ability to create and innovate (Cross & Parker, 2004). Thus, leaders will view these social networks in terms of achieving organizational goals and not necessarily the vast amount of tacit knowledge that is contained within them; the organizational goals cannot be achieved effectively or efficiently without this knowledge being transferred throughout the social networks.

Another interesting point about social networks in organizations is that the knowledge that is being shared in these networks is morphed as it is transferred from person to person based on their own experiences, interpretations, and meanings. We see this metamorphosis of information like that of the telephone game, which we have all played at one time or another in training or team-building activities (Cross & Parker, 2004). What was shared by the initial person does not always end up the way it was intended, creating a kink in the lines of communication and the flow of tacit knowledge between team members. Additionally, when leaders have a disproportionate say, or in this case, they regulate what is being shared and which interpretation of the information is to be followed, then the connectivity of the social networks can be stifled and ultimately broken, which is devastating to not only the team but also to the organization. As a leader, it is a fine line between regulating the social networks and how they communicate and share information versus allowing these networks to organically grow, which is optimal for these networks to develop and share their tacit knowledge, leading to greater creativity and innovation. Some regulation or "pulse" on the networks is important for leaders to have as it can help to reduce redundancies, inaccuracies, and miscommunications from occurring. Although some of this is inevitable as people are humans and misunderstandings and miscommunications will happen, the degree to which regulation of activities occurs is important to help mitigate problems that may arise.

The problem with leaders not being involved in or having a pulse on the social networks is that these networks can take on a life of their own. Providing the strategic goals and then standing back to allow the networks to accomplish these goals could have risks for the overall performance of the organization. For instance, the leaders should develop a community of practice or implement some collaborative technology to support these networks, as well as know what is going on within the networks. However, when left unattended or supported, tacit knowledge is being transferred between these social networks and not captured by the organization in any way. This oversight could be very costly for an organization (Cross & Parker, 2004).

One thing that leaders need to be cognizant of as well is that these social networks can be strong and highly collaborative. Furthermore, the collaboration within the social networks may surprise the senior leadership and, often, may not follow along with the formal organizational chart, which is great for collaboration to thrive, transferring tacit knowledge and increasing creativity and innovation within the organization. However, just as these social networks are strong and collaborative, it is important for the leadership to have their pulse on them, as this helps with decision-making and ensures that these networks do not go astray from the goals and objectives of the organization. Another advantage of these social networks that leadership can tap into is that senior leadership can leverage these insights within the social networks to address critical challenges or disconnects that have been developed deep within the organization, creating a "sense-and-respond" capability (Cross & Parker, 2004). An important caveat will be that even though the leaders will get involved enough to have their pulse on these social networks, they also need to understand that they cannot take over, and more importantly, they need to truly understand the inner workings of these social networks so decision-making does not get delayed and the employees can seize opportunities for creativity and innovation to occur. One way in which to help facilitate collaboration without interfering to the point of stifling progress is to target strategic points within these social networks, resulting in quickly increasing an organization's effectiveness (Cross & Parker, 2004).

Works Cited

Chow, I. H.-S. (2009). The relationship between social capital, organizational citizenship behavior, and performance outcomes: An empirical study from China. *SAM Advanced Management Journal*, 44–53. Retrieved from Business Source Complete database.

Cox, T. H., Lobel, S. A., & McLeod, P. L. (1991). Effects of ethnic group cultural differences on cooperative and competitive behavior on a group task. *Academy of Management Journal*, 34(4), 827–847. Retrieved from Business Source Complete database.

Cross, R., & Parker, A. (2004). *The hidden power or social networks: Understanding how work really gets done in organizations*. Harvard Business School Publishing.

Fliaster, A., & Spiess, J. (2008). Knowledge mobilization through social ties: The cost benefit analysis. *Schmalenbach Business Review, 60*, 99–117. Retrieved from Business Source Complete database.

Gudykunst, W. B. (1983). Uncertainty reduction and predictability of behavior in lowand high-context cultures: An exploratory study. *Communication Quarterly, 31*(1), 49–55. Retrieved from ABI/INFORM Global database.

Gupta, A. K., & Govindarajan, V. (2000). Knowledge flows within multinational corporations. *Strategic Management Journal, 21*, 473–496. Retrieved from Business Source Complete database.

Hall, E. T. (1959). *The silent language*. Doubleday & Company.

Hatch, M. J., & Cunliffe, A. L. (2006). *Organization theory: Modern, symbolic, and postmodern perspectives* (2nd ed.). Oxford University Press.

Inkpen, A. C., & Tsang, E. W. K. (2005). Social capital, networks, and knowledge transfer. *Academy of Management Review, 30*(1), 146–165. Retrieved from Business Source Complete database.

Kalling, M. (2003). Organization-internal transfer of knowledge and the role of motivation: Qualitative case study. *Wiley Interscience*, 10(2), 115–126. doi: 10.1002/kpm.170

Lei, H., Thi Lan Ha, A., & Ba Le, P. (2019). How ethical leadership cultivates radical and incremental innovation: The mediating role of tacit and explicit knowledge sharing. *Journal of Business & Industrial Marketing. Emerald Publishing Limited, 35*(5), 849–862. doi: 10.1108/JBIM-05-2019-0180

Lin, C.-P. (2007). To share or not to share: Modeling tacit knowledge sharing, its mediators and antecedents. *Journal of Business Ethics, 70*, 411–428. doi: 10.1007/s10551-006-9199-0

Lopez-Cabarcos, M. A., Srinivasan, S., Gottling-Oliveira-Monteriro, S., & Vazquez-Rodriguez, P. (2019). Tacit knowledge and firm performance relationship. The role of product innovation and the firm level capabilities. *Journal of Business Economic and Management, 20*(2), 330–350. doi: 10.3846/jbem.2019.9590

Mujtaba, R. G., & Balboa, A. (2009). Comparing Filipino and American task and relationship orientations. *The Journal of Applied Management and Entrepreneurship, 14*(2), 82–98. Retrieved from ABI/INFORM Global database.

Murray, J. Y., & Chao, M. C. H. (2005). A cross-team framework of international knowledge acquisition on new product development capabilities and new product market performance. *Journal of International Marketing, 13*(3), 54–78. Retrieved from Business Source Complete database.

Nonaka, I., & Takeuchi, H. (1995). *The knowledge-creating company.* Oxford University Press.

Polanyi, M. (2009). *The tacit dimension.* University of Chicago Press (Original work published 1966).

Rousseau, D. M., Sitkin, S. B., Burt, R. S., & Camerer, C. (1998). Not so different after all: A cross-discipline view of trust. *Academy of Management Review, 23*(3), 393–404. Retrieved from Business Source Complete database.

Slusser, B. E. (2012). *Establishing social networks to effectively transfer tacit knowledge within U.S. subsidiary locations of Japanese-owned MNCs: A case study.* ProQuest LLC, UMI Number: 3503079.

van Wijk, R., Jansen, J. J. P., & Lyles, M. A. (2008). Inter- and intra-organizational knowledge transfer: A meta-analytic review and assessment of its antecedents and consequences. *Journal of Management Studies, 45*(4), 830–853. Retrieved from Business Source Complete database.

Yang, Z., Nguyen, V. T., & Le, P. B. (2018). Knowledge sharing serves as a mediator between collaborative culture and innovation capability: An empirical research. *Journal of Business & Industrial Marketing, 33*(7), 958–969.

11

CAPTURING TACIT KNOWLEDGE IN HUMAN RESOURCE MANAGEMENT

Bren Slusser

Capturing Organizational Tacit Knowledge

Trying to capture tacit knowledge can be difficult, particularly when there are barriers between the different teams throughout the organization. Regardless of any barriers that may exist, how can an organization effectively capture tacit knowledge? This is a difficult question to answer, since capturing tacit knowledge is next to impossible. The only way to effectively capture tacit knowledge is to do so between efficient and effective teams within an organization. Generally, this is done through face-to-face interactions, regardless of whether the teams are in person or remote. As stated in the last chapter, when leaders nurture a positive working environment where employees feel safe to share their knowledge and ideas, tacit knowledge will freely flow from one person to another, allowing for a deeper understanding of both the individual and the organization. Human resources can develop HR practices and activities that help foster the work environment so that tacit knowledge can freely flow. An important factor is ensuring that HR helps nurture the culture by being involved in the hiring of key personnel, as the culture of an organization starts from the top.

How HR Helps to Capture Tacit Knowledge

Capturing both explicit and tacit knowledge is very important for successfully accomplishing strategic goals within an organization. Through effective HRM systems, this knowledge can be captured to drive organizational outcomes as well as employees' attitudes and behaviors. For

DOI: 10.4324/9781003322894-13

example, HRM systems are used in different industries to promote activities like workplace safety practices or reward service quality. Furthermore, if knowledge behaviors, such as the acquisition and sharing of knowledge, are critical to the performance of teams, then it stands to reason that strategic HRM systems should be designed to capture knowledge, promoting such behaviors to exist (Chuang et al., 2016). Capturing this knowledge is done through various HR activities or practices, together with employees' skills and motivation. Some of these activities include training and development programs, effective performance management systems, and opportunities for face-to-face communication (Lui & Lui, 2011). Through these HR activities and practices, and through the support of HRM with the leaders, it will help to provide a comfortable yet thriving work environment where employees will want to and naturally share their tacit knowledge.

Going a step further in discussing tacit knowledge, there are different types of tacit knowledge, which may help HRM capture this knowledge. For instance, according to Jeck and Balaz (2020), they discuss four different types of tacit knowledge. This is important to recognize because having this knowledge can be instrumental in developing HR activities to capture tacit knowledge effectively and efficiently. "Embrained" tacit knowledge is identified as the type of knowledge that "helps individuals to recognize underlying patterns and organize information according to specific narratives" (Jeck & Balaz, 2020, p. 99). However, "embedded" tacit knowledge can help individuals understand routines, roles, and procedures without even thinking about it (Jeck & Balaz, 2020). The third type of tacit knowledge is referred to as "embodied" knowledge. This is the knowledge that is developed by doing the job, doing things without thinking about them (Jeck & Balaz, 2020). The fourth type of tacit knowledge is "encultured" knowledge. This is the tacit knowledge that is shared between team members, the culture and norms that have been set by these teams, and what are acceptable and unacceptable behaviors. As discussed with social network theory, socialization, and acculturation are developed through the trust of working together, depending on one another, and sharing tacit knowledge. HR has a tremendous responsibility and opportunity to capture all tacit knowledge, but this can only be done with the help of the leaders that are working within the social networks and the willingness of the team members to share the knowledge that exists.

As indicated by Chuang et al. (2016), those working in knowledge-intensive settings require a breadth of knowledge and skills; competencies go beyond technical knowledge but should also include teamwork knowledge and skills. Thus, to effectively capture this knowledge, it will require members of the team who have good interpersonal relationships with both the team members and throughout the organization to have collaborative interactions so that the team can capture and share new and valuable knowledge. Having good adaptation skills also helps in capturing knowledge, as team members are constantly searching for new information and knowledge. Human resources can help with this endeavor by bringing in candidates who possess diverse skills and by developing training programs that improve the ability to learn from others. However, it is important to note that traditional training programs may not be fully sufficient for building these competencies. Instead, the training programs should be designed when they are needed, compared to a canned training program. Human resources can also help to foster a positive, working environment that encourages sharing tacit knowledge through recognizing and rewarding teams that do share information, as this can reassure others to share what they know so that knowledge flows within the teams and throughout the organization (Chuang et al., 2016). Through the encouragement from HR to build social networks, a byproduct is the development and improvement of communication skills, which enhance the sharing of information between team members and others within the organization.

One thing that is important to acknowledge is that culture plays a significant role in facilitating the capture of tacit knowledge. As discussed by Hofstede (2010), there are symbols, heroes, rituals, and values within an organization. Symbols are the most superficial of the four indicators of culture, which include words, pictures, objects, or even gestures. Heroes are described as people that are admired, either alive or dead that an organization may use as models of the behavior they want exhibited or emulated. Rituals, on the other hand, are collective activities that are deemed essential to achieving the goals and objectives of the organization. Finally, values are the deepest exhibition of culture and are the "broad tendencies to prefer certain states of affairs over others" (Hofstede et al., 2010, p. 9). Values are acquired early in life, so hiring individuals with similar values is important for the culture of an organization. This is not the same as experience, skills, nationality, etc. You want to have different "cultures" within an organization, as that is what makes up the diversity of people, which contributes to the differentiation of ideas, thoughts, and experiences where creativity and innovation can thrive.

As the team is developed within an organization, there will be "in-groups" and "out-groups" (Hofstede et al., 2010). This is also an important distinction to identify and understand because these groups are where tacit knowledge will be able to be transferred for the good of the team and ultimately the organization. However, as Hofstede (2010) points out, teams can run the risk of an "us versus them" mentality, which would not be conducive to transferring tacit knowledge for creativity and innovation to flourish. HRM's responsibility for curbing this tendency would be to create an inclusive environment where people feel comfortable sharing their tacit knowledge both within and outside of the group.

While HRM can affect cultural changes, it is essential to recognize that cultural changes take time. Some of an organization's culture can be changed quickly, such as the practices, which are ways in which to do things, shifting the symbols, creating new rituals, and meeting new heroes (Hofstede et al., 2010). However, values are the hardest and longest to change. As Hofstede (2010) points out,

> the social game itself is not deeply changed by the changes in today's society. The unwritten rules for success, failure, belonging, and other key attributes of our lives remain similar. We need to fit in, to behave in ways that are acceptable to the groups to which we belong. Most changes concern the toys we use in playing the game.
>
> *(p. 20)*

Instilling fun into the culture is another way in which HRM can positively affect the culture within an organization. This can be seen in many ways, such as through friendly competitions, wearing logoed items of the organization, volunteering together, and creating a culture where successes are celebrated. Friendly competitions can help to make creativity and innovation fun while also providing an opportunity for employees to be recognized for their ideas. Instilling fun in the workplace does not need to detract from living up to the values and expectations of the organization. It helps with creating a culture where people are proud of their workplace, have fun through working together, and celebrate each other's successes, as well as cope with the workload and demands of the job. One example of fun is to create a calendar of events that has different fun monthly events where people come together, interact, and have fun. This is usually best done through a cross-functional committee that is formed by a representative from each department across the organization so that everyone has an opportunity to get involved. Thus, HRM will be instrumental in the involvement in cultural changes that occur and affect not only the organization but also a team, providing guidance to the leaders of the team and ensuring that the norms, rituals, and values are consistent with those of the organization to help create consistency and inclusion for all members of the team and organization. The impact on the teams, either positively or negatively, will affect the flow of tacit knowledge, which ultimately affects the team's performance and the creativity and innovation within those teams.

Work Environment and Tacit Knowledge Transfer

Social factors are important when discussing the work environment and transferring tacit knowledge, allowing creativity and innovation to flourish, and propelling an organization to higher market share and become an employer of choice. As has been discussed, social factors include the culture, artifacts, symbols, rituals, and values of an organization. There has been a lot of discussion about culture, but what exactly is culture within an organization? It is the "mental software [to include] ... the patterns of thinking, feeling, and acting" (Hofstede et al., 2010, p. 5) that resides inside the organization. Again, culture is developed from the top and is a learned behavior that is demonstrated throughout the organization, such as the norms, values, and rituals, and is carried out by the employees. Culture is different from personality in that culture is assigned to an organization, whereas personality is assigned to an individual (Hofstede et al., 2010). However, an individual's personality will impact the culture of an organization through their behaviors and traits.

Additionally, we must acknowledge that values are the deepest part of the culture in an organization, outlining tendencies of behavior that are preferred over others. A person's individual values are developed early in life, shaping how they act or respond to different circumstances. We learn values from our parents on what is right and wrong, rituals of activities that are done, such as eating with utensils, and symbols such as the language we speak, whether verbal or non-verbal, based on our culture (Hofstede et al., 2010). While the culture of an organization is first developed by the top leaders of the organization, an individual's values help to either keep the culture going or destroy the culture of the organization. This is where HR can come alongside the leaders of the organization to ensure that the culture is maintained and changed as needed. An organization's culture is very important for the working environment, to include the sharing of knowledge, employee engagement, and job satisfaction.

Creativity and innovation in the workplace are affected by a positive work environment, and if the culture is suffering within the organization, then tacit knowledge cannot flow freely, thereby decreasing creativity and innovation in the workplace. There can be positive pockets within an organization, but it does need the whole organization to be healthy for a positive culture and working environment and the continued success of the organization. There are some who may argue that creativity occurs in an atmosphere where there are few resources. While this is certainly reasonable and possible, it is through positive management practices that the autonomy to be creative, along with providing challenging and interesting work (Schepers & van den Berg, 2007), will be seen and tacit knowledge can be shared. It has also been acknowledged that "resources are the least significant antecedent" (Schepers & van den Berg, 2007, p. 409) for creativity to occur. Regardless, employee participation is vital to the success of creativity and innovation; otherwise, there is very little tacit knowledge being transferred among the employees. Again, the opportunity to be creative and innovative is very much affected by the culture of an organization. Culture is much more of a realistic picture for innovation to occur than the working environment, which is objective by nature (Schepers & van den Berg, 2007). It is also thought that adhocracies foster a creative environment because they adapt to the environment. Additionally, people are more "motivated to learn, experiment, and take risks" (Schepers & van den Berg, 2007, p. 412) in an adhocracy. An innovative culture will help to enhance creativity whereas cultures that are more controlled will stifle creativity. Even though this is largely dependent on an individual's work environment, it will affect the whole organization in one way or another (Schepers & van den Berg, 2007). Furthermore, when there are shared gains for reaching an organization's performance goals, employees are much more likely to give it their all, along with sharing their tacit knowledge to achieve the goals and objectives of the organization. Employees want to know what's in it for them, not just how it will line the pockets of senior leadership. Personal goals and objectives can be difficult to achieve, let alone the organization's goals and objectives, thus employees are less motivated to achieve them if there is no implicit opportunity for them to share in the successes of the organization. This is shown through some sort of compensation, like a bonus, and other compensation-related items, such as company stock. Not only does this help to motivate employees to achieve their personal goals and objectives, but when they see the organization reach the targeted performance outcomes and receive some sort of compensation for helping in this endeavor, they become more motivated to work harder to reach increasingly difficult goals (Ulrich, 1997).

Another way in which HR can impact the working environment and allow tacit knowledge to transfer among the employees is by ensuring that employees are engaged, such as through setting goals, making decisions, and appraising results. A positive working environment necessitates that employees are participative and free to express their ideas, but it also requires a high level of performance standards. Participative management is instrumental in allowing creativity to occur, fostering a working atmosphere that is autonomous with a sense of ownership and control, allowing the freedom to find and test new ideas (Schepers & van den Berg, 2007), but also done with some regulation to ensure that everyone is working towards the same goals and objectives. HR can help in this endeavor by coaching leaders who are less willing to allow autonomy. When leaders are closely "facilitating" the teams' efforts, this can produce feelings of distrust, and their team members will become more guarded about sharing their tacit knowledge with others or with the leaders. This behavior by either the leaders or the team members can be devastating to the creativity and innovation that would naturally occur within the teams.

Additionally, when employees feel like they are free to share their ideas and feel valued, employee contributions go up (Ulrich, 1997). HR is instrumental in helping to achieve this by playing a "critical role in developing this employee-firm relationship" (Ulrich, 1997, p. 126) and by listening to and representing the employees' interests and needs. It is important to understand that HR is not the sole owner of employee engagement. This is a collective effort between leadership and HR; leaders have accountability for the employees' needs, while HR assists in these endeavors. More specifically, HR assists the leadership with knowing and understanding when employees are either underutilized or overwhelmed with their work. As Ulrich (1997) explains, the demand for employees has increased "to be more global, more customer-responsive, more flexible, more learning-oriented, more team-driven, more productive and so on" (p. 128). It is important to ensure that the employees' well-being is considered, because if you have underutilized employees, they will want to leave and find someplace that will value them more, taking with them their tacit knowledge, which would have a huge impact on the organization. Equally important is ensuring that those who are overwhelmed and/or have too much on their plate are supported so that they don't leave to find someplace where they won't feel taken advantage of, and when they walk out the door, all their tacit knowledge goes with them, impacting the organization. One way in which to do this is when there are organizational changes. Leaders need to not only focus on the "what" but also the "why" and communicate that to their team members. When team members feel like part of the process and are given knowledge about the business, they thus know and understand the "why" behind the decisions. This tremendously helps with buy-in, where the changes are more likely to be successful, resulting in greater organizational performance.

Furthermore, HR needs to have their pulse on what is going on and how people are feeling and share with leadership when there are problems arising. One way in which to do this would be through stay interviews. These are interviews conducted with current employees to gauge how they're feeling, what is going on, and to gather information to identify any problems that exist and then work with the leadership to fix them. Another way to gather data is through surveys. However, it is critical that when information is obtained, the organization share the results, including the plan for rectifying any problems that were discovered. Otherwise, people will not share how they are really feeling, which hurts the organization in the long run. Additionally, when people feel valued, there is more collaboration and teamwork, thus helping individual efforts to turn into extraordinary successes for the team. This is another example of how collaboration and teamwork leverage the team's talent in using creativity and innovation to turn something into a superior collective achievement (Ulrich, 1997), which also increases the team's tacit knowledge and is extremely important for the organization's long-term success.

Social Learning Theories

When looking at social learning theories, knowledge sharing is linked to workplace creativity. Thus, where there is a focus on employee interactions, there will be more opportunities and expectations to share knowledge, thus intensifying the creativity and innovation occurring (Schepers & van den Berg, 2007). As was discussed in Chapter 10, social network theory is an important theory to understand and is defined as the strength of the ties between individuals, such as the time spent together, reciprocity of knowledge, intimacy, and emotional intensity (Lin, 2007). Social networks are embedded within organizations and are a complex system of social relations amongst team members, whether in the same department or outside of the department, facilitating an environment for tacit knowledge to be transferred (Lin, 2007). The establishment of social networks is important for the transfer of knowledge to occur and is better than databases in transferring knowledge (Lodhi & Ahmad, 2010). Social networks will be established when there is mutual trust based on the interactions between co-workers, and trust is a prerequisite for tacit knowledge to be transferred (Lin, 2007). Managers need to recognize that the transfer of knowledge is important and is the "major portion of their organizational wealth" (Lodhi & Ahmad, 2010, p. 120), as are the knowledge assets held by the individuals within the organization, along with these assets being hard to "trace or control" (Lodhi & Ahmad, 2010, p. 120).

Social networks are a link to the employee's and organization's performance, providing advantages, such as assimilation, or disadvantages, where employees leave the organization with valuable knowledge (Sykes et al., 2009). A social network analysis was conducted by Cross and Parker (2004), identifying how all employees are affected by the social networks established and embedded within an organization. "These networks are not depicted on any formal chart, but they are intricately intertwined with an organization's performance, the way it develops and executes strategy, and its ability to innovate" (Cross & Parker, 2004, p. 3). These networks also have an impact on a person's productivity, learning, and career success.

Again, the establishment of these social networks often surprises executives as to the level of cooperation employees engage in within these networks (Cross & Parker, 2004).

In any organization, you have many varying levels of social networks throughout the organization. More specifically, Millar and Choi (2009) contend that it is through knowledge sharing in these varying levels of social networks within the larger networks that will develop the trust and shared norms in which tacit knowledge can be transferred. More specifically, through the establishment of social networks, they would naturally develop their own standards and set of norms to communicate for the transfer of tacit knowledge effectively and efficiently. These social networks would still be dependent on developing and maintaining trust (Millar & Choi, 2009), which is one of the most important requirements for successfully transferring tacit knowledge. It is advisable for leaders and HR to not leave the different levels of social networks to chance but rather to have a pulse on them, particularly to identify problems or disconnects that may occur within the social networks, along with the patterns of communication that naturally happen (Cross & Parker, 2004). As mentioned before, tacit knowledge is difficult to transfer and is done so through unconscious interaction through personal contact and trust (Schepers & van den Berg, 2007). Thus, the encouragement of face-to-face meetings, whether in person or virtually, allows for the development of those personal relationships where tacit knowledge can be transferred. The growth of communities of practice with the help and encouragement of HR will be instrumental in encouraging employees to share their experiences, insights, and tools within the organization. When experienced employees share their experiences, insights, and tools with inexperienced or newer employees, knowledge can be transferred to create shared experiences, which increases tacit knowledge. Additionally, supporting one another fosters creativity and innovation through open communication and trust, allowing individuals to be exposed to a variety of ideas and share information in a safe environment (Schepers & van den Berg, 2007).

Transferring tacit knowledge is part of the social network that is developed through organizational citizenship behavior (OCB) and may be part of social exchange processes among employees in organizations (Schepers & van den Berg, 2007). More specifically, employees are more likely to transfer tacit knowledge when their networks are social exchanges versus economic exchanges, or transactional in nature. Moreover, cooperation within the team enhances social exchanges, but everyone must be committed to being open, honest, and transparent (Schepers & van den Berg, 2007). Leadership and HR will be instrumental in ensuring that there are opportunities for social networks to be developed through a positive work environment, where team members are treated fairly by the organization; thus, the team members will be more open about sharing their tacit knowledge, leading to increased creativity and innovation.

Leader Involvement

Leader involvement in the transfer of tacit knowledge is very important. HR can help with this endeavor by training and providing development opportunities for leaders so that they know how to draw out tacit knowledge from their direct reports. However, this is not an easy task; transferring tacit knowledge is generally something that occurs without one consciously knowing that it is even being transferred. This is because completing tasks or collaborating with team members is subconscious but something where tacit knowledge is gained and shared. Leaders have the responsibility to draw out from their direct reports the knowledge that the team has so that tacit knowledge can be shared to provide a more effective and efficient workplace, not to mention a cohesive group working towards the same organizational goals and objectives. Again, it is important for the leaders to provide an autonomous working environment whereby there is a sense of freedom and control over the team member's work, which allows for creativity and innovation to occur and tacit knowledge to be transferred (Schepers & van den Berg, 2007). One thing that could impact the transfer of tacit knowledge is the hierarchy within an organization, as this can hinder collaboration, depending on the channels for communication (Slusser, 2012). More specifically, where some networks will operate similarly to those of the reporting relationships, such as top-down or bottom-up, some structures are more reliant on the informal development of social networks between team members, allowing for tacit knowledge to freely transfer between the cultures. Therefore, it will be important for organizations to establish less formal social networks that allow tacit knowledge to be transferred more freely between cultures. It will also be important to know the role of managers in social networks (Cross & Parker, 2004).

However, someone can share the knowledge that they have, but the person receiving the information or knowledge will form their own tacit knowledge "based on their previous experience, knowledge, skills, and mental models" (Matošková et al., 2013, p. 4). Some different ways to help with transferring tacit knowledge are done in both formal and informal ways. As was discussed above, some learning is done formally, but a lot of the learning and transferring of tacit knowledge is done in an informal setting. HR can help with the formal development programs, but it is through working together that the most tacit knowledge will be transferred between team members. When initiating formal development programs, it should be relevant to what the individuals need to learn and retain; otherwise, there is not going to be a lot of tacit knowledge transferred or remembered (Matošková et al., 2013). Matošková et al. (2013) purport that for the transfer of tacit knowledge to be successful, "it is important that bilateral knowledge fits the specific context…that the efficiency of the tacit knowledge used is influenced by context, concrete circumstances, and the setting" (p. 5). Another important factor is that when there is reciprocal trust, interpersonal relationships, and respect between the team members, particularly with the leaders, it allows for an easier flow of tacit knowledge to transfer to one another.

Other factors that come into play include physical proximity and social proximity. Physical proximity is important because it is not just the verbal information that is shared, but it is also the non-verbal information that is shared through observing and face-to-face contact (Matošková et al., 2013). This is particularly important when in a diverse workforce, such as low and high context cultures working together since they "communicate" differently, as was discussed in Chapter 10. When discussing social proximity, this is specifically referring to the shared values, such as norms, culture, and customs of the organization where tacit knowledge can be transferred. Furthermore, this is where HR needs to have a large presence by helping to foster the culture, whereby norms and customs of the organization are developed and lived through the employees of the organization. According to Matošková et al. (2013), social proximity also helps with reducing communication barriers, where these barriers can create misunderstandings and fears of misusing knowledge. Thus, support for sharing knowledge, whether formal or informal, is important and something that human resources and leaders need to be cognizant of for tacit knowledge transfer to successfully occur.

Management effectiveness also affects a team's performance, which impacts organizational performance and competitiveness. The longevity of the leaders and the team members within an organization also impacts how much tacit knowledge has been transferred. For example, team members who have been around a while will have tacit knowledge from previous work projects and teams they have worked with where knowledge was shared. When a new member of the team is introduced, or a new leader, this changes the whole dynamic of the team; thus, trust and respect will have to be earned by the new members, which impacts the transfer of tacit knowledge and ultimately the effectiveness of the team. This is another great opportunity for HR to help the organization—by ensuring that the human capital is managed properly and that the teams have the personnel needed with the right mix of knowledge, skills, and abilities (Mostafa et al., 2013). A lack of expert personnel can create obstacles for the teams and the organization. Thereby, "evaluating and categorizing whole employees based on their tacit knowledge, [the] human resource management (HRM) department can determine the best or the most effective HR practices for management of them" (Mostafa et al., 2013, p. 377). As we all know, HRM cannot do this alone, but together with leadership, HR practices can be quite effective in evaluating and categorizing employees and their level of tacit knowledge. However, in doing this, HRM needs to be cognizant of not creating a stifling, too-regulated environment where people will not want to share their tacit knowledge.

Another challenge would be unintentionally creating a problem with equity and inclusion. For instance, when employees feel valued, safe, whether physically or emotionally, are engaged, and can be authentic, then the leader is creating an atmosphere for DE&I to flourish. As noted by Northouse (2021), this is a good blueprint for leaders and HRM to follow to provide inclusion within the organization. Otherwise, there will be repercussions within the team and ultimately the organization that could have been avoided. While a leader may not intentionally create inequity or inclusion problems, it is beneficial for HR to educate leaders on cultural differences and to know and understand what each person's ethical ideals are and that everyone is different. Specifically, "different cultures have different rules of conduct, and as a result, leadership behaviors that one culture deems ethical may not be viewed the same way by another culture" (Northouse, 2021, p. 319). Thus, it is imperative to know and understand the diversity of thoughts, ideas, and experiences within an organization. Otherwise, there will be less tacit knowledge transfer, resulting in less growth, less creativity, and less innovation, subsequently decreasing organizational performance.

Works Cited

Chuang, C.-I., Jackson, S. E., & Jiang, Y. (2016). Can knowledge-intensive teamwork be managed? Examining the roles of HRM systems, leadership, and tacit knowledge. *Journal of Management, 42*(2), 524–554.

Cross, R., & Parker, A. (2004). *The hidden power or social networks: Understanding how work really gets done in organizations.* Harvard Business School Publishing.

Hofstede, G., Hofstede, G. J., & Minkov, M. (2010). *Cultures and organizations: Software of the mind: Intercultural cooperation and its importance for survival.* McGraw Hill Corporation, 3rd ed.

Jeck, T., & Balaz, V. (2020). Geographies of tacit knowledge transfer: Evidence from the European co-authorship network. *The Czech Academy of Sciences, Institute of Geonics, 28*(2), 98–111. Journal homepage: http://www.geonika.cz/mgr.html; doi: 10.2478/mgr-2020-0008

Lin, C.-P. (2007). To share or not to share: Modeling tacit knowledge sharing, its mediators and antecedents. *Journal of Business Ethics, 70,* 411–428. doi: 10.1007/s10551-006-9199-0

Lodhi, S. A., & Ahmad, M. (2010). Dynamics of voluntary knowledge sharing in organizations. *Pakistan Journal of Commerce & Social Sciences, 4*(2), 120–132. Retrieved from Business Source Complete database.

Lui, N.-C., & Lui, M,-S. (2011). Human resource practices and individual knowledge-sharing behavior: an empirical study for Taiwanese R&D professionals. *The International Journal of Human Resource Management, 22*(4), 981–997.

Matošková, J., Řeháčková, H., Sobotková, E., Polčáková, M., Jurásek, M., Gregar, A., & Švec, V. (2013). Facilitating leader tacit knowledge acquisition. *Journal of Competitiveness, 5*(1), 3–15.

Millar, C. C. J. M., & Choi, C. J. (2009). Networks, social norms and knowledge sub-networks. *Journal of Business Ethics*, 90, 565–574. doi: 10.1007/s10551-010-0607-x

Mostafa J., Peyman, A., & Mozhden, N. (2013). Classification of human resources based on measurement of tacit knowledge: An empirical study in Iran. *Journal of Management Development, 32*(4), 376–403.

Northouse, P. G. (2021). *Introduction to leadership* (5th ed.). Sage Publishing.

Schepers, P., & van den Berg, P. T. (2007). Social factors of work environment creativity. *Journal of Business and Psychology, 21*(3), 407–428.

Slusser, B. E. (2012). *Establishing social networks to effectively transfer tacit knowledge within U.S. subsidiary locations of Japanese-owned MNCs: A case study.* ProQuest LLC, UMI Number: 3503079.

Sykes, T. A., Venkatesh, V., & Gosain, S. (2009). Model of acceptance with peer support: A social network perspective to understand employees' system use. *MIS Quarterly, 33*(2), 371–393. Retrieved from Business Source Complete database.

Ulrich, D. (1997). *Human resource champions: The next agenda for adding value and delivering results.* Harvard Business School Press.

12

HUMAN RESOURCE MANAGEMENT FOSTERS ENGAGEMENT RESULTING IN CREATIVITY AND INNOVATION

Bren Slusser

How Engagement Fosters Creativity and Innovation in the Workplace

Knowledge-based innovation is seen as a "super star" of entrepreneurship and is what most people think about when they are thinking about innovation—the creative ideas that get all the attention but have the longest lead time—from thought to fruition (Drucker, 1986). There are some that take years to perfect and get out there, but there are others that the lead time is not as long, and the reason for this is that ideas are generally not just one person bringing the creative and innovative ideas to life, as it is a conglomerate or convergence of ideas and knowledge that make it possible. This convergence of knowledge-based innovation and creativity (ideas) is what helps the magic to occur. Taking the tacit knowledge of those involved and putting them together (the convergence) is how it happens, through careful analysis and a clear understanding of the strategic vision of the organization. Otherwise, the energy and knowledge shared could be fruitless.

As Drucker (1986) indicates, there are three major focuses for knowledge-based innovation, which are: a complete system; market focus; and occupying a strategic position. The first focus is a complete system, and this is exactly what it sounds like, a complete system. This would be a clear direction, time to work together to develop new ideas by exchanging tacit knowledge, and then developing a plan and process to implement these new ideas. This leads to the second focus: market focus. Through the creation of new knowledge-based innovations, the organization can create a market

DOI: 10.4324/9781003322894-14

focus—identifying who will benefit from the knowledge-based innovations and creating a market for them. The last focus is to occupy a strategic position, thus focusing on a key function, such as mastery of the idea, marketing, or whatever the organization chooses to keep the market share developed by these knowledge-based innovations. Basically, what will keep or bring the organization increased engagement for better performance, resulting in achieving strategic goals and objectives and increasing market share? It is the responsibility of the leaders to create a positive atmosphere for the teams so that their knowledge-based creativity and innovation can flourish while ensuring that the direction they are going is in line with the strategic goals of the organization. HR's involvement is to coach the leaders to pay attention to the signals their teams give, such as not being engaged or when conflict occurs, as well as work with the leaders to ensure everyone is moving in the same direction, moving towards the same goals. You may be asking yourself what this has to do with engagement, particularly as it pertains to creativity and innovation. Knowledge-based innovation is extremely important, and if employees are not engaged or there is no focus or a direction that has been set forth by the strategic goals outlined by the organization, then employees become less interested, and engagement suffers, affecting the creativity and innovation teams can produce.

Engagement is incredibly important, and when it is low, then everything suffers, affecting the sharing of knowledge, creativity and innovation, and ultimately the organization's performance. In a recent article in the SHRM magazine written by Meinert (2023), there is evidence to show that engagement is low within organizations, with "just 31% of workers in the U.S. and Canada [who] feel engaged at work" (p. 77). Low engagement impacts morale, which ultimately affects innovation and creativity in the workplace. HR is working to try to rectify this problem by incorporating more creative ways of increasing engagement and morale. Some of these things include "celebrations, comedy, wellness programs and volunteer activities" (Meinert, 2023, p. 77); however, it has yet to be seen if the results of this are truly increasing morale and engagement. There are many ways in which to help with this effort, but valuing employees and treating them well is so important, which includes celebrating employees, showing them gratitude, and just being kind (Meinert, 2023).

Another area to discuss is remote employees. While there has been remote work available for some time, this way of doing business became a necessity when the world experienced the COVID-19 pandemic, where everyone was forced to stay home and work remotely. There is a lot of discussion about whether continuing this trend is good for teams as well as for the organization. Not being face-to-face can impact the development of the social networks that are so important for sharing tacit knowledge, whereby creativity and innovation can take place. However, there are many industries that have continued remote work, but there are many that are requiring employees to come back to the office, either full-time or on a hybrid-type schedule. It is important, though, to know and understand that workers want flexibility in their work schedule, where work needs to fit within their lives, not their lives to fit into work. This is a significant change from years past; when people were living to work, now they work to live—work is not where you are but what you do. Since the pandemic, many more organizations (approximately 73%) have or are creating a hybrid work schedule, with only 19% requiring employees to come back to work at a physical location (Agovino, 2023). With the hybrid work schedule, approximately 70% of employees have a stronger sense of loyalty to the employer, compared to 69% of in-person employees and 59% of complete remote employees (Agovino, 2023). While there is not much significance between the hybrid and in-person employee, it does indicate that 100% completely remote employees are not more loyal to their employers, which is significant given the backlash some employers are receiving for requiring either a hybrid or completely in-person work schedule. Even with this new type of working environment, while it does allow for more collaboration, fun, and flexibility for employees to balance their lives and work responsibilities, there are also some challenges that exist.

More specifically, technology is important when you have remote and hybrid workplaces. One way to do this is to change the way in which the office is structured to be more inclusive, such as by having half-moon-type tables so it looks like remote individuals are in the room, versus the traditional square table where video conferencing can be awkward and impersonal and it is hard to see everyone in the room (Agovino, 2023). A redesign of the workspace really helps to facilitate collaboration and flexibility, which lend themselves naturally to creativity and innovation. For instance, not having an office for each person but a workspace where teams can get together and collaborate creates a more engaging, fun, and flexible environment, even if some of the team members are remote. Another challenge is designing the schedule so that it is fair across the board for the hybrid workers. It will be important that team members can get together in the office to interact. A solution is to allow managers and employees to determine their own schedules. However, this could also create unintended inequity amongst the different teams, as there are some managers who embrace a hybrid schedule more than others (Agovino, 2023). Managers and employees need to also be cognizant that finding the right schedule for their teams may take some time and be flexible about shifting the schedules when necessary. Still, implementing a hybrid schedule provides the opportunity for teams to collaborate in a face-to-face atmosphere, versus only being on video calls with each other, whereby they can share their knowledge and experience through these collaborative meetings, deepening their working relationships. While it is possible for remote teams to collaborate and share their tacit knowledge, it could take longer to establish these relationships where trust is developed to feel comfortable enough to share their valuable knowledge. Having these teams get together face-to-face sometime during the year, whether it is once a year or once a quarter, some face-to-face interaction is preferable.

Managing remote employees could prove to be a difficult task for both the managers and HR, particularly when discussing engagement. When you have remote employees, tapping into creativity and innovation can be more challenging, but it is not impossible. One way to do this is to ensure that there are ways for teams as well as all employees to stay connected, whether this is through a chat program such as Google Chat, Slack, or any of the other instant messaging programs available. These different channels that are created within the organization are essential for staying connected, which encourages tacit knowledge to be transferred among all employees, not just the remote employees. Some ideas for HR professionals to engage employees through these channels to help them stay connected are doing fun activities, such as a question of the day, or promoting health and wellness through these channels, like friendly competitions with prizes (Meinert, 2023). These channels are to create a sense of belonging, which ultimately fosters an atmosphere for sharing tacit knowledge whereby creativity and innovation can be fruitful. Another one of the challenges that exists is how leaders can ensure that these remote employees are performing to the expectations set forth by the leader, while also ensuring that if any of these remote employees are hourly, they are not being overworked or not working their full scheduled hours.

One way in which to mitigate this is to monitor their work, and is done through technology-based programs. It is imperative that before a system is implemented, the employer be transparent in their communication and explain the reason for putting a monitoring system in place. This can reduce some of the resistance employees will naturally feel towards this type of system. There are many different types of systems, but the employer needs to assess the system that will be best for their organization, such as a system to identify productivity, performance, and employee engagement. There are some systems that can be as simple as having a computerized time-keeping system for hourly employees to clock in and out on a computerized time-keeping system. However, this does not necessarily ensure that the employees are working their scheduled hours, but it does help with making sure that the organization is not violating any wage and hour laws. Anyone can clock in and out of the electronic timesheet system but keeping them engaged to perform their daily tasks can be quite another obstacle to maneuvering around.

When implementing a monitoring system, this can help with increasing accountability, process improvement, helpful performance feedback, and workload management (Naegle-Piazza, 2023). In discussing the different ways monitoring can help, the first subject to discuss is increased accountability. Making the employees aware of the system is incredibly important, and when they know that there is a system in place, this can trigger employees to be more mindful about how they spend their time, engaging in work-related activities versus personal activities that take advantage of productivity. Another way monitoring helps is through process improvements by providing robust analytics to different processes, which would not otherwise have been identified or detected if the work was being done in-person. Monitoring can also help with providing timely and helpful performance feedback through the data that is captured, showing a comprehensive analysis of an employee's work contributions. One of the other important ways monitoring can help is through workload management, identifying when someone is overworked or does not have enough tasks to complete during the day. Regardless of how much or little an organization monitors the work activity of their remote employees, HR will need to ensure that whatever system is implemented, there is a lot of communication surrounding the system, how it will work, and what it means for the employees in their workday. The last thing employees want is to know that their employer is looking over their shoulder with every keystroke that is made, which reduces the trust between the employer and employees along with potentially and unintentionally capturing personal information from a protected class of employees, or activities that employees engage in after-hours (Naegle-Piazza, 2023). While keystroke monitoring is one type of monitoring that can occur, this is not the ideal way in which to monitor remote employees' work. Additionally, this may affect morale, as the employees are left feeling like they are not trusted, which could reduce the collaboration, productivity, and transfer of knowledge between team members. As mentioned above, there are many different types of monitoring, and the organization needs to choose the best system for their organization and employees, making sure that HR is involved in the decision-making process to ensure compliance is followed. Furthermore, HR will need to develop a strong privacy policy that discloses the type of data that is being collected so that employees know and understand that the information being collected is not designed to monitor what they do in their personal lives, but only the work-related data is being collected, and again, there must be transparent communication about why the monitoring is occurring (Naegle-Piazza, 2023).

Another way HR can help an organization generate opportunities for tacit knowledge to be transferred for innovation and creativity to occur is by allowing time for innovation. This is particularly important for remote teams. For instance, one way is to allow the teams to meet in person at least once a year. Here, business problems can be presented, and teams can work on solving these problems together, which fosters an atmosphere for creativity and innovation to flourish. Fostering an atmosphere and culture of transparency, which starts at the top, allows for employees to share ideas and their tacit knowledge, strengthening trust and collaboration among the teams (Meinert, 2023). While meeting more often in person is ideal, this is not always an option for 100% remote employees to do or may not be affordable for the organization. However, with HR's help, this could be implemented into the strategic plan of the organization to embed this activity into the budget to ensure it takes place. Not only will this promote collaboration within the teams, but morale and engagement will increase, which also increases the knowledge being transferred within the team.

Activities to Help Foster Engagement

Activities that HR is involved in and develops based on organizational needs and strategic goals include updating organizational design and development; compensation and benefits; updating policies and procedures; the development of both the employee and the leader; and ensuring that the recruitment and selection process is inclusive and diverse. These activities focus on aspects of an organization's capabilities and are aligned with organizational goals (Lawler & Morhman, 2003). Thus, the activities that are developed reflect the importance of designing organizations to reach the potential of their employees' knowledge which is reflected in the creativity and innovation produced. This knowledge adds value to the organization in the sense that if employees leave the organization, they are taking with them valuable information that cannot be retrieved. Developing positive working relationships with leaders to increase engagement is also critically important. HR's focus needs to be on the alignment of HR activities with the organization's strategic goals. Building on the tacit knowledge within the organization increases employee competencies, creativity, and innovation, which has an overall impact on the organization's performance.

It is common knowledge that an employee's knowledge and skills are known as human capital. This is very important and valuable to an organization. Organizations invest in their employees through training, education, and well-being programs. It is also the most expensive aspect of an organization. So, you may be asking yourself what the relationship is between HR, knowledge management, and organizational performance.

They are all interrelated and acknowledging this as an organization is crucial to harnessing the tacit knowledge that employees have, as it has a tremendous impact on an organization's performance. More specifically, this is accomplished through a high commitment to HR practices, leading to improved personal performance, higher engagement, and wasting less time and resources, with increased creativity and innovation directly impacting the organization's performance (Kokkaew et al., 2022). It is also critical for HR activities to be aligned with the organization's strategies; otherwise, these activities will work against everything that the organization is trying to achieve. These activities include things such as cross-training, sharing of tacit knowledge and ways in which to do this, competitive wages, and promotions from within the organization. This is not an exhaustive list, but these are ways in which HR can help engagement, which ultimately affects creativity and innovation. As indicated by their research, Kokkaew et al. (2022) contend that HRM has a significant and positive impact on knowledge management. Tacit knowledge is difficult to share, but for the creation of innovative ideas to occur, there needs to be a large amount of tacit knowledge that is shared (Lui & Lui, 2022). This can be done through uninhibited brainstorming and collaborative problem-solving, creating the opportunity to be creative and innovative by sharing their tacit knowledge amongst the team.

As we have discussed, it is important to ensure that whatever activities are developed for engagement, it must align with the strategic goals and objectives of the organization. HRM should be involved in the strategic planning of the organization to ensure that whatever HRM's goals have been identified are aligned with the overall goals of the organization and help the organization achieve these goals through the activities implemented. HR cannot develop plans in a vacuum; otherwise, they will not mean anything to anyone other than those within the HR department, creating frustration all around. The outcome of integrating HR activities within the overall strategic goals and objectives is part of the framework for ensuring the success of strategic business planning and ultimately positively affecting business results through higher engagement. However, it must be acknowledged that there are no quick fixes, and engaging in such activities to try to create immediate results will backfire, as improvement activities take time and commitment (Ulrich, 1997). Benchmarking is an activity that has been around for quite some time but does not necessarily provide organizations with the best way in which to change or improve, as benchmarking is a snapshot of a single item versus what it took to get to that spot, or how it fits within the overall strategic goals of the organization. Furthermore, what works for one organization may not work well for another. It is like jumping from fad to fad in trying to lose weight—you need to stick with what works best for your organization versus trying to ensure a quick fix, or just because it is the "rage" right now does not mean it is the best way forward for the organization. Change is inevitable, and identifying and adapting the activities that work best for the organization will allow employees to be creative and innovative, which may be unique to the organization and ultimately increase engagement.

Leadership Engagement Responsibilities and HRM Guidance

Leadership's engagement responsibilities are very important within an organization. As one respondent indicated, "my manager encourages open communication and expects respect between all team members, along with celebrating engagement, correcting disrespect, and sharing learning materials." This type of behavior from leadership is critical for the sharing of tacit knowledge and to keep team members engaged at work, as well as for the team members to know and understand the behavior that is acceptable, and that leadership is fostering a mutually beneficial working atmosphere. Tacit knowledge plays a critical role in creativity and innovation in the workplace, which occurs mainly through face-to-face interactions, sharing tacit knowledge to solve problems, and increasing innovation and creativity (Deyong et al., 2007). By engaging in these knowledge-creation activities, this will help to create commitment to the team, the department, the division, and the organization. Thus, leaders and HR have an important role in fostering an atmosphere where team members feel confident and comfortable sharing their tacit knowledge, forming effective social networks, and guiding the direction of the teams to ensure that they are aligned with the department and organizational goals and objectives.

The leaders' role and their involvement in social networks that are developed within teams can be viewed differently by the leaders themselves, and their team members. Some leaders believe that they foster effective communication, such as face-to-face first, then telephone, and then email/instant messaging. When there is a language barrier, leaders should encourage their team members to follow up on any verbal communication with a written form of communication. This can help to reduce the opportunities for misunderstandings to occur, since misunderstandings could lead to bigger problems in both the long and short term. Leaders also need to ensure that they are setting expectations regarding communication and the sharing of tacit knowledge. This can be done through cross-training and cross-functional teams, confirming that the sharing of tacit knowledge is imperative for the success of the project or task.

Another area that HRM can help with engagement and the leaders' role in engagement is understanding how the leaders view their roles in establishing these social networks whereby tacit knowledge is transferred. These teams should also be cross-functional, providing for a diverse background of individuals sharing their experience, knowledge, and skills with and within the team (Nonaka & Takeuchi, 1995). More specifically, in the research conducted, the leaders, regardless of culture, took different approaches to helping establish these social networks. For instance, some leaders believed that communication was very important in helping to establish social networks, while other believed that teaming individuals together would be most helpful (Slusser, 2012). However, many of the team members did not believe that the leaders were all that involved in the development of social networks, indicating that the manager is only for work distribution and that they do not focus on the cultural differences within the teams. Taking a secondary role for the leaders in the development of social networks could be seen as a positive, as they only step in when communication between team members has been interrupted or problems arise (Slusser, 2012). Another way of looking at this is that leaders hire individuals who are self-motivated and proactive, allowing the team members to develop these relationships, stepping in when there are issues or problems, helping them through these challenges, and then releasing them to continue to develop the social networks, sharing their tacit knowledge, which increases engagement. HRM's involvement is to coach the leader through these challenges, but to get more involved when there are some of the more difficult challenges, as well as provide professional development to both the leaders and the team members on an ongoing basis, which helps to solidify teamwork and these social networks, reducing opportunities for stifling challenges. It is important, though, that the leaders and HRM do not micromanage or be completely involved in solving problems, but to keep a pulse on the dynamics of the team to ensure that everything is cohesive.

It must not be diminished though that leaders play a large role in the development of social networks, as they possess the lines of communication between lower-level employees and upper-level management, communicating project expectations and organizational goals. The role of the leader is not to be the only one providing great ideas, but to create an environment that fosters an atmosphere where ideas can flow through their team members. The leaders also need to ensure that the teams are not moving in a direction that does not line up with the organizational goals, but to help maintain the integrity of the knowledge being shared, the ideas that are flowing, and the social networks that are being developed. While the autonomy of the teams would allow them to perform many different functions, many times the teams will set their own task boundaries by which they will perform at higher levels, achieving the goals set forth by the leaders. One thing to also point out is that knowledge will be shared with those outside of these social networks, creating a redundancy of information and maybe with individuals who do not need the information at the time, such as the leaders of the social networks. While some may think this would be an inefficient business practice, it is quite important. Redundancy of information means "the existence of information that goes beyond the immediate operational requirements of organizational members" (Nonaka & Takeuchi, 1995, p. 80). Sharing redundant information promotes the transfer of tacit knowledge—not only is someone getting the information, but they are also learning and receiving the knowledge that the person delivering the redundant information is trying to convey. As the message continues to be repeated, more tacit knowledge is captured by the person receiving the information. The redundancy of information also helps to facilitate the exchange of information between lower-level and upper-level employees (Nonaka & Takeuchi, 1995).

HRM's Guidance to Right-Size Engagement

HR has an obligation to the employer and the employees to create a better experience. This occurs through many different types of activities. You may be asking yourself what this looks like. Some of these activities have already been discussed, but to implement needed activities for the organization, HR needs to guide leaders to right-size engagement. For instance, HR must prioritize activities to create a positive employee experience. This may require some changes to occur within the organization. Whatever change needs to occur, HR must not only demonstrate the need for the change but also align the systems to support the change (Merlini, 2023). One way in which to do this and prove to the senior leadership of this need is through data. Not only does HR need to convince the senior leadership of the change, but HR needs to get them to feel the need for change, not just understand it. When there is data tied to the rational and emotional sides of leadership, then they are more likely to embrace the ideas and support the changes needed (Merlini, 2023). HR has the tools and data to determine what is needed to increase engagement and the employee experience. By leveraging the data, HR can ensure that professional development programs are targeting effective leadership skills to align with the training and development needed for the employees for effective change (Merlini, 2023).

One area that gets reduced when an organization is experiencing tough times is training and development. However, training and development are very important to an organization to attract and retain top talent, increase engagement, and ultimately increase the organization's performance. According to research conducted, if leadership does not allow adequate time to train others, spending that time to share their knowledge, then team members will become frustrated and disengaged (Lui & Lui, 2011). HRM's help in right-sizing engagement is to provide feedback to the leadership that carving out time for training, or simply showing others how to do something, is important as that is where the transfer of knowledge will occur, and if there is not allowable time, and training is just expected to occur, then the team members will not have faith in the leadership to provide opportunities for training and development, leading to reduced engagement. However, it is also important to be cognizant that the leaders can foster an atmosphere that is conducive for team members to share their knowledge, because if team members do not see the value in sharing their tacit knowledge, it will not occur. Due to the expectancy-value theory, individuals are aware of the goals to be attained, and are willing to share their tacit knowledge only if they perceive the benefit of sharing this knowledge, along with their belief that the knowledge that they possess is worth sharing with their team members (Lui & Lui, 2011). This is significant because even though HRM and leaders create an atmosphere for creativity and innovation to flourish amongst team members, if the team members do not feel their tacit knowledge is important or safe to share, then their knowledge will not be shared, thus all efforts will be diminished.

Another piece of the puzzle is to create an atmosphere where employees are not overworked or have unfocused goals. When there is too much on employees' plates, their focus is stretched, impacting their ability and time to be creative and innovative. One way to mitigate this problem is to make sure that the goals to be achieved are overarching, with one theme to focus on (Ulrich, 1997). Sometimes reducing the workload is not possible, so HR needs to work with the leaders to develop resources to help the employees manage their time and feel like they are in control without diminishing collaboration and communication within the social networks and the organization.

Fostering working relationships allows team members to naturally share information, leading to increased engagement, thus affecting creativity and innovation within the team. Communication barriers prevent this from happening, which includes cultural barriers, as well as different personality types. For instance, one respondent indicated that shy team members do not contribute much; however, when the leadership fosters a positive and engaging working environment, even the shyest person will share their information and knowledge. Of course, the attitudes of the team members can impact the transfer of knowledge, as the receiver of the information needs to be willing to accept the information that the sender is trying to provide. More specifically, sharing of knowledge and communication barriers exist due to time constraints, confidence, differing personalities, cultural differences, immaturity, fear of change, and egos. Even as discussed above, if the team member does not see the value of their tacit knowledge or is not confident or safe to share their knowledge, it does not matter if there are communication barriers; it simply will not be shared. Knowing this creates a whole new challenge for HRM and leaders alike. However, if team members observe HR and the leaders freely sharing their tacit knowledge, thus leading by example, and are then encouraged to share and benefit from sharing their tacit knowledge, people notice how you do things and then feel more comfortable and confident to do the same. HR needs to know the group of people that they support, along with knowing and understanding the challenges that each group faces. For instance, in a large organization, the executives can get together and develop strategy goals and objectives, but if these are far from the challenges that the different locations are facing, then the strategies will not be implemented or successful. HR's responsibility in this exercise is to ensure that the senior executives know and understand the different challenges that exist and help tailor the strategic goals and objectives so that each location will be able to successfully implement the goals and objectives. Otherwise, this would increase frustration for those outside of the boardroom, reducing engagement and increasing turnover and dissatisfaction; thus, valuable knowledge would be leaving the organization, ultimately affecting the organization's performance.

Recently, there have been many organizations that are right-sizing, down-sizing, or restructuring their organizations, resulting in layoffs. While this may be a necessity for the business to continue, the effects can be devastating to an organization, particularly for those who were not laid off—they often have "survivor's guilt." More devastating though are employees who stay but are only there physically and not mentally, going through the motions but not exerting more energy or engaging in sharing their tacit knowledge, either out of guilt, anger, or fear. HR will need to move swiftly and compassionately to keep these employees engaged and persisting at the organization, so their knowledge does not walk out the door. But it is important to keep in mind that it is not only layoffs that would affect the organization, but employees who have been with the organization a long time. As mentioned earlier, when employees feel safe sharing their ideas, they will do so, but the organization must do something with this information. It is just like the annual engagement survey that many organizations conduct to gather information about departments and the organization, but once this information is gathered, no one ever hears the results, and nothing is done with the information retrieved. Thus, employees do not feel that they are being heard, leaving them to feel that it is a waste of time to provide information. When the environment is such that the employees do not trust or feel safe sharing their ideas, tacit knowledge is not being shared between the employees. HR must ensure that information is shared, that there is training with leaders to help with engagement activities, and that someone is listening to employees, allowing them to feel safe to share and transfer their tacit knowledge. HR is not only a neutral party for all employees, but they are business partners ensuring that employee contributions and engagement remain high through the different strategically aligned HR activities that are developed and implemented (Ulrich, 1997).

Works Cited

Agovino, T. (2023). *Welcome to the new workplace.* HRMagazine, SHRM.org, Spring 2023, 72–83.

Deyong, X., Xiangyun, Z., & Quiyue, Z. (2007). Empirical study on innovation competence based on tacit knowledge. *Innovation Management and Industrial Engineering (IEEE), 13,*5860–5863.

Drucker, P. (1986). *Innovation and entrepreneurship: Practice and principles.* HarperCollins Publishing, Inc.

Kokkaew, N., Jokkaw, N., Peansupap, V., & Wipulanusat, W. (2022). Impacts on human resource management and knowledge management on non-financial organizational performance: Evidence of Thai infrastructure constructions firms. *Ain Shams Engineering Journal, 13,* 1–12. Impacts of human resource management and knowledge management on non-financial organizational performance: Evidence of Thai infrastructure construction firms - ScienceDirect.

Lawler, III, E. E., & Mohrman, S. A. (2003). *Creating a strategic human resources organization: An assessment of trends and new directions.* Standford University Press.

Lui, N.-C., & Lui, M.-S. (2011). Human resource practices and individual knowledge-sharing behavior: An empirical study for Taiwanese R&D professionals. *The International Journal of Human Resource Management, 22*(4), 981–997.

Meinert, D. (2023). *Rules of Engagement: HR professionals around the country are finding creative ways to reignite employee's passion for work.* SHRM.org/ HRmagazine, 76–83.

Merlini, PhD, K. P. (2023). *Taking the wheel.* SHRM.org: HRMagazine, Summer 2023, 89.

Naegle-Piazza, L. (2023). *The pros and cons of monitoring remote employees.* SHRM.org: HRMagazine, Summer 2023, 20–23.

Nonaka, I., & Takeuchi, H. (1995). *The knowledge-creating company.* Oxford University Press.

Slusser, B. E. (2012). *Establishing social networks to effectively transfer tacit knowledge within U.S. subsidiary locations of Japanese-owned MNCs: A case study.* ProQuest LLC, UMI Number: 3503079.

Ulrich, D. (1997). *Human resource champions: The next agenda for adding value and delivering results.* Harvard Business School Press.

13

QUALITATIVE RESEARCH IN TACIT KNOWLEDGE TRANSFER AND WORKPLACE CREATIVITY

Bren Slusser

Research Results

The research that was conducted was performed by sending out survey invitations to LinkedIn contacts of the researcher. There were 184 surveys sent out, with 31 responses received. The number of responses is sufficient for the researcher to quantify the data received, as the pool of participants is a cross-section of different industries, education levels, and years in their roles. More specifically, 51.6% of the respondents hold a master's degree, with 32.3% holding at least a bachelor's degree, and a smattering of higher degrees or no degrees of the 16.1% remaining respondents. The roles the respondents hold are from many different industries, but it is the longevity of their roles that is most intriguing. For instance, 71% of the respondents have only been in their roles for 0–3 years, with 16.1% having been in their roles for 4–7 years, leaving the remaining 12.9% respondents in their roles for 7–10 years, 10–15 years, or 15–20 plus years. Interestingly, there was no one in their role over the past 20 years.

The results of the research indicate that collaboration and an atmosphere of sharing information assist creativity and innovation to flourish within an organization. One respondent indicated that "the prohibition of knowledge transfer occurs with the polarization of any given topic, feeling, or idea needing to be communicated." They further explain that the development of communication processes and social networks takes time. Communication processes can be stifled or hindered by egos, misunderstandings, and distrust, which affects not only the development of social networks for

DOI: 10.4324/9781003322894-15

sharing their knowledge, but ultimately also the creativity and innovation that occur within these social networks.

The **first question** that is asked of the participants is as follows:

Tacit knowledge is the knowledge a person has by doing the job. It cannot be captured in a database or in a manual. As a member of a team, how do you transfer the knowledge that you have gained in your job to the rest of the team?

The responses varied depending on how knowledge is transferred between team members. Many indicated that the information is shared through meetings, sharing documents, and just dialoging with team members. One respondent indicated that "by using effective communication techniques such as maintaining eye-contact and emphasizing key words and key points, and then making sure the tacit knowledge was acknowledged by asking confirming questions." While this sounds like it would naturally occur, it takes the sender to be able to ask the confirming questions in such a way that the receiver will be able to receive the information so that the information is successfully transmitted. Asking confirming questions is good for the most part but keep in mind the cultural barriers that may exist and ensure that each party is clearly expressing and understanding what is being communicated. This diversity of cultures that exist within organizations can impact the successful transfer of any sort of communication if the team members are not in tune with these barriers. For instance, if it is a low context culture sender and a high context culture receiver, there could be some barriers to effectively sending and receiving the information, as we have discussed in previous chapters. One respondent shared that "repetition of needs/goals shared, continual engagement of self-awareness and improvement to better engage, lead, help, teach, etc." is a great example of the types of activities a person needs to do so that tacit knowledge can be transferred successfully.

Interestingly, a few respondents indicated that they transfer tacit knowledge by utilizing Teams, Outlook, WebEx, or meetings. While this is one way in which to send information, this response needs further clarification about how effectively the transfer of tacit knowledge is done through these means. Another respondent indicated that mentoring was a big part of the transfer of knowledge, and it is important to acknowledge that it is also through these types of working relationships that tacit knowledge can be transferred. The biggest way in which tacit knowledge is transferred is through verbal interactions with one another, such as just talking, sharing examples, brainstorming, and other verbal or written interactions that naturally occur throughout the workplace.

One idea that is discussed by a respondent is how former teammates have "left behind lessons learned documents throughout their careers" which is a testament that the person leaving is conscientious about sharing their knowledge that they may not have shared or to reinforce what has been shared by documenting it. Another respondent corroborated that mentoring/coaching is a baseline method used to transfer tacit knowledge, but also indicates that it is "more often than not dependent on the individuals and the particular experience in question." The way in which tacit knowledge is transferred by this respondent affirms that tacit knowledge transfer occurs through the relationships built and the opportunity to share information between team members.

Other respondents identified ways in which tacit knowledge is transferred, such as "in a formal way through peer review and sharing information about progress during staff meetings. In a more informal way, tacit knowledge is shared during conversations and just checking in throughout the week." This is echoed by other respondents who indicate that tacit knowledge is transferred through personal meetings, oral communication, offering guidance, telling examples, demonstrating for them, shadowing, and observing. Thus, there are many ways in which the respondents have identified ways to share tacit knowledge. This is extremely important and helpful for HR to know and understand, as this will be instrumental in fostering an atmosphere for all these communication types to occur and to reinforce to leaders that providing a collaborative working environment is instrumental in facilitating the transfer of tacit knowledge.

The **second question** that was asked of the participants was as follows: Do you believe that your manager provides an environment where knowledge can be easily transferred? Of the 31 respondents, 80.6% indicated that yes, their manager provides an environment where knowledge can be easily transferred, while 19.4% indicated that their manager does not provide this type of environment. Of those that answered "no," the reasons are somewhat similar, which was the **third question** asked. For instance, one respondent indicated that their boss does not "pass it along if they think it does not directly impact me or my team, or if there is no action for me to take," which could cause problems for the transfer of tacit knowledge and an unknowing and unintentional deterioration of the social networks. Another respondent indicated that their boss lacks "effective communication skills and does not like to share information." Another respondent indicated that their manager could "be clearer about what he wants and the deadlines, and not changing direction every week." This type of behavior lacks support from the manager and the manager's team, resulting in an unintentional negative impact on social networks and the sharing of information. One respondent said it best by stating,

> the prohibition of knowledge transfer occurs with the polarization of any given topic, feeling, or idea needing to be communicated. Successful development of communication processes, and in my experience, has happened over long periods of time. Yes, fear can hinder advancement of knowledge sharing, ego, distrust, etc.; simple misunderstanding of what one another is saying vs. what is meant.

It is through effective communication skills and processes that allow for the sharing of information and knowledge with one another, which all the respondents indicated is true and lines up with their experiences. As discussed by Lui and Lui (2011), tacit knowledge and sharing of this knowledge largely depend on whether the team members believe that they can share this tacit knowledge along with maintaining a proactive attitude toward the process of sharing, such as through collaborative brainstorming and problem solving. Sharing their tacit knowledge successfully also depends upon the individuals' belief that they can successfully share this knowledge while also deciding if they are willing to engage in it after assessing the cost and benefit (Lui & Lui, 2011). Basically, if it is a mutually beneficial act to share their tacit knowledge, then they will share their knowledge. This way of thinking is described as the expectancy-value theory and has been "recognized as a basic paradigm for the study of human attitudes and behavior in organizational settings" (Lui & Lui, 2011, p. 983). As we have discussed in previous chapters, people will engage in activities where they believe that what they share will be received back. As the expectancy of tacit knowledge sharing increases, so do the knowledge-sharing behaviors.

The **fourth question** asked: "Do you believe that your manager creates an engaging environment for the transfer of tacit knowledge to occur?" Of the 31 respondents, 77.4% indicated yes, their manager does create an engaging environment, and 22.6% indicated that no, their manager does not create an engaging environment for tacit knowledge to transfer. The **fifth question** asks respondents, if they answered "yes" to the question, to answer the follow-up question of how exactly their manager creates an engaging environment. More specifically, one respondent said:

> My manager emphasizes how important our collaboration is to the overall goals and intentions. Because we feel valued and appreciated, our level of communication is free-flowing and without tentative obstacles or hesitation. My manager meets with us in groups, followed up by

1:1 meetings as well. This combination of strategies increases the tacit knowledge that gets successfully transferred.

This example is echoed by several of the respondents and how their manager creates an engaging environment for the transfer of tacit knowledge to occur, to include asking for feedback, having group meetings where information is shared, pushing each other to grow by finding new ways of doing things to improve productivity, having open conversations regarding problems and solutions, and encouraging open communication and demanding respect between all team members. One comment by a respondent captures the essence of what this would look like in an engaging environment from which creativity and innovation can flow. Specifically, "My manager models the behavior of knowledge sharing and transparency between management and direct reports, which encourages direct reports to share amongst each other." This example truly encompasses an engaging environment. This corresponds with the contentions of Deyong et al. (2007), indicating that while technology is needed, it has stimulated the importance of these face-to-face interactions, whereby tacit knowledge can be shared and is imperative for engagement as well as the transfer of knowledge for creativity and innovation to flourish. However, while some indicated that they try to capture knowledge through different software tools, one respondent indicated that it can be challenging across the departments due to not everyone using the tool or having too many things to focus on, so the information does not get put into the tool for the knowledge to be accessed by others. Having too many key priorities an organization is focusing on is also a challenge, and if sharing information is not a priority, then it can impact the knowledge shared and used throughout the organization, which would create misunderstandings, miscommunication, and overall frustration within teams. Thus, it is extremely important for leaders to have the skills to draw out the creativity and innovation within their teams, so that tacit knowledge can be transferred. As discussed by Matošková et al. (2013), a well-developed tacit knowledge program for capturing tacit knowledge can help facilitate the transfer of tacit knowledge. But it requires the leaders to be committed to doing this, without interfering too much to stifle the transfer. As has been discussed earlier, too much regulated oversight by the leaders can have a negative impact on the team's willingness to share their tacit knowledge. The transfer needs to be organic, but with the help of the leaders in fostering the atmosphere, this organic transfer can occur. HRM can be instrumental in helping in this endeavor, since it is through training and skill development that HR facilitates helping leaders ascertain tacit knowledge from their teams.

The **sixth question** asked respondents: "How well do you believe your team shares information so that creativity and innovation can occur within your team?" Given that this was a Likert scale response, 25.8% responded with a "3," which is a neutral response, while 38.7% answered "4" and 35.5% answered "5." Those that answered "4" or "5" make up 23 of the respondent answers, indicating that their teams work well together, sharing information whereby creativity and innovation can thrive.

The **seventh question** is a follow-up question to the previous question. Specifically, even though there appears to be ample opportunity for knowledge to be shared so that creativity and innovation can occur, some of the respondents indicated that there are "communication barriers when it comes to specifics. When it comes to overall information… people are hands-on with sharing their feedback." Other respondents expressed that some team members are shy by nature, so they do not contribute much to the conversations, or that their team members are caught up in doing their own work but will eagerly share information when asked. One respondent indicated that "we work very well together. Other teams have issues such as a lack of communication, language barriers and a strong hierarchical structure, where information is not disseminated to individual contributors." This statement demonstrates exactly how tacit knowledge can get stuck between diverse cultures, such as high and low context cultures, due to communication issues and language barriers.

Other challenges that can exist for tacit knowledge to be transferred between team members are things like the lack of desire to do anything outside of a person's regular routine or where it requires multiple team members to accomplish tasks where everyone must be in unison to get these tasks accomplished. Communication barriers and/or an unwillingness to work together can inhibit the transfer of tacit knowledge, reducing opportunities for creativity and innovation to occur. Fostering a collaborative environment not only helps the team but the whole organization, as it allows for creativity and innovation to thrive. Where there is collaborative innovation, there will be increased organizational market competitiveness, which will increase the performance of the organization. These collaborative environments are seen through the social networks that have been developed within the work teams, whether department-specific or cross-functional and are imperative for organizational innovation and competitiveness (Xiaomi et al., 2014).

In discussing the **eighth question** answered by respondents, they were asked: "How do you believe the organization provides an atmosphere for diversity of thought to allow for creativity and innovation to occur?" One respondent indicated that an organization needs to honor "individual collaborator opinions and continually being mindful of the intrinsic value of fellow collaborators' contributions… [to encourage]… transparency, a growth mindset, responsibility, and building community." This is well said that while it only takes two people to transfer tacit knowledge whereby creativity and innovation can flourish, it is through the organization providing an atmosphere for a diversity of thought for creativity and innovation to occur. Many other respondents stated that through group meetings and the encouragement to share ideas and experiences, diversity of thought occurs due to providing an atmosphere for the sharing of diverse thoughts and experiences. It is much easier to share with like cultures, but it is through the experiences of working together on projects and learning more about one another, regardless of culture, that tacit knowledge transfers naturally and freely between team members. It is not just the sharing of tacit knowledge through working together that is important, but also by observing what others do, watching to see what the social norms are, what is acceptable, and what is not acceptable.

One respondent expressed that they believe that the organization needs to promote diversity of thought rather than only providing the atmosphere. More specifically, they responded:

> Many times leadership and managers tend to ask those below them to be the initiators, but I believe the ideal environment is best when initiated and promoted by the very leaders themselves. Additionally, when leaders bring an atmosphere of diversity of thought to themselves it models an environment that is encouraging of that.

This statement is the essence of how incredibly influential leaders are within an organization. In an article by O'Neill (2001), the author indicates that learning coaches are important for leaders and how they help these leaders learn from experience, which is done by using feedback and reflection, specifically critical reflection. This is very important for organizations dealing with change and how leaders help through the change process, learning from one another. When discussing action learning, as it relates to developing people and learning from each other, a learning coach (HRM) helps leaders and teams share their knowledge and experiences, creating an environment for the teams to learn from each other (O'Neill, 2001). This is an important point to mention, as learning in a group setting is where tacit knowledge flows, allowing creative and innovative ideas and suggestions to be freely shared between the team members.

Another respondent further explains that their organization is over 80% diverse, which is great for the diversity of thoughts, experiences, skills, and ideas. That

> people are given the chance to try things without worrying about failing. We allow people to transfer teams to ensure that they enjoy their work.

They can also propose ideas to the leadership and be allowed to work on them. Leadership is supportive of people's ideas and success.

This statement further supports that it is through ethical, consistent, and collaborative leaders within an organization that it allows for diversity of thought, transferring tacit knowledge, and thus promoting creativity and innovation to be present in the workplace. Being part of a non-homogenous group brings diversity of thought to the organization and allows for continuous improvement. It starts at the top, through all levels of leadership, by being open to receiving, thoughtfully considering, and/or allowing employees to implement their different ideas, thoughts, and experiences. This is where the ground is most fertile to grow, water, and see the blooms of creativity and innovation flourish within the organization.

Unfortunately, not all respondents have an organization that promotes diversity of thought and "does not provide an effective channel for this. Everyone has ideas, and there is plenty of creativity and innovation, but it is often disconnected and inefficient because there are several silos keeping departments from collaborating." This is a great example of how closed lines of communication, a lack of promotion of diverse thoughts, and the fact that no cross-functional teams are formed to collaborate, share ideas, and transfer their tacit knowledge can impact the whole organization. This type of environment is not only reducing the opportunity for the sharing of ideas and experiences, but it ultimately affects the performance of the organization, as no one is moving together as a team towards the strategic goals and objectives the senior leadership has developed. Sometimes it is not that the leadership is not willing to do this, but they do not have the vehicles in which to capture and collaborate within these different teams of diverse thoughts, ideas, and knowledge. Thus, the exchange and capture of ideas are lost. Human resources have a prime opportunity to help reduce turnover and increase the sharing of diverse thoughts, experiences, and skills, so that leadership will be able to genuinely and ethically create a diverse working environment that allows for the sharing of tacit knowledge.

HRM is an instrumental piece of the organizational pie. The development of the HR role has come a long way since its inception as personnel management to being a strategic partner of the organization, involved in all aspects of employee development, organizational goal development, and overall employee well-being (Kokkaew et al., 2022). While this is a very generic and wide-reaching description of the HRM role, it is HR's knowledge, experience, and expertise that can help to launch an organization's performance. Furthermore, being involved in all aspects of the organization and sharing their tacit knowledge with the leaders and employees alike has helped HRM develop the activities for training and development of the employees, which impacts the organization's performance and creates a welcoming environment where tacit knowledge can be shared for creativity and innovation to occur through the teams.

Another important factor to identify regarding leaders and their involvement in facilitating a workplace where tacit knowledge can freely flow also has to do with holding team members accountable for those who are not performing up to expectations. Specifically, poor performers hinder the effectiveness and efficiency of a team, whereby the transfer of tacit knowledge will not occur due to frustrations within the team because of the poor performance of some team members. Thus, it is the leaders' responsibility and moral obligation to the team to ensure that everyone is pulling their weight and sharing information. This also impacts the overall performance of the organization when poor performers are not provided the feedback and tools to improve their performance, which also impacts the morale of the team if nothing is done about poor performers. This impacts not only the transfer of tacit knowledge and morale but also leads to higher turnover, a loss of creativity and innovation with the teams, and ultimately impacts the bottom line of the organization. As discussed by Hernandez (2001), knowledge and the transfer of this tacit knowledge have become an important part of the organization, used to create a competitive advantage. O'Neill (2001) corroborates this by purporting that learning coaches (HRM) and leaders help to propel the organization through the shared learning and knowledge that each team member holds, and it is their responsibility to provide the atmosphere in which the transfer of tacit knowledge can occur. The process of knowledge transfer is the source of competitive advantage (Hernandez, 2001). As has been discussed, knowledge is hard to capture, and when the organization is truly a learning organization, where tacit knowledge flows to capture that creativity and innovation in the workplace, then the organization will see continued higher employee and organizational performance. However, this endeavor requires the leadership to be completely on board with the process, and by not fully regulating the "what, when, why, and how," tacit knowledge is transferred, but by facilitating the opportunities for the development of diverse social networks where the natural progression of team member sharing occurs.

The **ninth question** asked: "Does your organization have what you would consider to be high turnover?" This is an important question because when there is high turnover within an organization, there is tacit knowledge leaving the organization. Of the 31 respondents, 41.9% believe that their organization experiences high turnover. While this is less than half of the respondents, the percentage of those who believe their organization does have high turnover is significant, indicating a lot of tacit knowledge is not being captured by the organization, directly impacting the overall success and performance of the organization. The **tenth question** asked the respondents what they believed was the cause of the turnover. However, when looking at the different reasons for the perceived high turnover, there is no one reason given that can be identified as the exact reasoning. If the researcher had had the opportunity to follow up with the respondents about this question, it would have been a great question to seek further clarification and information on to get a clearer picture of the broad reasons for the respondents' perception of the cause of turnover in their organization.

The **eleventh question** asked respondents to rate, on a Likert scale of one (1) to five (5), how they think turnover affects the performance of an organization. The results of this question showed that 67.7% rated this a five (5), indicating that 21 respondents believe turnover to have a profound impact on organizational performance; while one of the respondents rated it a four (4), which is still fairly high; 6.5% (two) of the respondents rated it a three (3), which is neutral; and then 12.9% (four) of respondents rated it a two (2), which basically indicates that these respondent do not believe turnover has much of an impact on the performance of an organization. The follow-up question (the **twelfth question**) asked respondents to "please explain the ways you believe turnover affects the organization's performance." All 31 respondents provided an explanation for this question. The overwhelming majority of respondents discussed that turnover, whether it is voluntary or involuntary, points to low employee satisfaction, requiring more training as new employees are hired, which also means that tacit knowledge is leaving the organization, along with the rebuilding of relationships for tacit knowledge to be shared with the new employees. An interesting statement by a respondent said that "it corrupts legacy and longevity." While this is true, another respondent counters that argument, indicating that "turnover is part of the work environment and is mostly good in the long term. New people, new ideas, new attitudes, and the hope that the addition, or subtraction, of people is a new positive for the company." This may also be one of the reasons why there are some who do not believe that turnover has a huge impact on the overall performance of the organization, as you insert new creativity and innovation when there are new thoughts, experiences, and skills infused into the organization.

The elephant in the room, though, is that when there is a significant amount of turnover that occurs within an organization, there tends to be a lot of tasks that the workers who still work there have to pick up, which reduces the opportunity for the sharing of knowledge and ideas, thus creating a gap in creativity and innovation which ultimately affects the organizational performance in the long run. This is supported by the research, such as: "…when someone leaves it is a huge dagger to morale." Not only is morale impacted, but the bottom line is impacted by turnover, as the organization is constantly training new employees. One way to calculate employee turnover is indicated below, and is something that the HRM should be calculating, know where the problems exist and a plan to reduce turnover.

Employee Turnover Rate Formula

$$\text{Employees turnover rate} = \frac{\text{Employees who left the organization}}{\text{Average \# of employees}} \times 100$$

Sample

$$13.33\% = \frac{20}{150} \times 100$$

As the sample provided above indicates, the average percentage of turnover is 13.33%. The organization would need to identify what percentage of turnover they are comfortable with, knowing that tacit knowledge is leaving the organization. Knowing what their ceiling will be is essential in determining how to reduce turnover. Not only is there tacit knowledge leaving the organization, but the average cost of turnover is 1.5 to 2 times the position's salary, and depending on the types of positions that are leaving, the cost of turnover increases, impacting the performance of the organization and its bottom line.

Some of the reasons that have been identified as potential reasons for turnover are things like the constant movement of the organization's mission and vision, which makes it hard to keep employees for a long time. As discussed, turnover impacts morale and can create an uncomfortable atmosphere, which impacts the culture because of the turnover, reducing trust and confidence among the employees with leadership. Everyone has heard the term "people do not leave their jobs, they leave their managers," which supports how much turnover impacts teams, their relationships, and ultimately the performance of the organization as the tacit knowledge walks out the door. It is important to mention, though, that not all turnover is bad for the organization, as there is some turnover that raises morale and positively affects the culture, resulting in more collaboration, the transfer of tacit knowledge, and increased creativity and innovation, which have a profound impact on the organization's performance.

Regardless of whether the turnover is positive or negative for the organization, as has been discussed, tacit knowledge is leaving the organization. The **thirteenth question** of the survey that respondents were asked was: "when turnover occurs, people take with them their tacit knowledge, which is valuable to the organization. What would be the best way to capture this information before the person leaves?" While capturing tacit knowledge may seem like an easy endeavor to undertake, it is quite difficult to capture since tacit knowledge is the knowledge that someone gains from doing the job. Even with the uptick in AI software, there are a lot of nuances that cannot be put into a database effectively to replace the person who has the tacit knowledge.

One way in which to capture the tacit knowledge is through designing more elaborate exit surveys in which to capture this knowledge, trying to gather as much information as possible in written form, but also through meeting with that person, taking notes, documenting what they say, how they executed tasks, and ways they did things. As one respondent indicated, capturing tacit knowledge is "more difficult than it sounds because if a person is about to leave, their number one priority is probably not their former company." This was corroborated by another respondent, who indicated that if you try to capture "what they have in their head as they are leaving you will get half-hearted answers and very little knowledge transfer." Developing some sort of way to capture this knowledge while these people are still employed is essential to trying to obtain the tacit knowledge, such as documenting their processes through standard operating procedures requiring the manager to ensure that this information is kept up to date, hopefully to minimally impact the tacit knowledge leaving the organization when the person leaves. Another respondent gave a suggestion of perhaps incentivizing or compensating the person leaving to document their knowledge, trying to memorialize their tacit knowledge.

Another way to think about this is through cross-training in sharing tacit knowledge; that way, when someone does leave the team, all their knowledge is not walking out the door, and there is no way of capturing this information. As one respondent shared, "this also creates bench strength, allowing for specific knowledge to stay within the organization's ecosystem." Succession planning was voiced among a couple of the respondents, saying that when tacit knowledge is shared amongst many members of the team, developing the successors for different positions, particularly key positions, then the organization is not flailing about trying to make sense of things in the wake of the person who vacated the position. Sharing knowledge with others within the different departments and within the organization only creates more success than the fear of being replaced. The more a person knows, the more valuable they are to the team. When people are cross-trained, have shared responsibilities or teams, and develop a succession plan, this creates a culture of trust, knowledge, comradery, security, and ultimately, retaining tacit knowledge within the organization, even when there is turnover.

As we have discussed, holding onto the tacit knowledge, even amidst turnover, helps with the overall performance of an organization. More specifically, the **fourteenth question** asked participants: "How do you think that the transfer of tacit knowledge helps with overall performance of the organization?" As one respondent stated: "the system is built around continuously learning...always trying to grow knowledge." Human potential is limitless; therefore, when employees find more efficient and/or more effective ways of doing things, the organization benefits when this knowledge is shared. This contributes to the continuous improvement and evolution of a company's culture and effectiveness. Another respondent indicated: "tacit knowledge is oftentimes associated with the culture of a company, and it's how they do things. Without this tacit transfer, a company would be without what makes them, them." This is a poignant statement, as during my initial research on tacit knowledge, the organization that was researched on how high and low context cultures transfer tacit knowledge identified this knowledge as "tribal knowledge" by being in the organization and the various teams learning from each other through shared experiences and discussions (Slusser, 2012). Interestingly, one of the respondents to this research also called tacit knowledge "tribal knowledge," as it is something that cannot be written down and is key for the overall performance of an organization. Thus, it is these shared experiences and the transfer of tacit knowledge that add to the culture and success of the organization. One person's idea or knowledge could be a major asset to the organization's success. When we can share knowledge, we are able to gain perspective and insight that we might not have had otherwise, growing, and developing in the teams as well as the organization. Tacit knowledge is experiential and assists with the continuity of the organization's performance. It helps to build the organization and reduce the risk of stagnation and redundancy. Sharing tacit knowledge helps to build microcosms of norms and expectations that create efficiency in a closed system. Gaps in this knowledge can cost the organization time as employees work to gain the knowledge that was lost by an employee leaving. This transfer of tacit knowledge can help keep the entire organization informed and equipped. In a high-turnover organization, the transfer of tacit knowledge helps seal the gap between employees; however, this is not always possible, and valuable knowledge is leaving the organization. This is critical to acknowledge, particularly when there are layoffs, as there is not generally time to capture the tacit knowledge that will be leaving the organization with the exodus of the individuals being laid off, leaving a gaping hole where the tacit knowledge once filled. Thus, as one respondent conveyed:

> if an organization can do a solid job of the transfer of tacit knowledge, they are able to effectively move the team forward faster and achieve the desired goals. An analogy would be a barn raising event that happened

in previous years. Once the neighborhood put up two or three barns, they would have learned all the little tricks that needed to be done to effectively raise the barn quickly and efficiently to get back to their own farms.

This is a great analogy that when the team works together and shares their experiences, skills, and knowledge, building trust and understanding between team members, tacit knowledge can be shared and used to get projects and tasks accomplished, even if someone leaves the organization. The organization will not come to a screeching halt if someone in a key position leaves the organization, provided that tacit knowledge is transferred in the teams and succession planning is performed to close the gap of opportunity of tacit knowledge completely leaving the organization, which ultimately impacts the overall performance of the organization.

The **fifteenth question** asked: "Do you believe that creativity and innovation affect an organization's performance?" Of the 31 responses, 96.8% indicated that they in fact believed this to be the case. This concludes that only one (1) respondent does not believe that creativity and innovation affect an organization's performance. While this is not a large enough sample size to indicate a trend, having a follow-up conversation about why someone would have this perception could provide some insight about their reasons for answering the way that they did, as they would not be the only ones in the workforce that would have this thought. The follow-up and **sixteenth question** asked: "If you answered yes above, please explain how creativity and innovation affect an organization's performance?" While this may seem like a natural, but silly follow-up question, it allows the respondents to explain why they chose "yes" to the previous question. More specifically, one respondent indicated that:

> There's nothing more important than creativity and innovation to a company's success. The world/environment that all businesses exist in is constantly in a state of flux, therefore the only way to thrive is by embracing continuous creativity thinking and encouraging innovation.

One respondent indicated that creativity and innovation should be regulated by the organization, because if they are allowed to be unregulated, then these activities could have devastating consequences. While this may be true and some regulation is needed by the leader, it could also hinder the teams from indulging in creativity and innovation, and a byproduct of regulating creativity and innovation may result in employees having a lack of trust in the leadership, which is not the direction an organization would want to move. Creativity and innovation allow for new and efficient operations, increased feelings of belonging and purpose, and enhanced quality of work and health among employees and the organization. Furthermore, when these efforts are highly regulated, this could stifle creativity and innovation since organizations are always looking for new ways to accomplish something and move the organization ahead. One respondent indicated that creativity and innovation "could be a time or money saver, could be a morale saver, maybe it improves customer service," regardless, they all benefit the organization. New marketing strategies could be developed, which may be the next big trend or viewpoint businesses use to increase their market share. As we have discussed, creativity and innovation are closely linked to an organization's culture. If the ability to be creative and innovative is stifled by the organization, this could greatly diminish and negatively impact the organization, which may have once been seen as flourishing with creativity and innovation.

Creativity enhances an organization's solutions and gives them a chance to succeed in multiple ways. As one respondent said: "The more diverse a team, the more life experiences they can bring to the table to come up with a variety of solutions." Having a diverse team greatly impacts the transfer of tacit knowledge. Organizations must continue to innovate to stay relevant and retain their market share. This is important to the bottom line. When organizations stifle creativity and innovation, what was once a market leader ends up reducing their human capital, with all that tacit knowledge leaving the organization. Static organizations do not survive, and the more organizations allow for creativity and innovation to flow through their teams, they will be able to drive change, which is critical in the world market. Furthermore, as one of the respondents indicated, "creativity and innovation can bolster an organization's ability to be adaptable, lead industry advancement, and improve overall business function." Fostering an open and positive culture while ensuring that the organization's values are followed makes employees feel more secure and loyal to sharing their knowledge, where creativity and innovation freely flow. As one respondent's answer sums it up: "it provides the organization with the opportunity to grow and develop past any perceived hindrances either within the organization or the market structure outside of the organization." Creativity and innovation help an organization move forward, resulting in higher performance and growth.

Research Opportunities

While engaging in the writing of this book, conducting the research, and analyzing the results, there are a few areas that have percolated to the top, needing further research. First, the second part of the book focused on tacit knowledge and how it affects creativity and innovation from a cultural perspective, how HRM can affect positive change and activities throughout the organization, and the leaders' involvement with these activities and how it impacts organizational performance. The participants in the research were from varied backgrounds and industries, which gave a good perspective given the sample size of 31. However, a deeper dive into specific industries would elicit further information for organizations, such as focusing only on technology-based organizations, the healthcare industry, or the educational industry, as these are some of the industries that can and have shared tacit knowledge and arguably stand to lose the most with the loss of tacit knowledge. This would give a wider perspective about specific industries.

Another research focus would be on DE&I. While it is addressed in part two of the book, there is a lot of ground to cover, and the researcher only touched the tip of the iceberg on the subject. DE&I impacts every part of the organization and would absolutely impact team development so that tacit knowledge can freely flow for creativity and innovation to occur. As has been discussed, when team members feel safe and trust has been developed, tacit knowledge will be shared and learned amongst the team members as well as through the organization. Leaders and HRM have a significant opportunity to help facilitate this endeavor through activities and people feeling like they belong. This also impacts commitment to the organization, reduces turnover and increases the sharing of tacit knowledge for creativity and innovation to occur.

A third area to focus on would be artificial intelligence (AI). This is a hot topic right now in business, and there is so much that we do not know about it, other than what is input by a human that AI is able to regurgitate. Everyone one of us has experienced calling customer service or getting on the chat feature of a company only to not have our questions answered because the system does not understand what we are asking, thus needing to talk to a live person. As such, AI does not and cannot consider tacit knowledge and the loss of human thinking to work around challenges or obstacles. Additionally, when thinking about HRM and recruiting, AI would not pick up on a highly qualified candidate if they had not inserted the key words that AI is looking for, thus creating the opportunity for discriminatory practices to occur and passing over on highly qualified candidates, which could impact hiring employees who would have a lot of tacit knowledge about the industry to share with their new team. There is a lot to learn about AI and how it would truly impact an organization, given the lack of the ability to learn tacit knowledge.

Another research focus area is to take a deeper look at the changing landscape of more remote and hybrid employees and 100% in-person employees, the impact that each of these has on team development, how easily tacit knowledge is transferred between these types of employees, and what, if anything, can be done to help facilitate opportunities for learning and sharing of tacit knowledge for increased creativity and innovation in the workplace. While having the flexibility to work remotely or even in a hybrid environment is great for employees, this also impacts the time it takes to develop those working relationships where tacit knowledge will freely flow. With completely in-person employees, these teams can generally develop trust and natural social networks quicker through face-to-face interactions, sorting through challenges, and sharing their tacit knowledge, whereby ideas lead to creativity and innovation. With remote and hybrid employees, the perception is that these working relationships can take longer, impacting the effectiveness of a team, their development, and subsequently the transfer of tacit knowledge, which leads to the creativity and innovation that occurs within the team. However, further research would be able to identify the impact, if any, and the true effectiveness of remote and hybrid teams.

A fifth research idea that became clear from the results of the survey is by following up with the participants of the survey and asking additional questions to gather more information and evidence to better understand why there is high turnover in these organizations and why six (6) of the participants did not feel or had a neutral response that turnover affected the organization's performance. More specific information and to inquire with more probing questions about the turnover, whether it has had a positive or negative impact on the teams and overall organizational performance, are needed. One reason could be due to the participants' role within the organization and not seeing or knowing how turnover has impacted the organization, or whether the turnover that has occurred was a positive benefit for the organization. Regardless of the reasons, this subject area warrants further research.

Yet another area for further research would be on the different generations, how they work together, the impact of having a cross-generational team for transferring tacit knowledge, and how creativity and innovation occur. Additionally, looking at the different ways in which HRM can focus activities that would not only draw out creativity and innovation across generations but also globally and how these activities are shifting due to the aging workforce, along with the differences between the generations and what is expected for retention and well-being. Every day, new research comes out about taking care of the whole employee, but further research is needed to really understand what all levels and generations of employees want from their workplace and environment.

There continues to be discussion about the involvement of HR within the senior leadership ranks, particularly as it pertains to strategic goal development. There still seems to be some thought that senior leadership does not value the input given or needed from HR on strategic decisions that are made, and how they impact the organization, thus just expecting HR to implement the initiatives set forth without vetting how they will impact the organization and the organization's overall performance. Therefore, further research is needed to peel back the onion on this line of thinking, and truly identify what senior leaders believe and how, or if they do, utilize HR during the strategic planning process.

Works Cited

Deyong, X., Xiangyun, Z., & Quiyue, Z. (2007). Empirical study on innovation competence based on tacit knowledge. *Innovation Management and Industrial Engineering (IEEE), 2*, 5860–5863.

Hernandez, M. (2001). *The impact of the dimensions of the learning organization on the transfer of tacit knowledge process and performance improvement.* Coaching and Knowledge Transfer. Symposium 8, AHRD Conference, Volumes 1 and 2; CE 081 829.

Kokkaew, N., Jokkaw, N., Peansupap, V., & Wipulanusat, W. (2022). Impacts on human resource management and knowledge management on non-financial organizational performance: Evidence of Thai infrastructure constructions firms. *Ain Shams Engineering Journal, 13*, 1–12. Impacts of human resource management and knowledge management on non-financial organizational performance: Evidence of Thai infrastructure construction firms - ScienceDirect.

Lui, N.-C., & Lui, M.-S. (2011). Human resource practices and individual knowledge-sharing behavior: An empirical study for Taiwanese R&D professionals. *The International Journal of Human Resource Management, 22*(4), 981–997.

Matošková, J., Řeháčková, H., Sobotková, E., Polčáková, M., Jurásek, M., Gregar, A., & Švec, V. (2013). Facilitating leader tacit knowledge acquisition. *Journal of Competitiveness, 5*(1), 3–15. doi: 10.7441/joc.2013.01.01

O'Neill, J. (2001). The Role of learning coach in action learning. *Coaching and Knowledge Transfer. Symposium 8, AHRD Conference.* Volumes 1 and 2; CE 081 829.

Slusser, B. E. (2012). Establishing social networks to effectively transfer tacit knowledge within U.S. subsidiary locations of Japanese-owned MNCs: A case study. ProQuest LLC, UMI Number: 3503079.

Xiaomi, A., Hepu, D., Lemen, C., & Wenlin, B. (2014). Knowledge management in supporting collaborative innovation community capacity building. *Journal of Knowledge Management, 18*(3), 2014, 574–590, Emerald Group Publishing Limited.

14

QUALITATIVE RESEARCH IN TACIT KNOWLEDGE TRANSFER AND ORGANIZATIONAL PERFORMANCE

Bren Slusser

Tacit Knowledge Transfer and Performance of the Organization

HRM is important to organizational performance. As has been discussed in previous chapters, the HR practices that are developed and implemented within an organization have been proven to lead to the improvement of the organization's performance (Kokkaew et al., 2022). Through the research conducted, the previous statement is corroborated, where Kokkaew et al. (2022) indicate that sharing tacit knowledge has a profound impact on an organization's operational efficiency, affecting its performance. This means that whether tacit knowledge is successfully transferred or hindered from being transferred, this impacts the overall performance of the organization. Furthermore, Kokkaew et al. (2022) contend that learning throughout the organization plays an important role in tacit knowledge transfer and overall organizational performance. This was validated by the research conducted, as human potential is limitless, and when the organization provides a positive culture where employees feel comfortable and secure sharing their tacit knowledge, employees find a way in which to become more efficient and effective, discovering creative and innovative ways of accomplishing projects and tasks. As one respondent indicated, "this contributes to the evolution of a company's culture and effectiveness."

While many will indicate that recruitment and selection efforts followed by training and development are important for operational performance, HRM's aggressive selection and development of people will ultimately lead to learning and growth, which then positively impacts the operational performance of the organization (Kokkaew et al., 2022). It is also important

DOI: 10.4324/9781003322894-16

to acknowledge how tacit knowledge transfer impacts the organization's performance. While some organizations may concentrate on knowledge creation and the storing and retrieval of this knowledge, others may tend to focus on knowledge utilization (Kokkaew et al., 2022). Regardless of how an organization uses the knowledge that they have, the fact that tacit knowledge is important and ultimately impacts the performance of the organization is an important discovery. Tacit knowledge is experiential and assists with the continuity of the organization's performance. However, an important aside is that turnover greatly affects an organization, the depth of the tacit knowledge held by its employees, leading to the continuity of performance. When there is turnover, whether expected or unexpected, this creates a gap in knowledge.

More specifically, turnover is inevitable within any organization. However, when turnover is high within the organization, this valuable knowledge also goes with the individual that leaves. As one respondent purports, "gaps in this knowledge can cost the organization time as employees work to gain the knowledge lost by an employee leaving." As we discussed in Chapter 13, the research shows that 41.9% of the respondents indicated that turnover was high in their organization. While this percentage is across many different types of industries, the number is staggering to think that organizations in general are experiencing higher than normal turnover. There is some belief that turnover has increased since the pandemic, and as indicators continue to point out, loyalty to an organization has dwindled making retaining valuable tacit knowledge that much more difficult. With 67.7% of the respondents citing that turnover affects the performance of the organization, many would naturally assume this to be the case because tacit knowledge is leaving the organization which impacts the structure of teams for creativity and innovation to occur as teams are having to go through the stages of development again as they re-develop the social networks that were disrupted due to the turnover in order to get to the point of sharing knowledge and ideas where creativity and innovation can once again flow. Employees will continue to find more efficient and effective ways of doing things, but the organization is impacted when knowledge is not shared. Turnover can also affect the willingness of employees to share their knowledge. This could be due to uncertainty about their place within the team and organization or a natural response to hold onto what they know so that they will be seen as valuable to the organization. When this does occur, it has a tremendous impact on the team, affecting cohesiveness; thus, the team deteriorates, affecting creativity and innovation and ultimately the organization's performance. However, when a team continues to share their tacit knowledge, this contributes to the continuous evolution of the organization's culture and effectiveness. As we have discussed, tacit knowledge is oftentimes associated with the culture of an organization, as it is how "they" do things, their tribal knowledge. This transfer of knowledge is what makes the organization what and who it is, infusing creativity and innovation that impact the organization's performance. HRM and leadership have a tremendous opportunity to help with the continuity of social networks so that tacit knowledge continues to be shared.

HRM has an important role to play in capturing this knowledge and helping to create the opportunity for tacit knowledge to be transferred, knowing that different HR practices profoundly impact organizational performance, such as employee engagement and succession planning. It is how these practices are operationalized that is important. When there are no processes in place or the senior leaders do not value the knowledge that is possessed by their employees, it can negatively impact the organization's performance. For instance, one of the respondents lamented that when people exhaust themselves, this can lead to a lack of guidance and empathy, thus leading to burnout and turnover, reducing the opportunity for skill development and the acquisition of tacit knowledge. Turnover, whether voluntary or involuntary, can be a sign of poor employee satisfaction, which necessitates more re-training and the loss of tacit knowledge, impacting morale and the culture.

However, as has been discussed, turnover is not always bad, as it can be a way of infusing new experiences, skills, ideas, and knowledge while eradicating poor attitudes, a lack of motivation, and an unwillingness to share knowledge and ideas, which can stifle an organization's growth and performance. Furthermore, turnover will also increase morale and change the culture of the organization in a positive way. Unfortunately, there is still tacit knowledge leaving the organization. For instance, as one respondent discussed, a recent layoff caused a huge knowledge gap as information was not captured before the layoff occurred. If there is an opportunity to have a transition from the layoff, the organization can try to capture the tacit knowledge of the person leaving the organization. This would not only expedite the transition to allow less of an impact, but it would also allow for greater emphasis on supporting the culture, earning stakeholder confidence at an exponential rate that would otherwise take months or years to accomplish. Regardless of the reason for turnover, tacit knowledge is still leaving the organization, corrupting legacy and longevity, which can result in extra time needed for new team members to become part of the team and organization whereby tacit knowledge freely flows between the employees.

One area to also consider as there is turnover is those that are "left behind" after a layoff or even a termination. Those who are still with the organization also possess tacit knowledge, which is very valuable to the organization. It is critical to understand the impact, at a psychological level, of still having a job. There is guilt and questioning why they were not laid off, or even when someone has been terminated, questioning what caused the termination and if "they will be next." Regardless of either of these scenarios, the employees who are still with the organization will feel insecure and unsure of their position within the organization. Thus, there could be some who leave the organization because they are feeling insecure and unsure about their place within the organization. This type of turnover will have a negative impact on the organization, as not only will the organization be losing top talent, but they will also be losing the tacit knowledge these team members possess. Trying to rehire for these positions could prove to be difficult, as candidates may not want to apply for these open positions at the organization after hearing about the layoffs.

Additionally, the employees who are still with the organization will want to hold onto their tacit knowledge and may not share it due to this insecurity and not being sure what their place is within the organization. This may be done for self-preservation to show value to the organization, but it could also be done out of spite to not share their tacit knowledge to prove that they have value to the organization. Either way, this will negatively impact the team and organization, not to mention the culture of the whole organization. HR and the leaders must be ready to intervene when turnover occurs, reassuring those who are still with the organization. They cannot always relay why someone was laid off or let go but communicating with the employees who remain of value to the organization is incredibly important, as the organization still needs to operate and perform, and helping to keep team members engaged through these changes is critically necessary.

In Chapter 13, it was discussed that the research showed that all but one of the respondents believe that creativity and innovation affect an organization's performance. While this is not a surprising result, some of the reasons provided for how it is impacted are worth noting and diving into. The business environment is always changing to stay ahead of or with the changing market; thus, the only way to really thrive is by embracing continuous creative thinking and encouraging innovation. As has been previously discussed in Chapters 11 and 13, regulated creativity and innovation can have both a positive and a negative outcome for organizations. However, it is the level of involvement of the leadership team that can have a profound impact. When there is unregulated creativity and innovation occurring within the organization, this can significantly influence the organization, but it may not necessarily be in a positive manner. Therefore, some regulation or oversight by the leadership team is imperative to keeping the teams moving in the right direction, which is towards the organization's goals and objectives. Otherwise, when teams are running rogue, they increase the chances of veering off the path of the organizational goals, which could negatively impact the organization's performance, and ultimately their market share.

As has been discussed throughout these chapters, creativity and innovation allow for new and efficient operations, increasing feelings of belonging and purpose, which is critical for the persistence of employees and overall performance. It has also been acknowledged that an organization needs to be careful that there is not too much regulation that stifles creativity and innovation. A good example of too much regulation by leaders is that an organization's performance could be greatly diminished and negatively affected if a once vibrant culture of creativity is turned into order and efficiency. If creativity and innovation live in an organization, the team will continue to grow in experience and knowledge, which in turn allows the organization to be successful through this growth, and employees will feel like they are contributing to this growth. Motivation to contribute more to the organization is essential and encourages employees to do their best, which helps with reducing turnover. As one respondent voiced, "the challenges of today and opportunities of tomorrow require a break from the past." Innovation helps in getting more out of current resources and creativity in developing new solutions to needs and challenges of the organization. As another respondent concluded:

> always seeking improvement is a value found in all high performing organizations. The people doing the work know how to best get it done better if they receive the tools and support. Decentralizing the capture and transfer of tacit knowledge would allow for more effective process improvement and greater efficiency.

Thus, a balance needs to be struck, and HRM's involvement can greatly help.

HRM can help employees at all levels stay engaged and draw out their tacit knowledge through the different activities that are developed, particularly after turnover occurs. However, different cultures may want different activities to stay engaged. More specifically, one area that should be discussed is the generational workers in today's workforce. With the older workforce, there is a lot of tacit knowledge that exists and can be captured within the teams. As we have discussed, some turnover is good as it infuses the organization with new ideas and innovations. However, this does not necessarily mean that it is due to younger workers with fresh ideas. Perhaps these new ideas will come from hiring a seasoned candidate who has years of experience where this tacit knowledge can be integral to the creativity and innovation of the work environment. There have been a lot of recent articles and publications discussing trying to develop a work environment that is conducive to the well-being of all employees, and some of this has pointed towards the younger workers; however, if this truly is the case, then organizations are missing out on some valuable tacit knowledge of hiring and retaining those candidates who have a vast amount of experience and skills that would infuse the work environment with fresh, yet tried and true ideas that have worked in the past. It is important to caveat this vein of thinking that there will be ideas bouncing off all the members of the team, both seasoned and less seasoned employees, creating and innovating new ideas. However, this will only occur when there is mutual respect between the team members and not a "push and pull" type of communication.

Any team will have conflict, which is healthy and expected, but conflict that is not resolved and allowed to fester will have an opposite effect, impacting the efficiency and effectiveness of the team, thus resulting in groups of employees feeling like they do not matter as much as another group, when this may not be the case at all. These are the types of situations that manifest themselves to give the appearance of inequity and discriminatory practices, which would have a negative effect on the teams and the organization. Leadership and HR involvement are the keys to ensuring that the teams are working together, helping to resolve conflict when necessary, and developing activities and practices that are for the benefit of all employees, not just one group of employees.

Another way of looking at this is that we are already seeing a shortage of skilled employees, where hiring more seasoned candidates can add to the team and organization with their vast tacit knowledge, experience, and skills. The HR practices that are implemented should look at all the generations within the workplace and identify what is important to employees through activities such as surveys or town hall discussions. Retaining and motivating all employees is important, and implementing HR activities to help with retention and motivation across generations is equally important. There must also be a global approach to this as well. For instance, in Thailand, the retirement age is typically 55, with some industries extending the retirement age to 60 if the employee is in good health (Napathorn, 2022). Here in the United States, this way of thinking about retirement age would not be tolerated, and it is in fact against the law to force someone to retire at a specific age. There will be exceptions to this based on industries, such as pilots or other professions where physical and mental capability will be tested to ensure the performance and safety of the person and others. In essence, when approaching this through a global lens, HR must ensure that all laws, regulations, and cultural norms are reviewed and incorporated as appropriate into the HR activities and practices that are developed. Furthermore, as is discussed by Napathorn (2022), "the relationship between HR practices and employees' job satisfaction and the relationship between HR practices and employees' affective commitment changes with employees' age" (p. 4). Therefore, what may work for retaining one generation of workers will not necessarily work for another generation. Gathering data from the employees will be instrumental in effectively developing and implementing HR practices and activities to capture each employee's tacit knowledge, which benefits the whole organization.

Additionally, a way in which to capture seasoned employees' tacit knowledge but also to try to meet them where they are in their professional lives would be to have flexible work such as part-time opportunities, reduced workloads, or even semiretirement (Napathorn, 2022). While this may seem on the surface to not be very effective in terms of utilizing human capital and organizational efficiency, organizations need to think outside the box as the aging workforce starts to leave, taking with them their tacit knowledge, or looking at hiring those that still want to contribute but may not want to be at the level that they once were, but still want to work and provide their tacit knowledge. As the working landscape changes, it is important to consider all the employees, regardless of age, experience, or knowledge that they possess, as all employees bring something to the table, and capturing the tacit knowledge for and from each other will have a positive effect on the team and the organization's performance alike.

HRM's Part in Organizational Performance

As discussed by Sanders and Frankel (2011), HR best practices improve engagement, motivation, and abilities in the workplace, which leads to greater organizational performance. More specifically, when there is collaboration and consensus between HR and leadership, this will encourage employees to make "strong cause—effect attributions" (Sanders & Frankel, 2011, p. 1612), which results in employees being more likely to conform to expectations set forth by their managers, such as expectations of high performance. Challenges exist when senior leadership does not see the HR leaders as strategic partners, and as Sanders and Frankel (2011) contend, the "contemporary HR director typically lacks the authority to challenge senior management decision in the name of profession, who…should be representing the highest standards of people management" (p. 1612). This realization could have a profound effect on the effectiveness of HRM in implementing best practices, which then affects engagement and ultimately organizational performance. One way that HRM can help with this endeavor is by fostering opportunities for employees to transfer their tacit knowledge through growth and leadership development. It is important to note that the continued challenges for HRM to help affect organizational performance through best practices can be seen from the top of the organization to the bottom. When senior leadership does not value the strategic opportunities that HR can provide and should be involved in, this lack of acknowledgement and dismissal sends a message to the rest of the organization that HR is not an important piece of the senior leadership team; thus, the organization can falter in performance because there is no uniformity of communication about the direction the organization is moving, which results in a lack of cohesiveness of the senior leadership team and ultimately creating an opportunity for individual departments to set about on their own agendas, regardless of what the strategic goals and objectives may be. Without the involvement of HR in developing these goals and objectives, to ensure that these goals are inclusive, compliant, and utilizing the organization's human capital to its fullest potential, there could be ramifications that senior leadership may not be aware of if they are not involving HR in the decision-making process.

Furthermore, if senior leadership is not involving HR in the decision-making process, they could be making decisions about the teams, which could impact the performance of not only the teams but the whole organization. More specifically, innovation competence and performance are directly linked to tacit knowledge and innovation. Knowledge is the most important piece of strategic resource within an organization; tacit knowledge is at the center of the actions and resources used by the organization (Deyong et al., 2007). A model that provides more specific information about tacit knowledge is the Knowledge Fermenting Model and its use in showing how tacit knowledge is utilized throughout the organization and how individuals learn from tacit knowledge. Basically, the model uses renewed tacit knowledge, resulting in applied competence and innovation, along with learning between team members, helping with organizational learning and impacting the overall performance of the organization (Deyong et al., 2007). This model is an important discovery as it can be extremely useful for organizations in identifying, capturing, and utilizing the tacit knowledge within the organization.

As tacit knowledge travels throughout an organization, this can help the organization identify and document knowledge for the purposes of organizational performance. When organizations help facilitate the transfer of tacit knowledge, some results will include higher working efficiency, increased team innovation, fewer errors in work production, and improved morale. However, as we have discussed, the involvement of leadership and HR in this endeavor through regulated activities can be positive, ensuring they do not interfere with the natural development of social networks, which could impact the transference of tacit knowledge. More specifically, the first step in the model is identifying the knowledge "bacterial strain," as described by Deyong et al. (2007), which is the conduit for the creation and transference of tacit knowledge whereby creativity and innovation are generated. Deyong et al. (2007) identify six different items within this step of the knowledge fermenting model, which include matters such as whether the team members understand the direction or goal of the organization and how to accomplish these tasks or goals, along with how these activities align with the organization's strategic goals.

The second step, the knowledge body, identifies a few different dimensions focused on the knowledge body, as indicated in the model. The knowledge body is used for the learning functions of the knowledge base of innovation (Deyong et al., 2007), which is one of the most important steps in the model as it identifies the how and why of tacit knowledge transfer within the organization. These items specifically address not only the effect on individual knowledge within the organization but also the activities that are associated with organizational experience. Furthermore, it is important to discuss that knowledge does not just come from the organization in which the person works but also from the experience that they bring to the organization and their willingness to share this knowledge with others. None of this will mean anything if there is no opportunity to share and discuss the knowledge brought into the organization with the team. The rest of the items identify the depth to which the members of the team are concerned with the sharing of knowledge and who will be the one to interpret the information as it pertains to the technology that may be used in gaining this knowledge (Deyong et al., 2007). This is an important piece of capturing tacit knowledge for HRM's because if the employees do not trust the system or feel that it is too invasive, then they will not be as willing to share their tacit knowledge and allow it to be captured.

As we continue to discuss the knowledge fermentation model, the next factor in the model is the knowledge enzyme. The knowledge enzyme has several factors to use in facilitating innovation, and whether the organization's help in coordinating these efforts plays a role in the creation of innovation (Deyong et al., 2007). This factor has to do with leadership and their help in coordinating activities. As discussed earlier, too many regulated activities by the leadership can stifle creativity and innovation; however, this factor discusses the degree to which the leadership is involved, their acceptance of such activities, and the amount of time the team members spend on the activities. Leadership involvement and team member focus on the activities that have been developed will be instrumental in the support needed for the creation of new ideas, whereby individual learning can occur, i.e., the transfer of tacit knowledge (Deyong et al., 2007). However, none of this can occur without the tools needed for the transfer of tacit knowledge.

The knowledge tools are the next factor and are the technological tools needed in the process of innovation and how these tools are used for prompting tacit knowledge transfer, along with how these technologies support innovation (Deyong et al., 2007). While this may sound innocuous, it is very difficult to capture tacit knowledge in a database. Thus, this would be the most difficult factor to accomplish as it pertains to learning someone else's tacit knowledge. Conversely, provided the HR activities that are developed to help with capturing tacit knowledge are effective, such as training and development of team members and opportunities for the teams to work together where sharing their knowledge is more natural, then the capturing of tacit knowledge will help with the creativity and innovation that occurs within the teams. Nevertheless, if the technology is capturing processes, this will be more likely to be successful, even knowing that when a person completes a process, they will be adjusting the process that is most effective and efficient for them. Knowing this will also allow for innovative ideas to flow and be shared with the team.

Allowing for a knowledge growth environment is the next factor and naturally follows the knowledge tools factor, as the knowledge growth environment allows for openness and equality, allowing for tacit knowledge to be shared and learned (Deyong et al., 2007). The environment is more commonly referred to as the culture of the organization, or, in this case, the degree to which innovation is open and encouraged through the organization's culture. As DE&I is very much present in today's workplace, this factor rests on equality and the opportunities the team members have within the organization, whereby candid conversations, and trust are developed through the teams. The organization's culture will largely depend on the openness of the teams, the leadership, and the organization to share, learn, and trust for tacit knowledge to be transferred. The degree to which team members are evaluated based on the learning activities they are involved in will also play a part in the equality of the teams and their effectiveness in transferring tacit knowledge (Deyong et al., 2007).

The next factor, which is the knowledge fermentation bar, discusses the process of transferring tacit knowledge through the influence of innovative activities within the team. The activities that occur within a cross-functional social network and how many there are within an organization will help with the fermentation process of knowledge. More importantly, the frequency of use of these cross-functional social networks is critical for learning and innovating, as their diverse make-up and the stable degree to which groups and teams are formed (Deyong et al., 2007). Once these social networks have been formed and trust has been developed, the influence within these networks is very important for the transfer of tacit knowledge, which plays a large role in allowing creativity and innovation to flourish within and through them. This leads into the last factor of organizational competence or advantage, where the transfer of tacit knowledge and innovation developed increases the performance of the organization, impacting its competitive advantage within the market, which is the goal of any organization—to have a significant share of the market in which they reside (Deyong et al., 2007). Tacit knowledge is closely related to innovation where the creation of high-performance teams and the support of the leadership in these creative and innovative activities increase the performance of the organization and ultimately increase its market share.

HRM's influence is through helping with cross-functional social network development, along with the leadership's involvement with the assistance of fostering an atmosphere for creativity and innovation to occur through the transfer of tacit knowledge, particularly as it pertains to organizational performance. High-performance HR practices have been proven to impact an organization's performance. HR best practice perspective is a view where HR practices significantly impact the opportunities for participation in the workplace, motivation to want to participate, and the ability to do so, which leads to higher work performance which also affects organizational performance (Sanders & Frenkel, 2011). While there may be some skepticism if HR truly does impact an organization's performance through HR activities or best practices due to the validity of research where only HR participants are surveyed, it is HR's seat at the proverbial senior executive strategic table that allows for these best practices to truly impact the overall success of the organization, but it largely depends on the support of the senior leadership. There is further research conducted where the process perspective is used in conjunction with the best practice perspective, where the process perspective asks the "how," which helps to validate the reliability of research on HR best practices and their impact on organizational performance (Sanders & Frenkel, 2011). Basically, the process perspective shows how employee attitudes and behaviors align with the improvement of employee performance, which positively impacts the organization's performance. Much of this has to do with job satisfaction and commitment to the organization, which occur through HRM's best practices implemented within the organization (Sanders & Frenkel, 2011). These best practices cannot thrive without the buy-in of the organization's leadership, resulting in employees being more committed to the organization, which can be seen through increased performance in both the employee and the organization.

Additionally, these best practices must align with the organization's strategic goals, with the support of all levels of leadership. A concern is that research continues to point to the fact that HR may still not be sitting at the strategic table; thus, any initiatives that are developed may not have HR input, which could result in the initiatives not working or never getting off the ground. This view of HR's strategic value starts at the top, and there is a lack of acceptance that HR should be a full strategic partner. The fact that HRM may not be seen as a full strategic partner impacts the authority or input to contribute to decisions that are made by the senior leadership on strategic goals and objectives for the organization. The extreme pace at which organizations are moving and changing also has an immediate effect on whether the organization succeeds or fails. Major decisions that are made at the top determine whether there are career opportunities, positions will change, or whether the organization will be sold off, merged, or go public. Whatever decisions are made at the top, HRM needs to be involved in these decisions to ensure that changes are lawful, equitable, and communicated properly (Pfau & Kay, 2002). Additionally, there is more expectation that HR and lower-level leadership will work together and that HR will be an advisor to middle- and lower-level leadership. Even though these relationships may seem stronger than those with senior leadership, employee and organizational performance are still occurring, even with the challenges of HR's role ambiguity and the conflict of lower-level leadership bending rules as they see fit (Sanders & Frenkel, 2011).

As has been discussed in previous chapters regarding Social Network Theory, Sanders and Frenkel (2011) discuss another theory, social capital theory, which is supported by social network analysis, and its relevance to HRM's relations and their effectiveness within the organization. Social Capital Theory takes a similar viewpoint as Social Network Theory in that it focuses on the social relationships that employees establish within the organization and the collaboration and sharing of tacit knowledge, which ultimately affects the organization's performance that results from these relationships. Building trust and going through the stages of development of the teams is the same, whereby sharing and learning of tacit knowledge naturally occurs through the team, increasing both team performance as well as job satisfaction. It is the collaboration of HRM and the leadership team that affects performance, both individually and organizationally, transferring the tacit knowledge needed for creativity and innovation to thrive. HRM needs to continue to show value to senior leadership through outlaying the data and the results of employee and organizational performance through the HR activities implemented, along with the increased job satisfaction and commitment because of HRM's involvement and effectiveness. While there has been a shift in recent years towards HRM being seen as a strategic partner, there is still room for improvement in this area, and HR can increase their strategic value by being adept in business and providing the data and analytics of the decisions being made for the organization. In essence, HR must equate business decisions with data and analytics and the effect these decisions has on employees as well as the bottom line.

Works Cited

Deyong, X., Xiangyun, Z., & Quiyue, Z. (2007). Empirical study on innovation competence based on tacit knowledge. Retrieved from IEEE Explore.

Kokkaew, N., Jokkaw, N., Peansupap, V., & Wipulanusat, W. (2022). Impacts on human resource management and knowledge management on non-financial organizational performance: Evidence of Thai infrastructure constructions firms. *Ain Shams Engineering Journal*, *13*, 1–12. Impacts of human resource management and knowledge management on non-financial organizational performance: Evidence of Thai infrastructure construction firms - ScienceDirect.

Napathorn, C. (2022). The design and implementation of age-related HR practices across firms in institutional contexts: evidence from Thailand. *Journal of Asia Business Studies*, *18*(1), 1–24. doi:10.1108/JABS-04–2020–0169

Pfau, B. N., & Kay, I. T. (2002). *Theories of executive human resource management*. McGraw-Hill Publishing, Capella University.

Sanders, K., & Frenkel, S. (2011). Introduction: HR-line management relations: characteristics and effects. *The International Journal of Human Resource Management*, *22*(8), 1611–1617.

INDEX

Printed in the United States
by Baker & Taylor Publisher Services